17

Comprehensive Planning and the Environment

Comprehensive Planning and the Environment

A Manual for Planners

John S. Willson
Philip Tabas
Marian Henneman

Abt Books
Cambridge, Massachusetts

Library of Congress Catalog Card Number 78-66683

Printed in the United States of America.

ISBN: 0-89011-515-X

Contents

Preface ix

Chapter One: Organizing Concepts. 1

Chapter Two: Planning Studies 11

Chapter Three: Development and Evaluation
                of Plan Alternatives. 91

Chapter Four: Plan Implementation. 155

Chapter Five: Plan Monitoring and Management 211

Appendix: Legislative Mandates 225

General Bibliography. 259

Preface

Passage of the Housing and Community Development Act of 1974 brought about important changes in the basic HUD Comprehensive Planning Assistance Program. Section 701 of the Housing Act of 1954, as amended, now requires that a federally assisted comprehensive plan contain, at a minimum, (1) a housing element designed to meet existing and prospective housing needs and (2) a land-use element for guiding major decisions regarding the location of future growth and the associated pattern and intensity of land use. HUD regulations issued in support of these requirements clearly call for inclusion of environmental-planning considerations in comprehensive planning and management. The regulations also require a separate environmental assessment of the comprehensive plan wherever an assisted work program will result in plans or policies affecting land use, community facilities, major utility and transportation systems, or the protection of natural areas.

The major purpose of this manual is to help comprehensive planners integrate these environmental-planning considerations. A second objective is to help planners develop the data needed for environmental assessment. Although the manual stresses the environmental-planning requirements of Section 701, it is intended to be of use to all agencies responsible for comprehensive or functional planning, regardless of whether Section 701 funds are involved. The manual is also designed to be useful at all levels: municipal, metropolitan, regional, and statewide.

This manual offers no original research or new theories of environmental planning. Instead, it brings together the most useful and interesting ways others have integrated environmental concerns into broader planning perspectives. Its intended users are mainly practicing planners, those with direct responsibility for relating environmental values to urban planning and development. Rather than emphasize formal integration at the conceptual level, the manual generally presents richly detailed "how-to" discussions of specific techniques. No doubt, this approach creates some repetition and occasionally mixes apples and oranges, but the authors hope that the loss of technical rigor is more than offset by the manual's usefulness for on-the-job planners.

Four important features of the manual, intended to ensure its maximum utility to planners, deserve special note.

Focus on the urban environment. It deals with problems of land use, water quality, air quality, noise abatement, hazard reduction, historic preservation, and social equity as they arise in built-up and developing areas.

Broad definition of environment. It defines the urban environment to include not only natural systems but also its man-made and social components.

Emphasis on directly useable information. It identifies relevant federal legislation, regulations, and standards; presents useful analytic and evaluative methods and techniques; and provides specific examples of the successful application of these methods and techniques.

Process-oriented approach. It presents these materials within the framework of a comprehensive planning and management process readily understood by local planners and officials. It treats the process in terms of planning studies, identification of the preferred plan, and on-going management and monitoring.

Although the manual is primarily intended for working planners, it also has certain value as supplemental reading for graduate courses in urban and environmental planning. It provides a thorough survey of current integrating techniques in planning, as well as a comprehensive bibliography. A separate appendix digests the major federal environmental statutes affecting urban planning.

The manual grew out of previous research done by Abt Associates for the U.S. Department of Housing and Urban Development, Office of Policy Development and Research, under Contract No. H-2175R. The manual is available in somewhat longer form as *Integration of Environmental Considerations in the Comprehensive Planning and Management Process*, under HUD cover. The authors express their appreciation to Paul Brace, Government Technical

PREFACE

Representative for HUD, and to George Winzer, Walter Prybyla, and Raymond Sherry for their guidance and support throughout the development and writing of this manual. The authors would also like to acknowledge the many helpful contributions made by Dr. Malcolm Rivkin and Goldie Rivkin of Rivkin Associates, Inc., in their review of early drafts.

Chapter 1
Organizing Concepts

A major criticism of comprehensive planning is that it has failed to adequately incorporate environmental considerations and values. This criticism has not been limited to Section 701 planning funded by the U.S. Department of Housing and Urban Development; it applies to the full range of comprehensive plans done at municipal, metropolitan, regional, and state levels. The objective of this manual is to help urban planners integrate important environmental-planning considerations into their comprehensive planning and management process. If proper integration is achieved, environmental impact statements will be much less likely to uncover unanticipated negative effects requiring costly plan changes and delay. More important, the resulting plans should be much more sensitive to *all* the needs -- social and cultural as well as physical — of the people who live in urban areas.

This first chapter presents the basic organization of the manual. It briefly summarizes the "environmental critique" of comprehensive planning and management as traditionally practiced. It then discusses seven specific environmental-planning considerations important to successful urban community-development and housing programs. Finally, it identifies four critical stages in comprehensive planning where increased sensitivity to these environmental factors would most likely result in beneficial change.

The Environmental Critique

Much of the criticism directed at traditional comprehensive planning and management has come from those who argue that it has ignored natural environmental processes as fundamental constraints to urbanization.[1] Land-use decisions, they say, have been made primarily on the basis of economic criteria, the objectives being to accommodate projected growth while minimizing development costs and maximizing economic accessibility. The major

1

planning concern has been to see that development is well nourished with the most extensive infrastructure the community can reasonably afford. Typically only limited consideration has been given to the effect of planned uses on natural systems. To the extent it is considered at all, nature is viewed largely as an economic constraint on use (for example, how soils, slope, and floodplains affect suitability and development costs). The result has been significant environmental degradation accompanied by hazard to human life and property, unanticipated social costs, and loss of amenity and diversity. Some of the specific problems resulting from development which ignores natural environmental factors have been:

Untreated sewage being discharged into receiving waters during periods of heavy rainfall because of combined sewers

Property loss from development on floodplains

Siltation of reservoirs from poor soil management

Pollution and depletion of groundwater supplies from development on aquifers and their recharge zones

Increase in frequency and severity of floods from extensive development in watershed areas, clear-cutting practices, and channelization programs

Destruction of wetlands by the disposal of solid wastes in land fills

Loss of agricultural land to urban sprawl

Air pollution resulting from poorly designed urban transportation systems

Property damage from building in active geologic zones

Destruction of the natural environment by recreation developments [2]

These critics argue that natural resource considerations need to be considered in comprehensive planning and management and used in conjunction with other criteria in determining rational land-use allocations. Land-use decisions should be based on land capability tempered by an appreciation of potential adverse environmental consequences.

There is evidence that many planning agencies have been moving toward increased "environmental" sensitivity. However, their response — much like the critique that gave rise to it — has concentrated mainly on problems of the natural environment. A national survey of urban and regional planning agencies conducted in 1973 found that, of the 40% of the sample agencies listed as doing some type of environmental planning, the great majority limited their planning to land use, open space, water and sewer, and solid waste. Much less likely to be included in environmental planning were those activities more directly related to the built environment, such as water quality and supply, air quality, noise, historic preservation, and urban design.[3] Nowhere, either in the survey instrument or the agency response, was there an indication of a perceived relation between natural and built environmental-planning considerations within any larger framework of such urban social problems as congestion, inadequate housing, decaying neighborhoods, poverty, and discrimination. If comprehensive planning processes are to be more sensitive to the environment, then that awareness must extend to include every influence on human life.

One of the major factors contributing to the lack of comprehensiveness in "comprehensive" planning and management has been fragmentation of the planning responsibility among specialized agencies. The result, in the absence of effective intergovernmental and interagency coordination, has been narrowly focused, single-purpose functional planning — for example, plans for locating highways, developing water resources, or building water and sewer systems. But measures designed to solve one problem often create or exacerbate problems in other functional areas. The examples of environmental problems resulting from a failure to plan comprehensively, listed in Figure 1,[4] generally include disruption and degradation of the natural environment, unplanned secondary development, and dislocation of people and whole neighborhoods.

Perhaps the most pervasive criticism of traditional comprehensive planning has been inspired by its apparent lack of concern for plan implementation. Yet planning agencies often lack statutory authority to impose their proposals, for comprehensive plans often have advisory status only. This criticism does reflect inattention to the job of translating physical-development plans into detailed, realistic capital-improvements budgets. But is also indicates a failure to recognize that "a multitude of individual . . . decisions made over time affect the form and function of the urban system and thereby

FIGURE 1

Some Environmental Consequences
of Single-Purpose Planning

Single Purpose of Plan	Resulting Problems
Highway Development	**Primary Impacts** • Air Pollution • Noise Pollution • Congestion **Secondary Impacts** • Induced growth, urban sprawl, strip development, leap-frogging • Restriction of transportation alternatives • Relocation of residents
Water Resource Development	**Secondary Impacts** • Control of natural waterways, loss of wildlife habitat • Water-quality problems associated with impoundments due to increased retention time • Development around reservoirs
Sewer and Water Systems	**Primary Impacts** • Water-quality problems associated with impoundments • Problems of sewage sludge disposal **Secondary Impacts** • Induced growth, urban sprawl, strip development • Inflation of land values, encouraging farmers to sell or subdivide their land • Rezoning or upzoning for higher densities

the environmental quality of that system. Most of these decisions are in fact private, but there are points of public intervention that must be used in a systematic and coordinated fashion if their maximum impact is to be affected."[5] Local governments have available a wide range of implementation instruments -- public investments, regulations, fiscal incentives — that can guide both public and private development toward a good urban environment. Local failure to adapt and redirect existing guidance tools has contributed to many of the undesirable features of "sprawl growth," i.e., the initial non-uniform improvement of isolated and scattered parcels of land on the urban fringe, followed by gradual urbanization of the intervening undeveloped areas. The "costs" of this growth pattern have already been well documented: waste of scarce land resources; higher costs of development for private and public sectors; higher levels of air, water and noise pollution; and unintended personal and social costs.[6]

Environmental-Planning Considerations

The Housing and Community Development Act of 1974 extended the scope of comprehensive planning and management to nearly all major planning concerns of local and regional government: the location of future growth and the resulting pattern and intensity of land use; housing needs as related to population growth; needed community facilities and supporting services; capital-improvements planning; and implementation of coordinated policies and programs to achieve these community goals while "taking into account appropriate *environmental* factors."[7]

In carrying out the act, HUD has adopted an equally broad definition of the urban environment. Sensitive to the environmental critique, this definition extends not only to natural systems but also to their interrelations with the built and social environment. Planning for the urban environment involves prevention and abatement of annoying or threatening nuisances such as water pollution, air pollution, and excessive noise. But it also has more positive aspects, like providing open space, developing aesthetically pleasing urban areas, and arranging areas for convenient living. All of these concerns must then be cast into a larger framework of human social needs, both present and projected. It is this broad conception of "environment" and "environmental planning" that underlies the discussion of specific integrating techniques and methods in the following chapters.

This manual groups environmental-planning considerations under seven major headings deemed especially relevant to comprehensive planning and management:

Land use

Water quality

Air quality

Noise abatement and control

Flood and other hazards management

Historic preservation

Social equity

Although this list could be extended to include many other environmental concerns, these seven are particularly critical to comprehensive planning as it is practiced in built-up urban areas. The following paragraphs define each of these considerations in terms of their relation to comprehensive planning.

Land Use. Decisions regarding use of land influence most other aspects of environmental quality, and land itself is now recognized as a valuable scarce resource. A number of disparate but related environmental concerns will be dealt with under this heading: land use according to land suitability; intermedia impacts of land-use decisions; land-use considerations for special areas, such as the coastal zone and other unique and pristine lands; land-use implications of special uses like solid waste disposal; interrelations between land use and energy conservation; and aesthetically pleasing urban design.

Water quality. The environmental-planning challenge is to protect against those factors that adversely affect water quality and quantity while ensuring that the community benefits from the water's use. Desired uses include public water supply, recreation, and visual and aesthetic enjoyment. Factors that can adversely affect the quality of water include municipal and industrial point source discharges, combined sewer overflows, urban runoff, on-lot disposal, and inappropriate development in environmentally sensitive areas. Needed complementary investments relate to physical access and the provision of facilities and amenities.

Air quality. The primary justification for including air quality as an environmental planning consideration is to safeguard human health; secondary objectives include protection of property and plant and animal life. Effective land use planning is the key both to predicting future air quality conditions and guiding future development so that these conditions will not violate mandated air quality standards. Air quality considerations need to be integrated into planning for location of industrial and residential development, utilities, highways, waste disposal sites, and recreational areas.

Noise abatement and control. Of increasing concern in congested urban areas are the adverse physiological, psychological, and economic effects of unwanted sound. A valid environmental consideration for urban planning is the limitation or reduction of noise that may cause hearing loss, interfere with speech communication, cause nervous tension or other disorders, or infringe on acoustical privacy in multifamily dwellings. Of the various types of bothersome noise, outdoor airborne noise (from aircraft, vehicular traffic, industrial plants) is the most amenable to control through comprehensive planning. Land-use planning that is sensitive to such noise can contribute to achieving acceptable noise levels by avoiding exposure of the population to its major sources. Indoor airborne, structure-borne, and impact noise must be dealt with at the level of design and source control ordinances.

Flood and other hazards management. Comprehensive planners are necessarily concerned with the protection of human life and property, including public facilities, from both natural and man-made hazards. Natural hazards include floods, tsunamis, earthquakes, tornadoes, and mudslides. Hazards originating within the built environment include explosions and fires from the storage, processing, or transport of hazardous materials and from the accidental release of large flammable and/or toxic vapor clouds. Development controls, more suitable use of hazard-prone lands, and the regulation of residential location near industrial sites are all effective and cheap alternatives to expensive structural solutions.

Historic preservation. Historic, archeological, commemorative, or otherwise culturally significant structures and places, including neighborhoods and natural areas, contribute a sense of time, scale, texture, and identity to the urban environment. The preservation and enhancement of these areas have come to be viewed as integral parts of environmentally sensitive urban planning. Comprehensive planning and management can contribute to historic preservation by identifying and mapping existing cultural resources and by coordinating preservation strategies with those for related community objectives, such as urban redevelopment and the provision of open space and parks.

Social Equity. The Housing and Community Development Act of 1974 contains a strong antidiscrimination clause covering, among other public actions, the determination of locations for housing and other facilities.[8] More positively, the act requires localities to respond adequately to the needs of minorities, women, the elderly and handicapped, and other segments of the low-income population when planning and managing community-development programs. This provision includes amelioration of the effects of past discrimination. Important environmental-planning considerations include assurance of open housing, nondiscriminatory land-use policies and practices, and equal access to employment opportunities and services.

This manual is designed to help planners integrate these seven environmental concerns, individually and collectively, into a comprehensive planning and management process. The central thrust of the manual is that conventional planning processes, carried on separately for each of these environmental concerns, do not necessarily add up to a comprehensive plan. Rather, the manual advocates that work on each of these components, from the first step to the last, be integrated into a single comprehensive plan.

Structure of the Manual

Comprehensive planning and management is defined in terms of goals and important activities rather than in terms of individual functions or levels of government. It must reflect heightened sensitivity to environmental-planning considerations, regardless of the level of public decison making involved. The objective of this manual is *not* to tell public officials what comprehensive planning and management is, but to provide them with the specific techniques and methodologies they need to undertake it.

For ease of presentation, the manual divides comprehensive planning and management into four major stages, namely:

Planning Studies

Development and Evaluation of Plan Alternatives

Plan Implementation

Plan Monitoring and Management

One chapter of the manual is devoted to integrating the seven environmental-planning considerations discussed above into each of these four stages.

Planning Studies covers that initial set of activities dedicated to goal formulation, data collection and interpretation, problem identification and analysis, and the establishment of planning priorities (chapter 2).

Development and Evaluation of Plan Alternatives covers refinement of community goals; definition of major alternative policies, programs, and specific project actions; evaluation of available alternatives according to various criteria, including cost-effectiveness, equity, administrative simplicity, and political accountability; and selection of a preferred policy or plan (chapter 3).

Plan Implementation covers the full range of public investments, regulatory tools, and fiscal incentives available to governments to carry out approved community-development and housing programs in environmentally sensitive ways (chapter 4).

Plan Monitoring and Management covers the on-going process of gathering and analyzing data on program accomplishments and effects, indicators of environmental quality, and trends in community sentiment regarding environmental goals and objectives (chapter 5).

REFERENCES

1. Edward Kaiser et al., *Promoting Environmental Quality Through Urban Planning and Controls* (Washington, D.C.: U.S. Environmental Protection Agency, EPA-600-15-73-015), especially chapters III and IV.

2. See U.S. Environmental Protection Agency, *Land Use and Environmental Protection* (Washington, D.C.: 1973), p. ii.

3. Kaiser et al., op. cit., pp. 77.

4. U.S. Environmental Protection Agency, *Land Use and Environmental Protection*, p. 12.

5. Kaiser et al., op. cit., p. 16.

6. *The Costs of Sprawl*, prepared by Real Estate Research Corporation for the Council on Environmental Quality, the Office of Policy Development and Research of the U.S. Department of Housing and Urban Development and the Office of Planning and Management of the U.S. Environmental Protection Agency (Washington, D.C.: 1974). See *Executive Summary* and Detailed Cost Analysis volumes, passim.

7. Housing and Community Development Act of 1974, Section 104(a) (2).

8. Ibid., Section 109. Also see applicable Community Development Block Grant regulations (Sections 570, 601).

Chapter 2
Planning Studies

This chapter takes up the first of the major steps in comprehensive planning and management — initial planning studies designed to determine the nature and significance of environmental problems. For ease of presentation, each of the environmental-planning concerns identified in chapter 1 will be addressed separately; however, since they are often related, these interrelations will also be identified and discussed. The planning studies require goal formulation, data collection and interpretation, problem identification and analysis, and the establishment of priorities. Depending on the particular problem, planning studies can include resource identification and mapping, development of pollution source inventories, measurement of current environmental quality, projection of future quality changes, and assessment of intermedia impacts.

The federal government has made a number of attempts to coordinate the various planning programs affecting the environment. Interagency agreements have encouraged program administrators to recognize that work performed to fulfill the requirements of one program can be useful in helping to meet the requirements of another. HUD's Comprehensive Planning Assistance (701) Program, with its environmentally sensitive land-use and housing requirements, is now interrelated with the NOAA's Coastal Zone Management Program, EPA's '208' Water Quality Program, and Interior's Outdoor Recreation Program, through a series of interagency agreements initiated by HUD. Not only reducing duplication of effort, this integration helps tie functional programs together in a comprehensive planning framework and allows more time for integrated environmental assessments.

Needs of the comprehensive planner are not, however, always the same as those of the functional planning specialist. The aim of comprehensive planning and management is to integrate individual environmental concerns into the broader context of urban land use, housing, and community development. This chapter concentrates on those types of planning studies most relevant to the comprehensive planner, that is, those that facilitate planning integration. For each environmental planning concern, as appropriate, this chapter (1) establishes the relevance of the concern for comprehensive planning; (2) presents the existing framework of federal legislation, regulations, and guidelines surrounding the planning studies activity; (3) discusses study approaches and techniques available to comprehensive planners; and (4) provides specific examples of where these approaches and techniques have been successfully applied.

LAND USE

This section deals with a series of five environmental planning concerns all related in one way or another to management of the urban land resource. Planning studies are discussed with reference to:

Land suitability

Coastal zone management

Solid waste management

Land use and energy conservation

Urban design

Land Suitability Studies

The standard critique of comprehensive planning has been that economic criteria have tended to dominate the local land-use decision-making process, resulting in environmental degradation accompanied by hazards to human life and property, loss of amenity and diversity, and other unanticipated social costs. The principal source of this criticism has been the natural sciences, with landscape architects playing an important intermediary role. They argue that traditional land-use planning fails to recognize that the urban environment is composed of a complex set of interdependent natural and man-made elements and that ecological processes are natural determinants of land use. A natural resource data base must be integrated into comprehensive planning and management and used in conjunction with other criteria for determining optimal land-use allocations. The goal is land use based on land capability and awareness of the potentially adverse environmental consequences of unsuitable urban uses. Actually, increased use of natural resource data in comprehensive planning makes sense regardless of whether the objective is to protect natural systems as social values in themselves or merely to protect development from its own adverse effects. This section concentrates on natural resource data useful in land planning, leaving aside the issue of whether natural systems represent "opportunities" or simply "constraints." However, although it is important to provide planners and decision-makers with scientific information which often has not been available to them, this is still only part of the problem; better information on the natural environment must be related to specific media impacts of development activities, as well as to important aesthetic, cultural, and social considerations.

Many approaches to natural resource analysis are possible. Most are roughly similar in respect to the basic inventory task; differences arise mainly in interpretation and evaluation. Natural resource analysis studies are expensive, calling for specialized expertise and costly computer and graphics services. Few comparative data exist on the costs of alternative approaches. However, most tend to make maximum use of available published data, so that the effort required beyond gathering and interpreting this data is largely a matter of limited field data checks and additional spot data collection where gaps exist. For an overview, it is useful to distinguish, as does Steinitz, between *static* and *dynamic* approaches to natural resource analysis, and further within these categories between *single-factor* and *multiple-factor* analysis.[1]

Examples of static, single-factor approaches include the Soil Ratings maps provided by the U.S. Department of Agriculture and the *Soil Development Guide* prepared by the Southeastern Wisconsin Regional Planning Commission.[2] They both draw on only one type of data, that is, soils, although the SWRPC *Guide* does incorporate more than one earth-science constraint related to soils. Still other examples of this approach are the visual analysis studies of forest landscapes pioneered by R. Burton Litton, Jr.[3] They too consider a number of variables (land form, spatial definition, light, distance from a landscape element, observer position, and the temporal/spatial sequence within which a scene is viewed), but all of these variables draw solely on the visual perspective.

This section concentrates on three major approaches to natural resource analysis which fall under the static, multiple-factor analysis category. This approach is the most highly developed one in the literature, and it has also proved the most applicable to comprehensive planning situations. The three variants that will receive detailed consideration are:

> *Land capability analysis*, developed jointly by the U.S. Geological Survey and the Association of Bay Area Governments;

> *Landscape analysis*, an approach associated with the "environmental corridors" work of Phillip H. Lewis; and

> *Environmental systems analysis*, the general approach developed by Ian McHarg.

Only brief mention is made at the end of this section of more advanced, dynamic approaches.

Land Capability Analysis

This approach grew out of a publicly funded effort to develop earth-science information in a form applicable to land-use planning and decision making. "Despite efforts in recent years to pay closer attention to geological phenomena, planners have not been totally successful in incorporating earth science information into the planning process . . . , the result of inadequate interpretation of earth science information by geologists and hydrologists and inappropriate resolution by planners of earth science [concerns] with other planning concerns."[4] The approach starts with data on geological conditions in an area, making maximum use of published data available from USGS, SCS, the Army Corps of Engineers, state divisions of mines and geology, and regional water districts. These data are then combined and interpreted for their implications regarding urban development. For instance, an important development consideration is slope stability. Geological data on slope and soil type are combined with local rainfall information to develop interpretive maps depicting slope stability and soil-creep potential for the whole area. Interpretive maps are also developed for earthquake intensity, ground-shaking potential, shrink-well potential, settlement potential, and potential for agricultural use.

Land capability analysis is ultimately intended to provide a framework within which to compare the total dollar costs related to geologic conditions for a specified parcel under alternative proposed uses. *Land capability* under this approach is defined as a measure of the probable cost of the presence of specific geologic properties/processes on a specific land parcel under a specific proposed land use. The land uses considered are single-family residential, multifamily residential, industrial, commercial, and agricultural. The three major costs elements taken into account are the costs of (1) engineering, design, and mitigation measures (current dollars per acre); (2) disaster or damage (dollars per acre times the damage frequency divided by the discount rate); and (3) development opportunities foregone (dollars per acre for a resource divided by discount rate). Interpretive maps are prepared for each land use, and a discrete dollar cost is assigned to each parcel for each geologic constraint present. When dollar costs for each geologic constraint are summed, the result is the total dollar costs for each parcel under the proposed land use. These totals are then displayed for the relevant region, color-coded by cost ranges (that is, $0 to $9 per acre, $10 to $99 per acre, $100 to $999 per acre, and so on) in a land capability map. The dollar totals associated with all the earth-science constraints/opportunities for a particular site under a given use are then regarded as indicators of the capability of that land to accommodate that use. The basic steps involved in land capability analysis are conveniently summarized in Figure 2.

In the San Francisco Bay Region Study, USGS and ABAG staff applied land capability analysis to the Santa Clara Valley area. This area, stretching from San Jose to Morgan Hill, was selected because it was experiencing intense development pressures, it presented a wide range of geologic conditions, and a wealth of existing data was available from prior studies. The study concluded that there are many important potential uses for land capability analysis, including (1) refinement of development policies and criteria; (2) evaluation — at least from the physical perspective — of alternative regional development scenarios; and (3) selection of specific implementation devices intended to reduce the expected costs associated with development. The study also mentioned one weakness of the approach: it is still rather expensive, given the effort required to assign expected dollar costs. A more important weakness, the developers of the approach concede, is that it is still limited to the physical aspect of the environment; therefore, its results must be weighed against other important economic, social, and aesthetic concerns.

FIGURE 2
Summary of Land Capability Analysis Procedure

STEP 1

BASIC DATA MAPS
Collect basic earth-science information on the land.

STEP 2

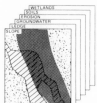

INTERPRETIVE MAPS
Compile maps for each earth-science concern directly from the basic data maps or by combining those maps.

STEP 3

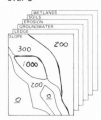

COST INDICES
Assign a numerical dollar value to the various categories of each resulting map to indicate the relative importance of that concern for each land use considered.

STEP 4

TOTAL COST
Add the cost indices for all the conditions found for each land use.

STEP 5

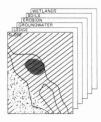

CAPABILITY MAPS
Divide these cost numbers into categories to be mapped for different land uses. Lighter shades represent lower costs and higher relative capacity.

Source: **Land Capability Analysis,** Association of Bay Area Governments, p. 45.

Landscape Analysis

This approach is associated with the work of Phillip H. Lewis, a noted planner and landscape architect. Its basic objective is to seek out and preserve natural and cultural patterns of "unique perceptual quality" within a landscape, harmonizing neighboring natural and man-made elements. It grew originally out of an effort in several Midwestern states to systematize recreation and conservation planning in the face of rapidly expanding demand for public outdoor recreation.[5]

A working definition of *perceptual quality* in a particular physical setting is visual contrast and diversity. On the one hand, a landscape contains certain "intrinsic" values (significant topography such as ridges, steep slopes, wetlands, surface water); on the other hand, it also usually contains so-called "extrinsic" values, that is, additional man-made elements (historic sites and structures, recreation facilities) or resources valued by man (wildlife, mineral deposits). Under this approach, intrinsic resources are mapped and composite overlays prepared. This mapping identifies "concentrations of value." Lewis discovered in his work that these concentrations of value tended to fall into identifiable linear patterns, or what he termed "environmental corridors." These environmental corridors became the basic units for his recreation/conservation planning.

Priorities among the various environmental corridors regarding future government action (such as purchase, development, management, and special protection) are established through use of a numeric point system. The points assigned to identifiable natural and man-made elements in each environmental corridor are totaled. The number of high-ranking areas are compared to estimated future demand for recreation/conservation lands, and specific uses are then assigned. Lewis's approach relies on a nonmonetary scale of values for comparing alternative land use patterns, and this is both a strength and a weakness. It recognizes the importance of nonmonetary social and aesthetic concerns, but it also introduces an element of arbitrariness and lack of replicability.

A recent example of the application of landscape analysis to an urbanizing area is the Dallas Ecological Study, undertaken by the city of Dallas in conjunction with Landscapes Limited, Inc. Rapid population growth in Dallas County since World War II had given it the highest population density of any county in Texas. The study objective was to examine "the various natural resources in the county in order to direct future urban development and to plan for needed urban centers with minimum destruction to the natural system."[6] The study, completed in 1973, was conducted at two levels: a regional study for the entire Upper Trinity River Basin, then a more localized study limited to Dallas County. It is the regional study that most closely approximates the landscape analysis approach. Planners identified "major resource patterns" by mapping and then overlaying five key environmental subsystems, their importance depending on their relative likelihood of responding adversely, in a directly observable way, to urban development. These five subsystems — botanic, zoologic, hydromorphic, edaphic, and geomorphic — were chosen to serve as readily identifiable environmental "indicators," physical landscape features that could be expected to show observable response to changes in the environment. The map overlays made major resource patterns — subsystem interactions and environmentally complex areas — clearly visible, and that helped planners to formulate general planning guidelines for the region and provided a means for indicating possible conflicts with proposed uses. The results of the Dallas Ecological Study have already been used to aid in the selection of transportation routes to the new Dallas-Forth Worth airport and in the development of land-use plans for the Upper Trinity River floodplain. Future plans call for similar studies to collect and map additional economic, social, and cultural data essential to comprehensive planning.

Environmental Systems Analysis

This general approach has been taken by a number of environmental planners, but it is most prominently identified with Ian McHarg, the landscape architect. Its basic premise is that we need to protect natural systems and processes because of their intrinsic value to society and individuals. The major social values at stake are the protection of human life, health, and property; preservation of irreplaceable unique and scarce resources; and avoidance of unnecessary social costs. Individual values to be furthered by environmentally sensitive development are heightened economic productivity of certain natural resources (food crops, forest products); minimization of on-site costs of development; maximization of desirable locations for development in terms of microclimate; view; recreation potential; and access to areas of historic, scientific, and educational interest.[7]

The first step in the procedure is to develop the ecological inventory. Typically, McHarg uses seven basic "indicators" of the natural processes to be protected: climate, historical geology, physiography, hydrology, soils, plant associations, and wildlife. Each indicator represents an environmental subsystem. The seven subsystems are mapped individually, and then judgments are made as to their suitability (plus, minus, neutral) to a range of specific land uses, including agriculture, forestry, recreation, and various intensities of urban development. The outputs of this process are "intrinsic suitability maps" showing the best use for each subarea within single environmental subsystems. Recognizing that coexisting compatible uses can be sustained in at least certain subareas, McHarg evaluates each environmental subsystem on a scale of from 1 to 5 (most desirable to least desirable) for each prospective land use, generating overall intrinsic suitability maps for each use. Optional is the making of a final composite map reflecting the relative importance attached to each land use by the community. Such maps are intended for direct translation into local regulations to protect the social and individual values inherent in natural systems. These regulations are formulated in terms of performance standards for all human activities relating to a particular value. If a proposed activity or land use meets the specified performance level, it is allowed. Conflicts can be resolved by the prohibition or redesign of the proposed activity.

The best recent example of the environmental systems analysis approach is the study done by McHarg's group at the University of Pennsylvania for Medford Township, New Jersey. Medford is located in a rapidly growing fringe area just east of the Philadelphia-Camden SMSA and south of Trenton. The study objective was to "identify with specificity the characteristics of [Medford's] lands and waters and the opportunities and constraints those characteristics indicate, so that the consequences, ecological and fiscal, of every future land use action may be anticipated. Uniquely, this study [is] directed toward production of rational, scientifically based, fair and reasonable land use regulations."[8] Data regarding surface waters, groundwater, runoff and erosion, geologic resources, unique vegetation, wildlife habitat, and microclimate were collected from existing sources and mapped. In addition to such natural resource data, data were also gathered on historic and architectural resources and on scenic and recreation areas. Using a combination of quantitative and qualitative criteria, land suitability maps were produced for agricultural production, forest production, and the following urban uses: rural-urban, clustered suburban, scattered suburban, and urban development. No final composite map was produced; instead, the planners went from the various suitability maps to land-use regulations specific to each area.

All three of these static, multiple-factor approaches to land planning — earth science, landscape, and social values — meet a very important planning need that is usually not satisfied by conventional comprehensive planning and management. They identify, quantify, and map natural resource data for an entire planning area and relate this data to its suitability for various urban uses. In the process, they provide the data "envelope" within which planners can examine and evaluate the potential consequences of alternative development policies and proposals on the natural environment. But they all share, to one degree or another, two major limitations. First, they are almost exclusively oriented to natural resources. Lewis provides for "extrinsic" or man-made elements in establishing major resource patterns, and McHarg includes areas of aesthetic and cultural importance in his ecological inventory; but for the most part, all three approaches leave out economic, social, and cultural data. These approaches are not necessarily incompatible with such information, but these data are not their driving concern. The second limitation is that all three approaches are static rather than dynamic. They rely primarily on map overlays and secondarily on point-rating systems for integrating multiple variables. Although overlays are the fastest way to identify zones that have all of a given set of conditions present, they do not easily identify suitability choices that are less than optimal. Overlays are unable to distinguish very many levels of internal scaling of variables, nor are they able to deal with large numbers of variables and weigh their relative significance. The basic problem with point-rating systems is that they involve an irreducible element of subjectivity that prevents replicability. Neither overlays nor point systems allow for treatment of inherently dynamic variables or for multiple analyses of the same problem under different technical or policy assumptions.

Dynamic Land-Use Models

Dynamic multiple-factor modeling represents the frontier in natural resource analysis approaches. One example, linking recreation and transportation models, can be seen in the Michigan RECSYS model.[9] This computer-based simulation model was designed to predict accurately the effect on the recreational experience of any changes in the condition of the resources themselves, the characteristics of population demand, and the transportation networks.

The RECSYS simulation model has three basic components: an origin model, which describes the characteristics and county locations of the populations who will participate in recreational activities; a travel model, which indicates the characteristics of the highway network that allows people to travel to places of recreation; and a destination model, which describes the attractiveness of the State Parks of Michigan for camping and boating.

Carl Steinitz and Peter Rogers have developed a multisector regional approach linking several allocation and impact-evaluation models that represent the various types of urbanization pressures in metropolitan areas. [10] Their simulation model begins with a projected population increase for five-year iteration periods. Four allocation models are then prepared: an industrial model, a residential model, a recreation and open space model, and a commercial centers model. A fifth model of transportation is also required if most of the transportation routes in the region remain to be established. Four evaluation models (political, fiscal, visual quality, and pollution) then all use a common data inventory organized by the GRID computer system.

In general, the choice between a static or dynamic analysis method is a function of the condition of the available data, the types of problems to be analyzed, the variety of planning alternatives to be considered, and the type and specificity of the planning response required. The local availability of time, money, technology, manpower, and expertise are clearly also to be considered. As noted previously, one critical area in which it has not been possible to make comparisons among alternative approaches is that of cost and efficiency. For a variety of reasons, most of which are obvious, the time, dollar, and manpower costs of resource analysis studies are never stated in their documentation.

Coastal Zone Management

Planning for the coastal zone is a special type of land-use planning, involving the most complex and environmentally sensitive of the land/water interfaces. Typically, it concentrates on the most sensitive of coastal areas — the estuaries and related coastal wetlands. *Estuaries* are areas where surface waters from streams or rivers mix with salt water from the ocean, under tidal influence. *Adjacent coastal wetlands* consist largely of marshes, mud, and salt flats. Estuaries are essentially "nutrient traps" and thus are highly productive biologically. The adjacent wetlands are also significant biologically: they are vital to the chain of marine life. Both areas are valuable to humans not only as fish and wildlife habitats, but also as unique recreational and aesthetic resources.

Coastal zone areas are sensitive to the pressures of urbanization. Roughly 50% of the U.S. population currently lives in coastal counties bordering the oceans, the Gulf of Mexico, and the Great Lakes. Coastal regions are in heavy demand for housing sites, for harbors and marinas, and for industrial uses, particularly power plants. Government plans for major new offshore oil and natural gas development can only intensify this demand. Urbanization brings damming, dredging, filling, water diversions, waste discharge, erosion, sedimentation, and polluted runoff. The planning challenge is to ensure wise use of coastal zone resources so as to maintain environmental quality while also accommodating community needs for housing and economic development. Furthermore, these two goals must be accomplished within the complex framework of federal, state, and local programs and agencies.

The chief federal legislation relevant to these areas is the Coastal Zone Management Act of 1972. Its principal objective is to encourage states to balance development and environmental protection by making deliberate choices among the myriad competing claims on coastal resources. Federal planning grants under the act support state efforts to:

Inventory valuable coastal zone features, such as fragile natural areas, essential wildlife habitats, prime beaches and open space, and historic sites

Establish priorities for land and water use

Plan for natural resource protection and orderly development, keeping in mind national as well as regional and local needs

The act also supports state efforts to preserve estuaries and wetlands, providing matching funds for establishing sanctuaries. The Secretary of Commerce can reject coastal zone management programs proposed by the states but, once approved, the programs apply to activities of the federal government as well.

The Marine Protection, Research and Sanctuaries Act of 1972 (Ocean Dumping Act) provides federal funds for establishing marine sanctuaries in areas of unique ecological, aesthetic, or recreational value. Still other federal programs deal with specific coastal zone problems. They include HUD's Comprehensive Planning Assistance activities, as well as its Flood Insurance Program; NOAA's Sea Grant and Marine Eco-System Analysis programs; Coast Guard efforts to minimize damage from oil spills; Corps of Engineers navigation improvements and erosion-control programs for beaches; and Department of the Interior regulations for development of oil and natural gas resources on the outer continental shelf.

A number of states have broad legislative authority over land use in the coastal zone. California, Delaware, Maine, New Jersey, Rhode Island, and Washington have particularly active planning and management programs for coastal areas. Because of the regional nature of estuaries and the strong pressures for economic development of these areas, local guidance and control programs have been largely ineffective. Individual communities competing for tax ratables have been very reluctant to give up important land-use powers to regional or state bodies and have proved susceptible to pressures from developers to dike and fill. Conflicts between economic growth and environmental quality have often been exaggerated, but genuine conflicts do exist. As the Sixth Annual Report of the Council on Environmental Quality notes, "The virtue of coastal zone planning is to make [these conflicts] explicit, to lay out the arguments on each side, and to help citizens make reasonable — and reasoned — choices."[11]

The critical planning task is to integrate techniques of coastal zone science into the broader land-use and comprehensive planning process. Comprehensive planners can contribute the following essential data toward this end:

Land use, by type of use (residential, industrial, utility, commercial, institutional, agricultural, recreational, and open space)

Population projections, in conjunction with analyses of vacant land, to determine zoning requirements and regional needs for transportation, recreation, and open space

Inventory of environmental features (resources, habitat)

Economic projections, for determining land-use mix needed to support expected jobs and population

Inventory and projections of public facilities, for parks and recreation, community services, educational and cultural facilities, and government facilities

Such data allow planners to define the special land-use problems of the coastal zone and place its special environmental sensitivities in the perspective of anticipated regional growth and development.

To support integrated planning HUD and NOAA have concluded a formal interagency agreement which allows HUD to accept coastal zone management programs approved by the Secretary of Commerce as meeting the minimum land-use planning requirements under Section 701. To the extent that the 701-assisted plan and the CZM program apply to the same geographic areas, approved management programs will be directly incorporated into the full HUD land-use element required of state and substate 701-grant recipients. The agreement includes provisions for communication and coordination between HUD field offices and OCZM at all important junctures, from review of initial grant applications through review and comment on plans prior to formal agency approval.

A recent example of successful estuary planning within a comprehensive planning framework is the Bay Conservation and Development Commission study of San Francisco Bay.[12] The BCDC study collected and analyzed data under twenty-five major headings, including water quality, pollution sources, fish and wildlife, recreation, ports, waterfront industry and housing, and urban design. The resulting development plan emphasized land-use controls, especially regulation of dredge-and-fill operations, in close coordination with local governments. Certain high-priority uses such as regional ports, transportation, and recreation facilities were identified; land was reserved for them, and filling was permitted. A special permit system was proposed to control dredge-and-fill operations. Specific policies were also developed for wetlands management, public access, and the visual appearance of shoreline development.

Perhaps the most methodologically innovative example of integrating coastal zone planning into comprehensive planning and management is provided by the work of the Nassau-Suffolk (N.Y.) Regional Planning Board. Assisted by HUD research funds, the Nassau-Suffolk agency developed an overall planning approach to their coastal zone consisting of twelve separate but closely related component methodologies (refer to Figure 3). This integrated approach was designed to assist regional planning, planning for individual communities, and even planning for localized watersheds and coastal reaches by providing both quantitative and qualitative tools to test goals and develop alternative solutions. The heart of the procedure is the COZMOS computer model. COZMOS enables planners to identify the location and significance of potential water-

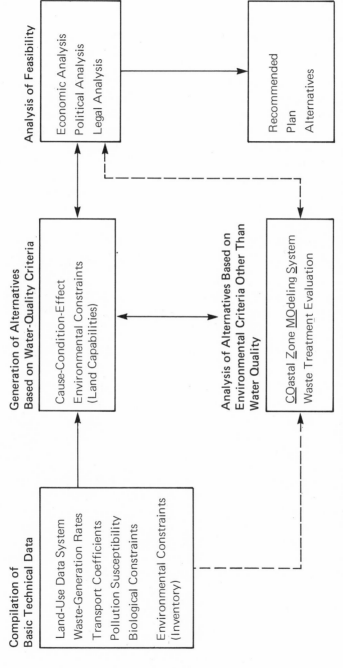

FIGURE 3
Nassau-Suffolk Integrated Methodology Flow Chart

Compilation of
Basic Technical Data

Land-Use Data System
Waste-Generation Rates
Transport Coefficients
Pollution Susceptibility
Biological Constraints

Environmental Constraints
(Inventory)

Generation of Alternatives
Based on Water-Quality Criteria

Cause-Condition-Effect
Environmental Constraints
(Land Capabilities)

Analysis of Alternatives Based on
Environmental Criteria Other Than
Water Quality

COastal Zone MOdeling System
Waste Treatment Evaluation

Analysis of Feasibility

Economic Analysis
Political Analysis
Legal Analysis

Recommended
Plan
Alternatives

Source: *Integration of Regional Land Use Planning and Coastal Zone Science,* Nassau-Suffolk Regional Planning Board,
June 1976.

quality problems resulting from projected types and densities of land uses. COZMOS is not a water-quality model in the sense of estimating short-term dispersions of pollutants from point sources; rather, it predicts average steady-state pollutant concentrations resulting from certain levels and distribution of land use. The cause-condition-effect framework is a supplementary tool for identifying the probable consequences of modifications to the resource base and for suggesting answers to other problems for which the established data base appears inadequate. Although the Nassau-Suffolk package is capable of predicting water-quality conditions under various patterns of land use, there are definite limits to its integrative power. For instance, the COZMOS model considers but does not explicitly take into account water supply, air pollution, and solid waste generation.

Solid Waste Management

Solid waste is anything thrown away, including garbage, rubbish, trash, litter, junk, and refuse from any source (residential, industrial, commercial, institutional, agricultural). This section will concentrate on the bulk of urban solid wastes: the garbage and general refuse usually collected by municipal agencies. Special wastes account for only a minor portion of all solid wastes; hazardous wastes, such as toxic chemicals, pesticides, acids, caustics, flammables, explosives, and biological and radiological residuals will be covered in a later section of this chapter.

Planning for solid waste management requires sensitivity to a number of important environmental considerations. Present options for solid waste management may entail the multiple environmental effects discussed below.

Land Use. Land is needed for transfer, processing, disposal, and resource recovery facilities, purposes which must compete with other urban land-use needs. If land is available, it is often unsuitable because of soil, geology, or topography. And if it is suitable, it may be so isolated from service areas as to be uneconomical.

Water quality. A dangerous by-product of both open dumps and sanitary landfills is *leachate*, a grossly polluted liquid comparable in inorganic content with chemical plant wastes, similar in organic content to food-processing plant effluent, and often containing hazardous concentrations of trace elements and heavy metals. Pollution of ground and surface waters can occur through two different leaching processes. Water moving through solid waste can dissolve solid and liquid pollutants and transport them to ground- and surface-water reservoirs. Also, the carbon dioxide given off by decomposition can dissolve in the groundwater adjacent to the dump or landfill.

Air quality. Refuse incineration, either by controlled munici- pal incinerators or by uncontrolled open burning at dump sites, is a volume-reduction technique widely practiced in many areas of the United States. Overall, the evidence indicates that the contribution of incineration and open burning to national air pollution is small.[13] But in some local areas incomplete combustion can lead to substan- tial adverse consequences due to a greatly increased volume of noxious effluents, especially particulates. These can cause deleterious physiological effects in humans and animals; structural damage and soiling of clothing, buildings, and vegetation; decreased visi- bility; and general aesthetic complaints. Comparison of open-burning emissions with those for controlled municipal incineration indicates that open burning results in significantly higher emissions of hydro- carbons, nitrogen oxides, and organic acids, but lower emissions of particulates.[14]

Noise. An almost neglected externality of sanitary landfill- ing is noise. Noise at landfill sites is generated by compactor and transport trucks unloading their cargoes and by the continuous use of heavy equipment for spreading, compacting, and covering the refuse. *Site location planning*, which locates noise operations away from noise-sensitive receivers and which considers both natural and man-made sources of attenuation, can significantly reduce noise from ground sources such as landfill equipment.

Hazards. When solid waste decomposes in a landfill, gases are produced. Over 90% of these gases are carbon dioxide and methane. Carbon dioxide, mentioned previously in regard to water quality, can lead to pollution of groundwater through leaching. Methane is dangerous because, in high concentrations, it is explosive. A danger of explosion and fire exists when methane seeps into enclosed areas such as adjacent sewer lines or the foundations of buildings located above completed fill sites. Also, methane seepage into the air from completed landfills can occur in sufficient quantity to produce a significant hazard. Although very few instances of explosions or fires have been traced to methane seepage, the potential danger is no less real.

The planning challenge is to anticipate and meet future solid waste management needs in ways that are not only economically feasible and politically acceptable, but also environmentally sensitive. As a first step, solid waste planners need to develop information on:

Existing solid waste management practices

Projected quantity, composition of solid waste

Available alternative management strategies

Facility location options

Relevant laws and ordinances

Existing state solid waste plans

Each of these planning data needs are discussed briefly below.

Existing management practices. Planners need to identify existing methods of collection, transport, processing, and disposal of solid waste, and then to assess their current effects on water quality, noise levels, hazard potential, and public health. Current waste-generation data are needed in terms of political subdivisions, major planning areas, and planning subareas; and the quantities and composition of these wastes must be identified by source types (residential, commercial, industrial, other). Data are needed on equipment and property (including trucks, transfer stations, disposal sites, incinerators, and resource recovery stations) according to type, location, capacity, and life expectancy. Planners also need data on agency finances, organization, manpower, regulations, enforcement, and existing relationships with private systems. A good deal of the data are available from EPA national surveys; the rest can be gathered through special local survey efforts.

Projected quantity, composition. Waste quantity projections are required as a basis for determining needed facilities and their capacity. An inventory of existing land uses, developed by local comprehensive planners, can be used along with current data on solid waste quantities to derive waste-generation rates based on land use. For instance, by dividing present residential acreage into the total solid waste generated by residents living on that acreage, a residential waste-generation rate can be estimated. By examining projected population and land use and by building in a waste "growth" factor, a fairly realistic estimate of future residential solid waste-generation can be made. Further refinement of this approach is possible by distinguishing between single and multifamily residential uses and deriving a generation rate for each. A similar approach can also be employed for estimating future commercial and industrial waste quantities. The advantage of this approach is that it yields not only projected total waste quantities, but also the location or "nodes" of generation. Expected amounts and locations can then be used to determine optimal numbers and locations of transfer stations, reduction and disposal facilities, and equipment.

Available alternative technologies. Comprehensive planners will also want to examine available technological alternatives to open dumping and sanitary landfills. Processing alternatives for which data might be collected and analyzed include size reduction and compaction, incineration with and without heat recovery, production of fuels from waste, separation of wastes for reclamation, mechanical separation, and pyrolysis. Alternatives should be examined in terms of system costs, required transport distances, potential environmental effects, and possibility for resource recovery.

Facility location options. Earth science and related land characteristics data gathered by comprehensive planners can be used to determine the availability of environmentally suitable locations for future landfill sites. Evaluation of a landfill site from the standpoint of the groundwater pollution hazard must take into account all factors that influence hydrologic conditions in the subsurface: depth of the water table, soil permeability, flow gradients, distance to wells, and the geological characteristics of the aquifer network. The hydraulic characteristics of the landfill boundaries are important determinants of the quantities of carbon dioxide and methane produced, so they are critical to groundwater pollution potential and explosion hazard. The level of noise experienced by those living near landfill sites can be reduced by ground characteristics and by wind and temperature gradients; available data on these area characteristics should be accessed.

A particularly important comprehensive planning input to facility location planning is the existing and planned transportation network. Solid waste cannot be moved for processing without using one or more modes of transportation. Transportation facilities contained in comprehensive plans should be related to future solid waste management needs. The transportation information that should be collected and analyzed goes beyond the location of streets and highways and includes such specialized characteristics as travel-way width, surface type, present and projected average daily traffic (ADT), and speed and load limits. A number of planning models help determine optimal locations for solid waste management facilities. Most of these models involve minimizing total system costs; some also incorporate other important management objectives such as minimizing total distance transported and total amounts shipped across designated boundaries. Data inputs typically include generation rates, haul distances, haul routes, transportation costs, facility capacity, fixed and operating costs, and volume-reduction factors. These various models have been evaluated in a recent MIT study done for the National Science Foundation.[15]

Laws and ordinances. Plans for solid waste management will affect and be affected by state laws and local ordinances. An inventory of all laws and ordinances pertinent to solid waste management should be assembled as part of all planning studies. Particularly relevant are laws and ordinances dealing with public health, zoning, subdivision regulation, building codes, air and water pollution, noise abatement and control, public finance, and permissible forms of intergovernmental agreements. The inventory will not only provide the legal framework for planning, but also the basis for proposing new legislation where existing laws are inadequate.

State plans. Regional and local planners must also now take into account state solid waste management plans mandated under the Resource Conservation and Recovery Act. State plans must address responsibilities, regulatory powers, and environmentally sound disposal practices within an organizational and regulatory framework designed to eliminate open dumps, prohibit new dumps, and promote resource conservation and recovery. Federal technical and financial assistance is available for states with approved plans. Guidelines issued under this act also provide for coordination of solid waste planning with groundwater assessments conducted under the Safe Drinking Water Act and with the areawide water-quality planning process funded under Section 208 of the Water Pollution Control Act.

Land Use and Energy Conservation

A new imperative for comprehensive planners is to take into account the consequences of land use changes on energy use. Figure 4 breaks down 1974's total national energy consumption by final uses. The three major sectors involved are industry, buildings, and transportation. Land-use decisions, over time, can affect consumption in each of these categories.

FIGURE 4
Total Energy Use

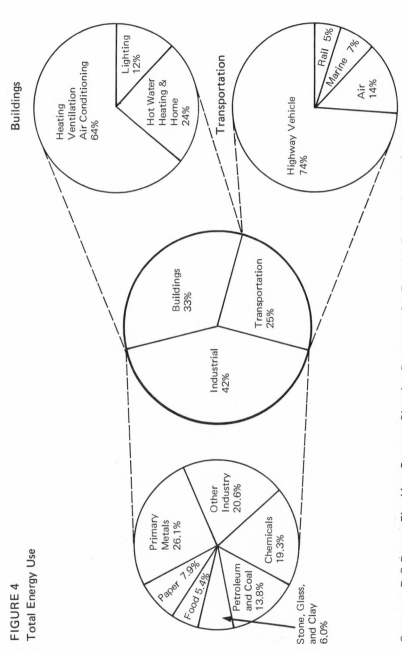

Buildings

Heating
Ventilation
Air Conditioning
64%

Lighting
12%

Hot Water
Heating &
Home
24%

Transportation

Highway Vehicle
74%

Rail 5%

Marine 7%

Air
14%

Buildings
33%

Industrial
42%

Transportation
25%

Primary
Metals
26.1%

Other
Industry
20.6%

Paper 7.9%

Food 5.4%

Petroleum
and Coal
13.8%

Chemicals
19.3%

Stone, Glass,
and Clay
6.0%

Source: D.G.Bauer, *Five Year Program Planning Document for End Use Energy Conservation,*
Research, Development, and Demonstration, Federal Energy Administration, 1974; p. 13.

Industrial energy use. Use of waste heat from utilities and industrial processes can conserve critical fuels by making for increased efficiency in their use and by allowing substitution of noncritical fuels for critical ones. Waste heat can be used in two ways. Process steam and electricity can be produced simultaneously, with substantial energy savings;[16] and waste heat can be used for district heating, sewage treatment, and aquaculture.[17] In either case, land-use issues arise because the considerable heat loss associated with moving steam and heated water from primary to secondary users makes it necessary to locate users next to one another. Land-use policy that encourages the development of such joint sites can promote energy conservation.

Building heating and cooling. Land-use patterns affect space-heating and cooling requirements for residential buildings. Two recent studies have examined the relations between housing density and space-heating and cooling needs.[18] Both studies indicate that higher-density housing, with its generally lower square footage per dwelling, requires less energy. The potential for energy conservation increases if a substantial number of households can be shifted from single-family detached housing and mobile homes to denser forms of housing. "Savings of 40 percent to 60 percent per housing unit seem possible; half due to lower unit size, and half due to the greater energy efficiency of dense housing forms."[19]

Transportation energy use. The amount of energy consumed for transportation is a function of a number of variables including trip length, trip frequency, and mode of travel. Each of these variables is, in turn, a function of other variables which are influenced by the availability of energy, distances among activity centers, and types of travel modes available. Thus, land-use decisions both take account of transportation availability and affect the need for and use of transportation systems. From the standpoint of energy conservation, the planner's task is to determine the transportation effects of proposed land-use changes and then to estimate their effect on energy consumption.

Local land-use patterns and their effects on energy use in transportation have been examined in three recent research efforts.[20] All three studies concluded not only that land-use patterns heavily influence energy use for transportation, but also that most energy-conserving land-use patterns involve clustered activity centers of industrial, commercial, and residential use that foster use of mass transit. Achieving these land-use patterns will require changes in technology (replacement of automobile travel by innovative modes such as Dial-A-Ride and PRT, more efficient internal combustion engines in lighter automobiles) and in life-style (clustering of residences near places of employment, clustering of people with common interests, increased sensitivity to the idea of energy conservation). In their evaluation of the effects on per-capital energy consumption of nine alternative scenarios for passenger transportation in the Trenton, New Jersey SMSA, Fels and Munson concluded that in the long run these life-style changes would be significant in achieving energy conservation.[21] According to their findings, vigorous introduction of new techniques alone would, at best, hold transportation energy consumption in the year 2000 to roughly its current level. But these technologies, if adopted in conjunction with the mixing of land-use types and the clustering of activities, could reduce current consumption levels from 57 to 80% by the year 2000.

Energy planning information. As energy conservation has emerged as a new concern for comprehensive planning, there has been a growing recognition of the need for improved energy information systems to support policy making at state, regional, and local levels. Although considerable work has been done to incorporate energy coefficients into existing models of the national economy, relatively less has been done at the subnational level.[22] Current subnational modeling efforts can be summarized under three major headings: those for direct and indirect energy subsystems and the more limited models of the relation between land use and transportation energy needs.

The major available tool for analyzing the direct energy subsystem of a regional economy is the Reference Energy System (RES).[23] It lists energy sources and end-uses and then relates them, assessing at each of several intervening steps source inefficiencies and storage and conversion losses. Although useful for projecting overall energy requirements and flows for a region, RES does not relate energy use to land-use patterns; that is, it does not trace out the indirect energy subsystem.[24] Input-output models, such as the one developed by Oak Ridge National Laboratory, have been the principal tool used to account for indirect energy demands in a region.[25] The Oak Ridge model can account for the energy sectors in terms of coal, crude petroleum and gas, refined petroleum, electric utilities, and natural gas utilities. However, the ability of the model to determine the energy intensiveness of alternative forms of housing and to answer other related questions about indirect energy costs associated with alternative land-use patterns is still quite limited.

Land-use transportation models have been used by planners to relate land-use patterns specifically to the energy requirements for local transportation. A recent example is a study done for the Metropolitan Washington Council of Governments, which made use of the Council's TRIMS model.[26] The basic limitation of such models has been that they have so far lacked sufficient detail to assess the residential energy impact of alternative development patterns. Also, they tend to be expensive to develop and costly in terms of data collection and processing. An excellent source of information regarding other models of the types mentioned here is a 1975 survey of the states undertaken by the National Governors' Conference.[27]

As for energy-planning coordination, under the terms of a joint DOE-HUD agreement the HUD 701 Comprehensive Planning Assistance Program has become the central federal grant program available for energy-related planning.[28] Through the 701 Program, the two agencies have cooperatively funded a number of demonstration projects designed, among other things, to "integrate energy requirements into comprehensive planning and increase interstate, state, areawide, or local energy-related planning capabilities." An extensive effort is currently underway to disseminate the results of the first round of demonstration projects through development of planning handbooks as well as seminars and training sessions.

Urban Design

The term "urban design" is intentionally broad and includes the full range of local government activities to enhance or preserve the appearance and amenity of the urban physical environment. These activities include:

Design and construction of public facilities

Development of policies, principles, and criteria to guide private-sector design efforts

Legal controls and design-review programs

Preservation of natural and physical environmental elements having historic or cultural value

Traditional concepts of urban design have been changing in the face of growing pressures for urban environmental quality. Public concern is no longer just with the physical or "built" environment; it extends to social, economic, and cultural components. A recent survey of urban design developments noted three particularly significant trends:[29]

> *More systematic approaches.* The major characteristics of recent urban design methods are greater explicitness of goals, objectives, and decision criteria; increased reliance on comprehensive, scientifically based data; systematic procedures for gathering, analyzing, and coding the data; provision for feedback and redesign; and integration of creative and analytic phases.

> *Shift to citywide concern.* There has been a trend away from the district-level focus toward analyzing problems and proposing solutions at the broader city level. This has grown out of a need and desire to develop an overall framework within which to coordinate private development and public urban design.

> *Process orientation.* Planners increasingly recognize that city-building activities gain maximum leverage by influencing private development. They may intervene in the private development decision-making process through framework plans, regulatory devices, and design review, seeking to guide and coordinate private decisions. Or, by implementing projects, renewal programs, and open-space programs within framework plans, they can alter the urban context for private development.

The logical culmination of these related developments is systematic integration of urban design concerns within the comprehensive-planning and management process. Figure 5 shows an initial attempt to accomplish this integration.

Two approaches to achieving planning integration are related to urban design. One involves an urban design study conducted independently, then integrated with social, economic, and technological studies to generate a comprehensive plan. Recent examples of this approach include studies done in San Francisco[30] and Seattle.[31] A second, more ambitious approach calls for urban design studies conducted simultaneously with other related comprehensive-planning studies, with integration provided for at critical points throughout the process. Examples of successful application of this approach include work done in Minneapolis[32] and Dallas.[33] Whichever course is adopted, comprehensive urban design "begin[s] with a process

FIGURE 5
Process-Oriented Urban Design

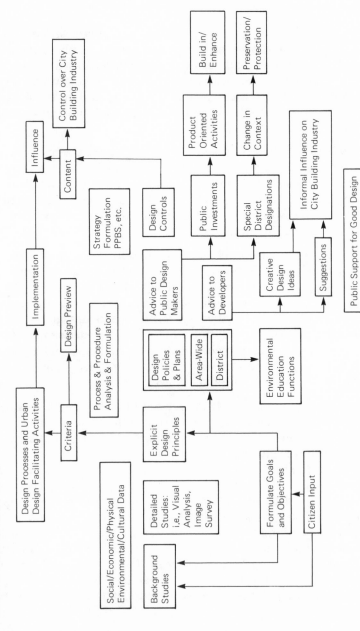

Source: Environmental Protection Agency, *Promoting Environmental Quality Through Urban Planning and Controls*, p. 307.

approach, developing an overall citywide framework with specific objectives, principles, and criteria. This framework is then used to develop policies, capital improvement programs, district regulations, and review procedures . . . as well as to develop design plans and capital improvement projects at the district level. Within this context, specific capital improvement projects, regulations, incentives, and educational programs are devised to influence the environment at the element level."[34]

Planning studies typically involve a visual inventory and analysis of the city. These studies concentrate on form and form-related elements: topography, transportation routes, open space, building mass, general building types, views, neighborhood boundaries, and historic sites. The recent Dallas and Seattle studies also incorporated additional ecological and cultural information. The San Francisco Urban Design Study extended the scope of traditional environmental form and image studies in a number of interesting ways. Four related surveys were conducted: (1) a Quality of Environment Survey; (2) an Internal Pattern and Image Survey; (3) a Road Environment Survey; and (4) an External Form and Image Survey. The Quality of Environment Survey evaluated nine factors: quality of maintenance; quality of view; visual interest of the street facade; block variation; distance to open space; presence of natural elements; compatibility with the natural setting; clarity of local image; and microclimate. The Internal Pattern and Image Survey entailed identification, evaluation, and mapping of important physical features that serve to structure and organize a city: focal points, viewpoints, landmarks, and movement patterns. An analysis of these factors, combined with the results of the Quality of Environment Survey, enabled planners to interpret design problems and opportunities by individual planning areas. The Road Environment Survey looked at roadway characteristics and evaluated them according to level of maintenance, spaciousness, order, monotony, clarity of route, orientation to destination, and safety and ease of movement. The final External Form and Image Survey looked at the city's existing skyline using selected photographs. The results of the four surveys were then displayed on two maps, one a summary map of visual elements of city form, the other a map of visual problems and potentials.

There are a number of other related approaches to the conduct of visual surveys. A convenient reference to these other approaches is provided by a recent HUD-supported study of the relation of urban design to comprehensive planning.[35]

WATER QUALITY

Planning studies for water quality have traditionally been one of two types: either river basin studies or studies focusing on urban water-quality management. The former emphasize broad objectives relative to the full range of water resource issues and cover a wide geographic area; the latter are more oriented to day-to-day management, geared to specific local demands and a narrow range of alternatives related to building and operating treatment facilities. River basin studies, because of their broad geographic scope, have not proven particularly useful to urban or metropolitan areas. On the other hand, more focused urban management studies have not fully examined the available alternatives, including nonstructural approaches, to dealing with complex land-use/water-quality interrelations. "What is needed is a combination of regional objectives and long-range planning perspective [with] urban management and operations expertise and more broadly focused urban land use guidance strategy and tools."[36]

The most promising vehicle for achieving this kind of planning integration is the Section 208 Areawide Waste Treatment Management planning process, funded under the 1972 amendments to the Federal Water Pollution Control Act. Section 208 plans are clearly intended to deal with urban and urbanizing areas where substantial water-quality problems exist "as a result of urban-industrial concentration or other factors." Their areawide scope is broad enough to encompass an entire metropolitan region, unlike some urban-oriented management studies, but it is not so broad as to preclude consideration of alternatives that basin-wide studies have addressed in the past. Substantively, Section 208 studies are intended to address controls on both point and nonpoint sources and thus avoid an overly narrow engineering approach. They are also supposed to retain the broad "issue focus" of basin studies. Section 208 studies are concerned not only with achieving the 1983 goal of "fishable-swimmable" water but also with related aspects of water-quality protection such as conservation and reuse, management of residual wastes, and protection of groundwater. Other community goals to be considered in selecting a final 208 plan include effects on other environmental media, recreation, housing, and economic development. "[Section] 208 planning should be viewed as providing the water quality component of the comprehensive plan for the areas," and "the relationship between water quality and other [community] goals should be understood from the outset of the planning process."[37] Thus, Section 208 planning studies represent a new middle ground in terms of water-quality planning. River basin and facilities-oriented planning are still provided for under PL 92-500, [Sections 303(e) and 201, respectively], but they must now be reconciled for major metropolitan regions with a consistent 208 areawide framework.

The Section 208 Plan

The substantive areas to be covered by a 208 plan can be identified conveniently under four headings: (1) treatment works; (2) regulatory programs; (3) processes for identifying and controlling nonpoint sources; and (4) identification of management agencies.

First, the plan must identify the collection and treatment works that will be needed in order to meet anticipated needs over a twenty-year period. It will be necessary, then, to coordinate expansion of collection and treatment capacity with expected growth and development. Section 201 facility plans completed or well underway before the 208 planning process begins must be incorporated into Section 208 plans.

Second, a 208 plan must establish a regulatory program (1) to assure the conduct of areawide waste treatment management and the control or treatment of all point and nonpoint sources of pollution within the area, including in-place or accumulated sources; (2) to "regulate the location, modification, and construction of any facilities within such area which may result in any discharge in such area"; and (3) to enforce applicable pretreatment requirements for industrial or commercial wastes. Such a program might establish special permit systems for sewer connections, subsurface disposal, land-disturbing activities causing runoff, and so forth, all backed up by monitoring and enforcement capabilities.

Third, a 208 plan must include processes for identifying specified types of nonpoint sources (runoff from agricultural and silvicultural activities, mines, and construction sites; salt water intrusion) and for deciding upon procedures and methods, including land-use requirements, to control such sources as much as possible. With a view to protecting the quality of ground and surface water, Section 208 plans must also specify processes for controlling the disposition of residual wastes (sludge or precipitates from treatment facilities designed to remove air or water pollutants) and the disposal of pollutants on land or in subsurface excavations (dumps and septic tanks). Since a 208 plan must be "applicable to all wastes generated within the area involved," it will likewise have to address itself to any other nonpoint sources beyond those specified here. Section 208 makes it possible, however, for the state to take over the regulation of nonpoint sources.

Fourth, the 208 plan must identify the agencies necessary to construct, operate, and maintain all facilities required to carry out the plan. Implementing agencies will include some with managerial, and some with regulatory, powers. The governors, in consultation with the planning agencies, will then designate the management agencies. They will be acceptable to EPA if they have all necessary managerial and fiscal authority to carry out appropriate portions of the plan.

Initial Section 208 plans must be certified by the governors and submitted to the EPA administrator not later than two years after the planning process is in operation or after the planning grant is received. After the management agencies have been designated and the plan for a 208 area has been approved, the law prohibits EPA from making any grant for construction of publicly owned treatment works within the area except to the designated management agency for works in conformity within the plan. Moreover, no permit may thenceforth be issued under Section 402 of the act for any point source that is in conflict with an approved 208 plan. These are the only means expressly provided in the law for enforcing implementation of Section 208.

The Section 208 areawide planning process, as defined by EPA, consists of seven generalized planning tasks:

1. Inventory of existing and potential discharges and characterization of possible problems
2. Data collection and projection of population, employment, and land use over the planning period
3. Projection of wasteloads over the planning period
4. Determination of effects of water quality
5. Determination of necessary wasteload reductions
6. Development of alternative strategies of wasteload reduction to achieve and maintain standards
7. Evaluation of strategies and selection of a preferred alternative

In carrying out these tasks, Section 208 planners are required to seek every opportunity to integrate water-quality planning into comprehensive planning and management.

Water Quality and Land Use

The most important integrating influence at work under Section 208 is the requirement to consider nonstructural pollution-control alternatives, primarily land-use and land management controls. It is stated EPA policy to "ensure that full consideration be given to attaining an appropriate balance of nonstructural . . . and structural . . . methods in order to achieve and maintain environmental quality standards most effectively and most economically,"[38] and further, that "land use controls may provide a means of preventing environmental damages and . . . may be used as alternative or supplemental measures to other pollution control methods.[39]

A particular land-use pattern is determined by characteristics of form, density, land mix, and rate of land conversion. These underlying determinants of land-use patterns can have significant impact on water quality in both developing and developed areas. In developing areas, certain environmentally sensitive lands play an important role in protecting or — if improperly developed — in degrading ground- and surface-water quality. The direct costs to the public of failing to protect these lands can be high, for lack of attention will eventually require expensive storm sewers, higher levels of water and wastewater treatment, and new sources of water supply. Some of the more important of these land types include:

Streams and creekbeds

Aquifers and their recharge areas

Wetlands

Woodlands

Steep slopes

Specific rationales for protecting each of these land types from inappropriate development are briefly summarized below.[40]

Streams and creekbeds. Streams and creeks play two important roles within the hydrologic cycle. First, they contribute major drainage systems carrying runoff and sediment from higher elevations to low-lying land and water bodies. Second, they contribute water to aquifers during the wet season and receive groundwater through springs or seepage during the dry periods. Development in these areas, by removing vegetation and introducing impervious surfaces, increases erosion and sedimentation which, in turn, increases stream turbidity and reduces available oxygen in the water.

The increased runoff introduces urban pollutants in such forms as petroleum products, fertilizers, and road salts. Removal of shading vegetation can increase thermal pollution of the streams. Development also can adversely affect the overall hydrologic balance within the watershed. Streambed siltation obstructs natural flows from surface to groundwater; streamflow becomes irregular, with lower base flows and high peak flows, raising the level of flooding.

Aquifers. Groundwater is carried by *aquifers*, formations composed of consolidated (limestone, basalt) and unconsolidated (sand, gravels) rock. This underground water supply is fed by seepage from streams and lakes as well as by precipitation which percolates directly to the aquifer. Groundwater is an important source of water for human consumption and helps regulate surface flow by absorbing water during wet periods and releasing it during dry periods. It also acts as a natural filter, since percolation of water through the soil and other formations removes certain impurities.

Inappropriate or unregulated development on or near aquifers can affect water unfavorably in a number of important ways. By covering recharge areas with relatively impervious surfaces that effectively seal them to percolation, development decreases recharge of the groundwater supply and increases runoff. Development that pumps water in excess of aquifer recharge rates will cause the groundwater reservoir to fall, not only reducing the available supply, but also causing land surfaces to sink. Where fresh groundwater is located near saline groundwater, overpumping can also decrease the natural flow from fresh to saline, resulting in saline pollution of the freshwater reservoir. The location of septic tanks or cesspools at or below the water table, subterranean disposal of wastes, agricultural activities involving concentrations of fertilizers or animal wastes, and poorly constructed chemical or petroleum storage tanks can also allow harmful substances to enter the aquifer.

Wetlands. The term "wetlands" encompasses a variety of ecological areas that are generally classified by their vegetation, water type (fresh, saline), and predominant water depth. These areas include fresh and saline meadows, marshes, swamps, bogs, bays, and open water. Performing a number of vitally important natural functions, these areas affect water quality by filtering out silt and other pollutants, slowing runoff, and changing inorganic nutrients into acceptable nutrient material. Wetlands also serve to stabilize water quantity by absorbing excess flows during flood periods and retaining water during droughts. They are particularly important for the maintenance of fish and wildlife habitats; they provide critical breeding, nesting, and feeding grounds for birds, fish, and other aquatic animals; and they contribute to the food chains of upland plants and animals. Finally, in addition to supporting general ecosystem health, wetlands have value as recreation, education, and aesthetic resources.

Development or alteration of wetlands can create serious water-quality and related environmental problems. Upland development can lead to nutrient and sediment inflows that exceed the natural filtering capacity of the wetlands. When wetlands can no longer efficiently transform nutrients into harmless inorganic matter and remove suspended sediment, the nutrients stimulate eutrophication. The increased turbidity resulting from the sediment reinforces the depletion of available oxygen in the stream, degrading water quality and killing fish. Wetlands may function as recharge areas for groundwater, groundwater discharge areas, or catch basins for overland flow. Development that increases upland runoff or affects groundwater levels can upset the intricate cycling of water among wetlands, groundwater, and surface water, thus impeding the wetlands' ability to counteract floods and droughts.

Woodlands. Woodlands help protect soil resources, moderating the effect of storms and wind by reducing erosion and sedimentation. Also important for water quality, forest vegetation slows runoff, allowing pollutants to be filtered out before water reaches groundwater reservoirs. Clearly, woodlands represent valuable resources to the community for a host of other reasons. Aside from the economic value of the timber, they present opportunities for recreation and aesthetic enjoyment. They are a diverse environment, home for a variety of plants and animals and thus a significant factor in wildlife conservation. Woodlands also moderate the local climate, since the shade and transpiration of the forest microclimate stabilize air temperature and buffer urban noise.

Steep slopes. Hillsides are biological features which, in combination with vegetation, soils, and precipitation, affect the natural balance of the hydrologic system. Hillsides move naturally as the result of gradual weathering and erosion. However, development that removes vegetation sharply increases soil and slope instability by increasing the amount of water in the soil. Construction that alters the natural formation of rocks, soils, and other components of a slope will make it more susceptible to slides and slumps. Development that removes vegetation or otherwise alters natural drainage patterns will increase runoff and erosion. Steep slopes and soils that are relatively less permeable (clays, for example) are particularly prone to this problem. Radical changes in hillsides due to erosion will, in turn, affect surface-water quality, groundwater quality and quantity, and stream flow.

Improper construction techniques can leave the landscape permanently scarred. The aesthetic damage is compounded where site planning and design ignore the natural contours of the terrain and obliterate the hillside itself; after all, slopes provide distinctive relief to the landscape and interesting settings for human activities.

In more highly developed areas, additional urban development can lead to reduced infiltration due to increased amounts of impervious surfaces and runoff of increasing volume and velocity. Such changes in an area's natural hydrologic balance can have serious consequences for water quality. The two major water-quality problems associated with more intensive urban development are (1) erosion and sedimentation and (2) surface and subsurface pollution.

Erosion and Sedimentation

The construction phase of urban development can result in significant alteration of the landscape, the extent of which usually depends upon the size of the development. One common construction cost is large-scale removal of vegetative cover. The result of this operation in terms of the hydrograph, is increased runoff resulting from increased quantity and velocity of flow. Both of these factors lead to significant erosion. The actual amount worked away from the site will depend upon the extent of surface area exposed to the runoff and the characteristics of the soil. The sediment washed from areas undergoing urban development is from five to five hundred times as great as that from undeveloped rural areas. The consequences of erosion are loss of productive topsoil and the deposition of the soil, including its organic constituents, in streams, marshes, lakes, and other water bodies. Streambed organisms and plants are smothered, the water bodies' storage capacity for water supply and flood control is destroyed, and there is an increase in the rate of eutrophication.

Sedimentation not only interferes with the functioning of the natural ecosystem, but also with the uses which mankind usually expects to make of water bodies. Sedimentation of streams and rivers with a heavy organic load decreases their aeration capacity and the ability of the water to assimilate discharges from waste-water treatment facilities. Furthermore, deposition of the sediment in reservoirs reduces their capacity for all uses — water supply, power generation, or flood storage. In due time these dams will retain only silt, and the original problem (water supply, power, and flood control) will still have to be solved. Sedimentation also interferes with the use of water bodies for recreational purposes. The destruction of bottom or bed life and the inflow of organic matter can result in an oxygen decrease that kills fish. Finally, the transport of sediment in streams and lakes reduces their aesthetic appeal.

Studies of river channels have shown that the natural forces inherent in periodic flows naturally construct and maintain channels with the capacity to carry a volume smaller than the average flood. This finding means that, on the average, such rivers overflow their banks every one and a half to two years. With runoffs of increasing volumes and velocity, the short-term result is flooding and the long-term consequence is an increase in the channel's cross-sectional area through erosion of its banks. This increase means additional deposits of sedimentation downstream.

Surface and Subsurface Pollution

The constituents of pollutants deposited on the surface of urban environments vary widely, ranging from common organic material to highly toxic metals. Some pollutants — road salt, insecticides, herbicides — are intentionally placed on the surface, only to be carried away by the runoff. Others — such as lead from automobile exhausts and oil drippings from trucks and cars — are the unintentional residue of man's activities. Such pollutants appear to vary according to the land use and intensity of land use.

For a given frequency of rainfall, increasing urbanization leads to greater removal of these surface pollutants due to the increased quantity and velocity of the resulting runoff. This becomes important when one realizes that the most significant pollution occurs when there is just enough runoff to carry pollutants to the receiving water but no further; such runoff guarantees minimal dilution in the streams. For the same frequency of rainfall occurrences, this means that urbanization will result more often in greater scouring or washing of the pollutants into the streams.

Leaching refers to the removal of soluble materials by percolating water. If these soluble materials are pollutants, this removal is harmful. Subsurface leachage is intentional in the draining of a septic tank. However, if a leaching field is blocked or otherwise fails, proper leaching does not occur and subsurface water containing pollutants often works its way to the surface. There it can be picked up by runoff and carried to nearby bodies of water, resulting in their degradation. Leaching often occurs at landfills, as rainfall percolates down through the site where wastes have been disposed. If water percolating through this waste picks up soluble materials or harmful virus and bacteria and later becomes part of the groundwater that augments streamflow, these pollutants may also be carried into the stream. Proper landfill location and operation minimizes leaching problems.

Planning Integration Under Section 208

Recognizing the importance of the relation between water quality and land use, EPA and HUD have concluded a formal interagency agreement to "ensure that land use planning undertaken for water quality purposes is developed within the framework of comprehensive planning . . . . In those geographic areas where both a 701 land-use element and a 208 areawide waste-treatment management plan will be developed, planning agencies will demonstrate in their work programs how activities under both the 701 and 208 programs will be coordinated so as to ensure that (1) there is no duplication of effort; (2) completed plans will be consistent; and (3) the objectives of both programs will be achieved."[41]

Projections/Modeling

A necessary starting point for such coordination is a common set of projections of future areawide population and economic growth. The EPA Program Guidance Memorandum regarding coordination of Section 208 and air quality maintenance planning, for instance, calls for a "coordinated search of existing economic, demographic . . . and other baseline data . . . prior to the development of the data base" for the two planning efforts and, further, use of "consistent economic and demographic projections" in developing projections of future land use and pollutant loads.[42] The Section 208 planning guidelines underscore the point that the resulting land-use projections "should be consistent with those used in other programs, especially air quality, coastal zone management, and HUD-funded land use elements."[43] To ensure such consistency the

EPA 208-AQMA Program Guidance Memorandum urges adoption of a "common classification system . . . for land use and economic factors so that the data will be compiled using a similar format."[44]

Section 208 land-use inventories and projections focus on the origins of potential nonpoint sources of pollution. Watershed parameters particularly important to NSP include:

Topographic and soil-series classifications

Bodies of water and related lands that would be beneficially or adversely affected by a change in water quality

Water supply, treatment, and distribution systems

Existing waste treatment and collection systems, including interim facilities and major urban storm drainage facilities

Solid waste disposal sites

Areas presently served by septic tanks and areas suitable for septic tanks at specified densities

Environmentally sensitive areas

Once the extent of nonpoint source problems has been determined in terms of loadings for specific pollutants, several planning approaches exist for tracing them to their origin within the watershed. These techniques are generalized predictive modeling, local monitoring, and sampling. Predictive techniques are advantageous because monitoring and sampling for NPS is costly and requires a long time to collect accurate data. The Section 208 guidelines suggest primary reliance on predictive approaches for this reason, with monitoring and sampling restricted only to those situations where more accurate estimates are needed than can be obtained by modeling.

Using regression techniques, the form of the relation between land use/economic activity and water quality in a particular watershed can be estimated on the basis of limited sample data. An excellent example of this approach is a study carried out for EPA in the Brandywine watershed in Pennsylvania.[45] The study set out to estimate a predictive equation for changes in water quality due to changes in patterns of urbanization in the watershed. Despite variability in urbanization patterns and the multitude of complex physical processes by which these activities affect water quality (including point source phenomena, nonpoint loads, contamination through the groundwater system), changes in water quality were treated as independent variables and data were gathered on selected water-quality parameters for fifty-eight streams on two consecutive days at low-flow conditions. The sample of streams, all of which were located in the piedmont portion of the Philadelphia metropolitan area consisted of watersheds ranging between one and six square miles in area. Due to the small size of the streams studied, the watersheds contained relatively few water-using industries. Therefore, the study focused more on water pollution caused by human residence than on industrial pollution. The dependent variables thus used to "explain" the observed water-quality levels were, with the exception of stream discharge, variables relating to watershed conditions, primarily conditions relating to land use and activity. These variables were all prepared using a watershed grid system, with grid squares forty acres in size. The values of the quantities in question were measured and recorded for each individual grid square and then summed over the entire watershed. In some cases, variables were weighted by other quantities observed for individual grid squares before being summed.

The analysis procedure was to enter the watershed variables into a step-wise multiple regression analysis routine, which estimated the statistical form of the relation between each of the land-use and activity variables and the measured water-quality parameters. Considerable experimentation was done with the exact analysis procedure, including adding and deleting independent and dependent variables in the regression. The results of the analysis were encouraging. The basic watershed activity variables showed a high level of explanation for each of the water-quality parameters.

Interagency Coordination

The Section 208 planning guidelines, as well as EPA guidance on continuing planning for water-quality management at the state level, recognize the possibility of conflict among separate environment-related planning programs. Thus they call for early and frequent coordination of efforts.

Conflicts can arise because of intermedia effects. An obvious example is the use of control technologies and equipment which, although reducing emissions to one medium, have the effect of transferring the pollution problem to another medium. Lime/limestone scrubbers, which are means for reducing SO_2 emissions, produce a liquid sludge which must be disposed of. Conversely, sewage treatment plants may try to dispose of sludge through incineration, thus increasing air-quality problems. Such problems can also affect energy production. A fossil-fueled electric generator may be undesirable because of air-quality limitations, but a nuclear generating plant may be unable to meet thermal pollution standards.

Conflicts can also arise over the issue of community growth. Where should it occur? How should it be distributed? And how much should be allowed? To continue the previous line of examples of potential conflict between water quality and air-quality management planning, the location of waste-treatment plants and sewer interceptors can induce and guide growth toward the serviced areas. But those areas planned for expanded sewerage service may already have air-quality problems which increased growth would simply exacerbate. In Ocean County, New Jersey, for instance, the combination of the expansion of the Garden State Parkway and a large proposed treatment plant would have permitted both a rapidly accelerating growth rate and more severe air pollution problems. Citizen objections finally resulted in a smaller plant. In the Washington, D.C. metropolitan area, a large interceptor was run out to serve the Dulles International Airport through land which was largely undeveloped. The combined attractions of the airport and sewer service put severe pressure on local communities to accommodate greater development and thus more pollution.

Water quality and air quality management programs may also consciously attempt to guide growth toward different distributions. In designing an air-quality maintenance (AQMA) plan, for example, the planning agency may want to use emission-density zoning and establish emission limits for different areas. An industrial zone might have a limit of three tons of total suspended particulates per square mile, while the limit for a commercial zone would be considerably less. However, wasteload allocations consistent with maintaining water quality may necessitate a diffferent land-use configuration which would not correspond to air-quality zones. For example, the location of additional heavy industry within an area may lower the quality of the receiving water below standards even though favorable meteorological conditions make it a desirable location in terms of air-quality maintenance.

On a larger scale, the two programs may favor different general growth patterns. In one area, for example, substantial immigration and a concommitant demand for housing might result from increasing job opportunities. New housing construction to meet the increased demand might occur primarily in the urban fringe, where excess treatment capacity exists. Indirect sources such as shopping centers would accompany the residential construction and, as a result, air-quality standards might not be attained or maintained. In addition, adequate mass transit might not be available, and the inevitable increase of motor vehicle use could cause substantial air-quality problems. Thus, the development pattern best suited to meet the requirements of a water-quality plan may indeed conflict with the needs for air-quality maintenance planning.[46]

EPA guidance to Section 208 planners stresses coordination, not only with air quality maintenance area planning, but also with:

Comprehensive local and regional planning, particularly land-use planning sponsored under the HUD 701 program

Water supply programs, particularly those set up under the Safe Drinking Water Act

Coastal zone planning and management, sponsored by NOAA and the various state departments of marine affairs

Solid waste management planning, regarding water pollution resulting from solid waste and residuals disposal

Soil conservation, forestry, and agricultural planning conducted by USDA and state departments of agriculture

Transportation planning carried out by FHWA and UMTA

Recreation planning, particularly the State Comprehensive Outdoor Recreation Plan (SCORP) developed with funding from the Department of Interior

The Corps of Engineers Urban Studies Program

AIR QUALITY

Air quality is an especially important environmental-planning concern for integration into comprehensive planning and management. Air pollution affects people in urban areas through (1) effects on human health (morbidity, mortality); (2) effects on other living organisms (which then influence humanity); (3) effects on materials (soiling, corrosion); and (4) aesthetic and nuisance effects (odors, smoke, fumes). The Clean Air amendments of 1970 directed EPA to establish primary and secondary ambient air-quality standards (NAAQS's) for various pollutants, essentially levels that must not be exceeded for longer than a specified period of time. Primary standards reflect protection; "requisite to protect the public health." Secondary standards, although more stringent, are less specific: they are designed to "protect the public welfare from any known or anticipated adverse effects associated with the presence of such air pollutant in the ambient air."[47]

Air Quality and Comprehensive Planning

The Clean Air Act and its supporting regulations recognize transportation and land-use controls as important means of attaining and maintaining air-quality standards. State Implementation Plans (SIP's) must include "emission limitations, schedules, and timetables for compliance with such limitations and other such measures as may be necessary to ensure attainment and maintenance of . . . standards, including but not limited to transportation controls . . . and preconstruction review of direct sources of air pollution . . . ."[48] The provision for preconstruction review can certainly be construed as a land-use control measure even though it is not identified as one. SIP's must include "a procedure . . . for review, prior to construction or modification of the location of new sources . . . [of air pollution which] shall provide for adequate authority to prevent the construction or modification of any new source to which a [federal] standard of performance will apply at any location which the state determines will prevent the [achievement] of such standard . . . ."[49] Moreover, the relative importance of transportation and land-use controls vis-à-vis source emission limitations is steadily increasing as the planning challenge shifts from initial attainment of standards to their long-term maintenance and to the prevention of "significant deterioration" in air quality in now-pristine areas.

A successful court suit brought by the Natural Resources Defense Council forced EPA to reject the first round of State Implementation Plans developed under the 1970 legislation because they failed to include adequate measures to maintain national ambient air-quality standards. Although most SIP's had adequate maintenance provisions to ensure that major stationary sources did not by themselves cause the standards to be exceeded, no plan had specific provisions to ensure that standards would not be exceeded due to (1) clustering of mobile sources; (2) clustering of small-point sources that were not subject to individual review; (3) rapid and extensive growth of area sources such as light industry;

and (4) major shifts in population centers with associated residential and commercial growth.

In response, EPA developed two new approaches: indirect source review and the preparation of Air Quality Maintenance Area (AQMA) plans. Under the first approach states, but preferably local governments, can review all new developments above a certain size that threaten to cause new, or exacerbate existing, violations of air-quality standards by inducing transportation-related emissions. Such developments include parking facilities, shopping centers, airports, and sports arenas. Although the review is intended primarily to require good design rather than to prohibit construction, the latter result is certainly a possibility. In July 1975, however, EPA indefinitely suspended those portions of federally promulgated indirect source review regulations covering parking-related facilities. The second response, the AQMA planning program, is aimed more at long-range planning solutions. It requires states to determine which areas, due to projected growth rates, may present threats to continued maintenance of air standards. Over 150 such AQMA's have been so designated, the vast majority representing the major urbanized areas of the country; however, a few AQMA's which are currently sparsely populated are expected to undergo massive development in the near future. AQMA analysis will project population and economic growth for at least the next ten years and determine the impact of that growth on air quality. The effects of existing controls are to be factored into the analysis and, if the results show that these controls are indeed adequate to ensure maintenance of standards, then no further action is necessary. However, it is anticipated that existing controls in most AQMA's will not be adequate because the combined effect of new large-point sources and the multitude of new small sources typical of high-growth urbanizing areas were not sufficiently considered in the development of these controls. In such cases, AQMA plans with additional controls have to be developed. The modifications and additions will be primarily land-use and transportation-control measures, including emission-density zoning and a requirement for EIS's prior to decisions on requests for land-use changes.

A second successful court suit, this one brought by the Sierra Club, challenged EPA's practice of allowing deterioration of air quality in relatively clean areas. As a result, no "significant deterioration" will be allowed in these areas in the future. Under EPA regulations, areas may be categorized by states as coming under one of three classes. Each class has a different allowable increase in total suspended particulates (TSP) and sulphur dioxide (SO_2). Class I applies to areas where almost any increase in concentrations of the two pollutants would be considered significant deterioration of air quality. Class II applies to areas where the air-quality deterioration which normally accompanies well-planned growth would be considered insignificant. Class III applies to those areas where deterioration to the pollutant concentrations established as ambient air-quality standards would be considered insignificant. Initially, all areas where significant deterioration is potentially an issue are designated by EPA as Class II areas. However, EPA regulations permit states, federal land managers, and Indian governing bodies to request that any such areas for which they have responsibility be redesignated as either Class I or Class III to accommodate social, economic, or environmental needs. A public hearing is a prerequisite to reclassification. An analysis of the effects of reclassification which considers regional and national as well as local needs must also be prepared and be available to the public prior to the hearing.

The EPA regulations are implemented through a preconstruction review of proposed developments in those areas which fall under one of nineteen major industrial and energy sources of air pollution. According to which class an area is assigned, any major new source in one of these nineteen industry categories that would violate that class's standard of significant deterioration would be prohibited from locating in that area. Other types of development are not affected by the regulations. Implicit in any local move to reclassify an area would be a conscious local decision regarding those areas to which major industry is to be attracted. Hence, the effect would be to provide guidance to industry regarding where to locate certain major new facilities.

Both maintenance of ambient air-quality standards and prevention of significant deterioration involve controlling the amount and location of future emissions. The fundamental process to be followed is a combination of emission limitations and land-use planning. In the past, air pollution control consisted of identifying the major sources of pollution and imposing requirements to reduce emissions, either to the lowest practical level or at least to that level that would protect the public health and welfare. Air pollution control did not involve any long-range planning and therefore did not get directly involved in the land-use planning process. With the new requirements, air pollution control will have to devote as much attention to where a source should and should not locate as to determining what emission limitations that source should meet.

As with water quality, HUD has taken a strong position that AQMA plans should "incorporate the benefits of advanced comprehensive land use planning — a process involving simultaneous consideration of community, social, economic, physical development, and aesthetic goals in the analysis of employment, housing, traffic, and other functions, as well as the use of land, water, air, energy and natural resources, and consideration of multiple 'quality of life' requirements." Further, HUD stresses that in the development of AQMA plans "greater reliance [be placed] on input from the ongoing comprehensive planning process of the land use planning agencies normally supported by HUD's Section 701 program" rather than on independent development of a land-use element by the AQMA planning agency or on uncritical adoption of the conventional land-use element contained in regional transportation plans.[50]

How this integration of AQMA planning and the land-use and transportation elements of local comprehensive plans will be achieved is a matter of great concern. Unlike regional water-quality planning, "little air quality planning has been conducted, and what has been done in preparation of SIP's has been the type to direct emission regulatory programs. It has been done mostly by state antipollution agencies. Very few local governments and COG's have conducted air quality planning, nor even included air quality as an element of a comprehensive land use plan."[51] HUD's concern extends beyond just regional land use and transportation planning to include physical design for air quality, that is, site design and construction considerations affecting indoor as well as outdoor areas.

AQMA Analysis and the Comprehensive Plan

AQMA planning follows the same general logic as that of Section 208 areawide water-quality management planning:

Inventory of existing and potential emissions and characterization of possible problems

Data collection and projection of population, employment, and land use over the planning period

Projection of emissions over the planning period

Determination of effects on air quality

Determination of necessary emission reductions

Development of alternative strategies of emission reduction to achieve and maintain standards

Evaluation of strategies and selection of a preferred alternative

Major elements of AQMA analysis include development of a current emission inventory; projection of emission patterns for a number of possible futures; measurement and interpretation of current air-quality and meteorological data; use of inventory and measurement data to develop appropriate simulation models; and use of these models to project future air quality associated with the projected emissions. The output of the analysis — projected future air quality— is then compared with national standards. If it appears that they will be exceeded without additional measures to control the type, amount, and location of future emission sources, then an AQMA plan that develops and evaluates alternative maintenance strategies and provides for implementation of the preferred strategy must be formulated.

Development of alternative maintenance strategies and evaluation of their impact on improved future air quality is reserved for the following chapter. The discussion here will concentrate on the AQMA analysis of future problems in the absence of additional control measures. Clearly, existing and planned land uses and transportation facilities are a critically important input into AQMA analysis. The emission inventory is constructed from a source inventory plus data on emission factors. The source inventory consists of a list of the number, size, location, and (in the case of large sources) emission release characteristics affecting the height of the source's effluent. Numerous small sources are listed collectively as "area" sources and may be aggregated on a county basis or disaggregated to a network of grid squares using such schemes as the Computer-Assisted Area Source Emissions Gridding Procedure (CAASE). Longer-range forecasting of emissions involves estimation of the number, type, and location of new sources; the attrition and modification of existing sources; and the emission factors applicable to both new and existing sources. These estimates are then used to alter the existing or base emission inventory. The important question from the standpoint of the comprehensive planning and management process is whether a land-use element being developed by an air pollution control agency with limited authority, limited staff, and limited roots in ongoing local land-use planning can be adequate to the AQMA job. The same question applies to the conventional land-use element contained in transportation plans, as it is frequently developed on straight-line extrapolation of previous growth trends. "There appears to be a tendency to equate land use planning, which is a comprehensive political process, with the land use element in transportation planning, which is only a carefully calculated technical hypothesis of growth, with limited political screening . . . . Only the land use alternatives developed by the land use [planning] agency, in close cooperation with the air quality staff and with other functional planning agencies, will have a high correlation with final implemented forms of growth and will represent a balance among the multiple objectives of the community."[52]

Air-quality planning should be closely integrated with comprehensive planning and management at all important points of contact, including not only the initial analysis but also plan formulation, evaluation, and update.[53] A model for implementing such coordination between AQMA and land-use planning already exists: it is the one already worked out between HUD and EPA regarding Section 208 water-quality planning.[54] According to this approach, the HUD 701 land-use element would provide the basic land-use planning including (1) long- and short-term policies regarding where growth should and should not take place; (2) the type, intensity, and timing of growth; and (3) studies, criteria, standards, and implementing procedures necessary for effectively guiding and controlling major growth location decisions. Land-use evaluation under AQMA planning would be more narrowly directed to (1) determining the most efficient air-quality maintenance strategies consistent with the basic land-use plan; and (2) analyzing land-use/air quality relations to determine what modificatons should be made to the basic land-use plan for the purpose of managing future point, line, and area sources of air pollution. Further integration in planning along the lines of this approach is possible given EPA's stated policy intention to "designate, when possible, the same agency to do both 208 and AQMA planning."[55] Nearly all designated Section 208 agencies are Councils of Government (COG's), which typically perform HUD 701 comprehensive planning. Some Metropolitan Planning Organizations (MPO's), which conduct DOT-supported regional transportation planning, are also COG's. These multiple-purpose agencies would be able to integrate air-quality, water-quality, comprehensive land-use and, in some cases, transportation planning.

AQMA Data and Analysis Needs

As part of conducting AQMA analysis, planners must: (1) measure/estimate current emissions; (2) project future emissions; (3) measure/estimate current ambient air quality; and then (4) project future ambient concentrations. Data on matters other than land use are also important to these planning tasks.

Emissions inventory. Although air quality is the final measure of success of a pollution control program, the emission inventory (and changes therein) is the base on which control measures and strategies must be developed. Hence, an accurate, up-to-date inventory is essential. Measurements or estimates of current emissons levels need to be obtained for point sources, stationary area sources, and mobile area or line sources. EPA has developed well-documented procedures for compiling an emission inventory covering these sources. For point sources, given the high costs of source monitoring, the most practical method for ascertaining the quality and quantity of emissions is analysis of fuel consumption and raw material use. When multiplied by standard emission factors, these indicators will provide estimates of aggregate emissions. Data on fuel and raw materials can be obtained either from point-source surveys, records of local distribution, or statewide data on consumption collected by the air pollution control agency or the U.S. Bureau of Mines. Most area sources are groups of point sources which are too small to investigate individually, so secondary sources of information are frequently used. For residential area sources, local fuel distributions can be consulted for data on the amount and mix of fuels used for space heating. Most emission inventories treat line sources as area sources by aggregating and then uniformly distributing them throughout the analysis area. The data base for estimating emissions from line sources is usually available from local transportation departments, which maintain detailed information on street capacities, traffic volumes, and vehicle mix by age and type. When these data are not available locally, such indirect data as total gasoline sales and motor vehicle registrations can be helpful.

Emission projections. Projections of emissions permit estimation of future air quality by application of relationships between current emissions and existing air quality. For AQMA purposes, the emission projections of concern are those that account for the increases in emissions attributable to all aspects of community growth and development. Estimation techniques exist for aggregate or large-area analysis, as well as for smaller subareas and even individual developments. For large areas, emissions from existing sources are first modified to reflect mandated future reductions. Then "growth factors" for the various categories of sources are derived from the land-use plan and other sources being evaluated. These growth factors, modified by applicable new source emission standards promulgated by EPA, are then applied to the current level of activity within each category to obtain estimated emissions for the desired future year. Projection of future emissions for particular subareas can be based on (1) distribution of expected aggregate growth and (2) estimates of growth for each subarea. Project plans for major new point sources are usually specific enough to allow estimates of their future emissons. It is harder to estimate the additional emissions these sources may induce in transportation-related pollution. General sources of local data for refining emission projections include not only land-use studies, but also studies relating to transportation, energy use, and utility expansion.

Current ambient concentrations. Recognizing that the costs of an ideal monitoring system are prohibitive, EPA guidelines emphasize placement of sampling stations where the potential for pollution problems is highest. Criteria for identifying "hot spots" include population distribution, location of sources, and areas of expected future growth. Where the number of monitoring stations is still insufficient, diffusion models will be needed to obtain isopleths of current ambient concentrations.

Future ambient concentrations. Drawing on the three preceding sets of calculations and on data on meteorological and surface features, the planner can make estimates of future ambient concentrations for each of the relevant pollutants. Manual techniques as well as those requiring computer support are available. A recent publication by HUD conveniently describes, in terms local planners can understand, each of the major techniques for predicting future air quality. Accompanying the descriptions are brief summaries of the advantages and disadvantages of each technique.[56]

NOISE ABATEMENT AND CONTROL

Only recently has urban noise, or unwanted sound, come to be viewed as integral to environmental quality. Noise previously was seen in the limited context of industrial health hazards or community nuisances. The change is directly linked to the drastic increase in urban noise levels. The major urban noise sources are aircraft operations, ground vehicular traffic, and construction and other heavy equipment. Aircraft produce the most intense noise, and vehicular traffic noise is the most prevalent source. The aircraft noise problem has been accentuated by the rapid increase in the volume of air traffic since the mid-1950s and by the replacement of propeller aircraft by much larger, noisier jets. Vehicular noise is closely related to the volume of truck traffic, and trucks represent the fastest growing component of ground traffic.

As with other forms of environmental pollution, the long-term effects of excessive noise on people are difficult, if not impossible, to determine with scientific precision. Numerous studies have, however, established a causal relation between noise and various physiological and psychological effects, such as hearing loss and impairment, interference with speech communications, sleep disturbance, general anxiety, irritability, and annoyance. Other less well established effects include physical fatigue, unsociability, and inefficiency in the performance of complicated tasks. As can be seen in Figure 6, many everyday occurrences in urban areas produce noise levels that could cause hearing loss and other physiological effects. Note, however, that these adverse effects are likely to occur only after frequent and extended exposure. In 1974, EPA estimated that 13 million Americans resided in areas where continuous exposure to urban environmental noise levels averaged above 70 $dBL_{eq.}$ [24], the equivalent A-weighted sound level over a twenty-four-hour period. This level may be harmful when combined with shorter, more intense noise exposure in the workplace, during travel, or in recreational areas. Furthermore, an estimated 100 million people reside in areas where the L_{dn} (A-weighted day-night sound level) exceeds 55 dBL, a level clearly identified with marked annoyance.

The Planning Context

Noise phenomena consist of a well-defined set of related components: (1) a source or noise generator, (2) a path of transmission, and (3) a receptor. In turn, a noise-management strategy may include any combination of measures to (1) reduce noise generation, (2) modify noise transmission, and (3) provide protective measures at various receptor sites. Reducing noise generation can include changing the timing and location of activities as well as decreasing their noise levels.

The major thrust of the Noise Control Act of 1972 is source control, developing noise emission standards for new products which

FIGURE 6

Typical Noises:
Their Noise Levels and Human Reactions

Subjective Impression	Noise Level [dB(A)]	Typical Noises (distances and decibel levels given for some)	Hearing Effects
	130	Machine gun; pneumatic riveter; air raid siren	
Deafening	120	Siren (100 ft.); sonic boom	Threshold of pain
	110	Jet take-off (200 ft.); rock band (108 ft.); auto horn (3 ft.)	
	100	Jet take-off (2000 ft.); loud street noise	
Very loud (Shouting at 2 ft.	90	Heavy city traffic; unmuffled truck; kitchen blender	Hearing damage if prolonged
Loud (Very loud conversation at 2 ft.)	70	Average street noise; vacuum cleaner; electric typewriter; freight train (100 ft.)	Contribution to hearing impairment begins; Speech interference begins
	60	Window air conditioner (20 ft.); normal conversation	
	50	Quiet street	
Moderate/Faint	30	Quiet conversation	Annoyance, sleep interference

Source: Gregory Houle, "Toward the Comprehensive Abatement of Noise
Pollution," Comment in Ecology Law Journal, Winter 1974, p. 112.

are major noise sources, such as motor vehicles, construction equipment, and other kinds of motors and engines. The act did not provide for federally assisted regional or local noise abatement planning along the lines of Section 208 areawide waste treatment management planning or AQMA planning. Nor have any standards been issued under the act to define maximum acceptable noise exposure for particular land uses and human activities.

HUD policy, expressed in Circular 1390.2, while seeking "to encourage the control of noise at its source in cooperation with other federal departments and agencies," concentrates on two other objectives: "to encourage land utilization patterns for housing and other municipal needs that will separate uncontrollable noise sources from residential and other noise-sensitive areas, and to prohibit HUD support to new construction sites having unacceptable noise exposures."[57] In support of these latter two objectives, Circular 1390.2 places particular emphasis on the importance of compatible land-use planning in relation to airports, general modes of transportation other than air, and other significant sources of noise. It supports the use of planning funds to explore appropriate ways of reducing environmental noise to acceptable exposures. Interim standards for external noise exposure for HUD-sponsored construction were promulgated as part of the circular. HUD is currently reviewing the effect of these noise standards, and changes in policy and/or standards may result.

Department of Transportation Policy and Procedure Memorandum 90-2 provides noise standards and procedures for state highway agencies and the Federal Highway Administration in order "to assure that measures are taken in the overall public interest to achieve highway noise levels that are compatible with different land uses, with due consideration also given to other social, economic, and environmental effects."[58] FHWA views the design noise levels, to be implemented "at the earliest appropriate stage in the project development process," as maximum values, although it recognizes that in many cases highway agencies should "strive for noise levels below the values . . . when the lower levels can be achieved at reasonable cost, without undue difficulty, and where the benefits appear to clearly outweigh the costs and efforts required."[59]

Finally, under the Air Installation Compatible Use Zone (AICUZ) program established in 1973, the U.S. Air Force promulgates planning guidelines for land-use activities adjacent to its air bases to assure compatibility with the noise and accident potential of aircraft operations. Air Force policy is to work through the local land-use planning and control process. It applies noise compatibility guidelines to noise zones identified through a systematic mapping and measurement procedure and then recommends compatible land uses to responsible community officials. The AICUZ program and its land-use compatibility guidelines are generally consistent with the policies of the Department of Housing and Urban Development. The two programs reinforce each other.

Defining the Noise Problem

For purposes of comprehensive planning and management, defining the noise problem in a given urban area consists of the following three tasks: (1) describing the noise environment, (2) identifying the noise sensitivity of activities, and (3) establishing the nature and extent of conflicts between noise-sensitive activities and the noise environment.

Describing the noise environment. Data collection efforts for defining ambient noise environments should first include identification of all known previous noise surveys of the area. Where previous surveys are nonexistent or otherwise inadequate, original data collection is necessary.

The Washington, D.C. Council of Governments' comprehensive environmental noise study exemplifies the use of previous survey material. The Council of Governments found and made use of forty such surveys which had been done for a variety of purposes — highway EIS's, residential development, rapid transit, sewage treatment plants, sanitary landfills, and others. For each of these surveys the study team summarized the location and characteristics of the measurement sites, the measurement methodology, the results, and an overview of the data generated.[60]

Where original data collection is necessary, planners may choose any of several methodologies for estimating noise, or they may elect actual field measurement. One fairly simple methodology for approximating minimum ambient outdoor sound levels is based on a general assessment of land-use patterns. The output of this approach is not much more than an "educated guess," but can be useful, if for nothing more than planning subsequent field measurement surveys.[61] An urban noise survey methodology developed for HUD takes into consideration the number and type of noise sources, their location, intensity, frequency, content, and time-history. These categories are important because community response will be a function of these sound characteristics. Applied in New York City, this approach divided up the study area into units corresponding to those land-use classifications under the zoning regulations that appeared to have different noise climates.[62] In this way, information on noise levels may be more easily integrated into a land-use regulatory scheme.

Since traffic noise generally controls the ambient noise climate of communities not located near airports, another method for determining their ambient noise environment is to model traffic noise based on vehicle counts. The Federal Highway Administration has developed a model that will predict noise levels at various distances from highways. The Department of Housing and Urban Development, in its *Noise Assessment Guidelines*, has incorporated these models into a simplified pencil-and-paper method for determining noise exposure at various distances from roads.

Field measurements are another method of determining the ambient noise environment. Such measurements involve use of a hand-held sound-level meter at a number of locations. An obvious problem the sound surveyor has to cope with is the variation in observed sound level with time; however, procedures have been developed to approximate the minimum sound level (variously known as the "residual" or "background" level) during the time of observation. Other procedures can be used to obtain some measure of the central tendency of the meter readings or of the entire distribution of observed sound levels.[63]

Noise environments can be measured using several different statistical noise descriptors. These include: (1) L_x [the noise level, L, in A-weighted decibels exceeded for x amount of time]; (2) L_{eq} [the average sound level or the constant level of sound that exposes the ear to the same amount of acoustical energy as does the actual noise pattern that varies with time]; and (3) L_{dn} [the average sound level (L_{eq}) weighted with a ten-decibel night-time penalty to account for the fact that the same noise level is more disturbing at night].

For areas located near airports, noise descriptors designed specifically for aircraft noise are most useful. These include Composite Noise Rating (CNR) and Noise Exposure Forecast (NEF), which rate aircraft noise based on maximum sound pressure level of flyovers, frequency and duration of flyovers, time of day, and other variables related to community response. L_{dn} can be used as a descriptor of aircraft noise as well as of other community noise, so its use simplifies combining measurements of a variety of noise sources.

Identifying sensitive activities. In order to identify the noise sensitivities of various activities, descriptors must be related to standard threshold values above which indoor and/or outdoor environments are no longer suitable for specified uses. Several federal agencies including OSHA, HUD, DOD, FHWA, FAA, and EPA have identified such thresholds, either in the form of enforceable standards or suggested guidelines, after making social surveys to assess people's reaction to noise. Most surveys consider activities affected or interrupted by awareness of noise, annoyance or hostility resulting from interruption, and complaints about the annoyance.[64]

Identifying conflicts. To map noise conflict areas, *noise contours* (which identify areas within which similar noise levels exist) should be overlaid on a land-use map on which noise-sensitive land uses and activities are identified. NEF, CNR, or L_{dn} contours developed for most airports should be used for aircraft noise, and contours measured by an appropriate noise descriptor and separated by appropriate decibel intervals should be used for other sources. Areas where the noise levels exceed the standards applicable to each land use and activity should be identified. In these areas of conflict, various land uses are incompatible with the noise environment.

Long-range planning considerations. An important adjunct to existing community noise description is the determination of anticipated changes in the noise source inventory, particularly such major sources as airports and highways, and of anticipated changes in noise-sensitive land uses and activities. For airports, the comprehensive planner will want to take into account projected levels of flight operations and corridor use and/or redesign. Regarding highways, the planner will need to be aware of projected increases in vehicle usage on existing roads as well as of extensions planned for the existing network. Anticipated noise-sensitive land uses and activities should be documented in community plans.

Integrating Noise Abatement Into Comprehensive Planning

Until very recently, planning for noise abatement and control had not been recognized as an integral part of areawide comprehensive planning and management. Where such planning had been undertaken, it tended to focus almost exclusively on the noise source; controls on the path or the receptor were rarely considered, except in planning for control of aircraft noise. For both aircraft and highway noise, a three-pronged approach to noise planning is required: (1) reducing noise at the source through quieter engines and vehicles, (2) revising aircraft operational procedures and highway designs to lessen noise impact and avoid populated areas, and (3) planning land-use controls to achieve compatibility between the noise source and its neighbors.

Again, planning for control of aircraft noise has made the greatest strides in terms of integration with more general comprehensive planning and management. A number of excellent planning studies dealing with airport expansion in the context of larger urban growth issues have recently been completed. These include studies at Chicago's O'Hare Airport, New York's John F. Kennedy Airport, Hartford's Bradley Airport, and the Cape Kennedy Airport at Melbourne, Florida. All were funded under HUD's Aircraft Noise Abatement Policy Studies Program.

FLOOD AND OTHER HAZARDS MANAGEMENT

Given such circumstances as heavy rains, hurricanes, and snow melts, rivers and streams may overflow their banks causing loss of human life and damage to buildings and property. Within an urban environment, floodplains compose a significant portion of the land area, an average of 16.2%.[65] Urban growth pressures have led to wide-scale development of floodplains. These areas, flat and economically attractive to developers, were generally considered safe from flood hazard because of the presence of dams and levees, but structural controls have proven inadequate. Total annual flood losses are increasing, as are the dollar costs of relief and rehabilitation. The potential flood hazard is increasing as population growth and development patterns increase development in flood-prone areas, thereby increasing the potential flood hazard area.[66]

This situation has led to a reexamination of the range of adjustment measures available to mitigate flood hazards. Available adjustment measures include:

Structural controls (protective works, floodproofing)

Warning systems

Flood insurance

Relief and rehabilitation assistance

Land-use management

By and large, the least-used of these measures have been those most directly related to comprehensive planning and management, that is, land-use controls in natural hazard areas. These controls include land acquisition, restricted development policies, and assorted regulatory programs. Often overlooked are three important social benefits that can be expected from their implementation. First, a substantial reduction in the population and economic investment at-risk can be attained. Second, the expenditures of private and public agencies for evacuation, relief, and rehabilitation can also be cut drastically. Third, dependence upon protective works can be decreased.

In addition to reducing losses from floods, restricting development in flood-prone areas can further more general environmental goals. Flood hazard areas are often areas of valuable natural processes and unsuited to intensive human use: marshes, wetlands, and dunes commonly found in coastal hurricane storm-surge areas. Also, where it is possible to accurately delineate hazard zones, it is often feasible to locate open-space uses, such as floodplain parks. In response to increasing public demand for outdoor recreation and open space in urban environments, governments are placing more emphasis on providing such areas. Overall, the effect of most land-use management schemes is to produce less intensive uses of land in the hazard zone and less modification of the natural environment.

Recent legislation has recognized the growing importance of the land-use management option for reducing flood hazards. One of the stated objectives of the Flood Disaster Protection Act of 1973, which modified the existing federal flood insurance program, is to provide wise land-use policies for flood-prone areas and to regulate future development so that the potential for flood damage will not increase. The Disaster Relief Act amendments of 1974 specifically included land-use and construction regulations as hazard-mitigation measures to be encouraged. The Water Resources Development Act of 1974 recognized this need for basic land-use adjustments by requiring in the planning of any federal project involving flood protection that "consideration shall be given to nonstructural alternatives, including but not limited to . . . floodplain regulations; acquisition of floodplain lands for recreational, fish and wildlife, and other public purposes; and relocation with a view toward formulating the most economically, socially, and environmentally acceptable means of reducing or preventing flood damage."[67]

At one time, various units of government may not have had the legal authority to enact regulations guiding land use in hazardous areas, including floodplains; however, most of these legal impediments no longer exist.[68] But, despite the lessening of legal obstacles, there has been no great rush to adopt regulations controlling land use in these areas. Opposition to governmental restrictions on land use comes primarily from property owners. Managing hazard zones to minimize the loss of life and property can run counter to the forces that attract people and activities to these areas; economic and aesthetic enticements create intense pressures to develop in floodplains and other hazard zones. Also, political officials are often reluctant to impose regulatory measures that reduce, in effect, any land's property tax. A particularly important problem of adjusting land use to reduce flood hazards is the length of time required for the full benefits of the program to accrue. In areas that are already urbanized, the period may be twenty to twenty-five years.[69]

At the planning studies stage, accurate hazard zone mapping is a critical component of the comprehensive planning process. Mapping is necessary if a local ordinance regulates the use of land in hazardous areas. Without a map delineating the area and the intensities of risk within it, public opposition to land-use measures will be particularly strong, and a legal attack on the validity of the ordinance would probably succeed in the courts. The following two sections deal with mapping as a part of local flood insurance studies and with more general efforts to identify natural hazard zones. Planning to reduce man-made hazards in urban areas is treated in a third section.

Flood Insurance Studies

Under the Flood Disaster Protection Act of 1973, flood insurance studies are required as an evaluation of a community's existing flood damage potential. The completed study identifies areas within the community subject to flooding, how often they can be expected to be flooded, and to what depth. Thus, the flood hazard for individual properties in the area can be determined and actuarial insurance rates established. The study is designed to be the basis for floodplain management measures for mitigating or eliminating future flood damage. The typical flood insurance study involves (1) ascertaining the scope and magnitude of the flood problem; (2) estimating the flood flow frequency; (3) establishing flood elevation frequency profiles for ten-year, fifty-year, one hundred-year, and five hundred-year floods; (4) computing flood hazard factors; and (5) identifying the floodway for one hundred-year floods. For purposes of defining the flood hazard area, the federal Flood Insurance Program has adopted the one hundred-year flood, that area immediately adjacent to the stream which is necessary for the passage of the flood flow. A high-hazard coastal area is also identified for regulatory purposes, and it is defined as that portion of a coastal floodplain with special flood hazards that is subject to high-velocity waters, including hurricane wave wash and tsunamis. The Department of Housing and Urban Development can contract with various federal, state, regional, and local agencies as well as with private consulting engineers to conduct flood insurance studies.

The HUD procedures provide for extensive coordination and consultation with community officials at every stage of the study process and allow for written appeal of the proposed flood elevation determinations within ninety days.

The requirements of the federal Flood Insurance Program are oriented more toward controls on construction than toward general land-use controls. The HUD regulations do not require the restriction of any land use per se, except that structures within the hazard zone must be flood-proofed or elevated to minimize flood damage. However, the HUD regulations do recommend that each community, in formulating its development goals and adopting floodplain control measures, consider the following factors which are directly related to land-use management: [70]

Importance of diverting future development to areas not exposed to flooding

Possibilities of reserving flood-prone areas for open-space purposes

Possible adverse effects of floodplain development on other flood-prone areas

Need to provide alternative vehicular access and escape routes to be used when normal routes are blocked or destroyed by flooding

Need to establish minimum floodproofing and access requirements for schools, hospitals, nursing homes, penal institutions, fire stations, police stations, communications centers, and other public or quasipublic institutions already located in the flood-prone area, in order that they may withstand flood damage and facilitate emergency operations

Possibilities of acquiring land or land development rights for public purposes consistent with effective floodplain management

The need in riverine areas, for subdividers to delineate floodway limits before approving a subdivision

The need in coastal areas to establish programs for preserving natural barriers to flooding, such as sand dunes and vegetation

Proposed revisions to the Federal Insurance Administration regulations also emphasize the need to assure consistency among state, areawide, and local comprehensive plans (particularly the land-use element) and floodplain management and conservation programs.[71]

Identifying Other Natural Hazard Areas

Local priorities for hazard mapping should be based on potential adverse effects and related in turn to their likelihood of occurrence. For the United States as a whole, earthquakes (including tsunamis), floods, and hurricanes have a very high priority. Avalanches, coastal erosion, drought, frost, hail, landslides, and tornadoes are generally of a lower priority, while still lower would be lightning, urban snow, volcanoes, and windstorms. For particular localities, of course, these priorities may be ordered somewhat differently.

Transferring known hazard occurrences to a map can be done for all hazards for which accurate data on occurrence exist. Even where historical data are not available, sophisticated statistical techniques involving correlation of the existing physical properties of an area to the hazard occurrence potential are now employed in some cases. Federal agencies do most of the mapping of hazardous areas, often at the request of or in cooperation with state and local agencies. The Department of Housing and Urban Development, the Army Corps of Engineers, and the Soil Conservation Service of the U.S. Department of Agriculture have been mapping flood hazards for several years in virtually all areas of the United States. The National Oceanic and Atmospheric Administration (NOAA) and the U.S. Geological Survey have ongoing programs to map areas susceptible to earthquakes, tsunamis, landslides, and volcanoes. NOAA is also mapping hurricane storm-surge areas along the Atlantic and Gulf Coasts.

Available mapping techniques rely principally on either on-site investigation or remote imagery. On a national or regional scale, remote imagery techniques are adequate for the accuracy required; on the state or particularly the local level, a combination of both remote and on-site techniques is usually required to obtain the needed accuracy. At the local level technical accuracy is paramount, for local regulations governing land use must be very precise. At this level site-specific verification ("ground truth") is required for dependable maps. With the launching of the ERTS-1 satellite, high-altitude imagery (multispectral photography) has become available for certain types of hazard mapping. The most innovative aspect of ERTS is the ability of the imagery to provide large-area perspectives which are especially useful in identifying regional faulting relations. More detailed imagery from low-altitude aerial surveys is used extensively in the United States for identifying floodplains, faults, avalanche paths, landslides, and other hazards accurately. Generally, aerial photography is most useful for mapping geomorphic and hydrologic hazards, while atmospheric hazards such as tornadoes are more suited to use of historical data.

Application of hazard mapping to land-use management requires sufficient data substantiation for use by a political decision-making body to create a defensible hazard zone area. Legal defensibility depends on predictive capability: if the predictive capability of a hazard map is low, the use of the map for regulatory land use is questionable. Predictive capability is based mainly on the probabilities within which variation of occurrence exists. Thus, accuracy is relatively high for delineations of floodplains based on past flood histories and reliable hydrologic data; for the natural hazards where assignment of probabilities of occurrence is less reliable (earthquakes, volcanoes, tsunamis, avalanches, landslides), mapping is less defensible as a basis for land-use management. However, hazards within this latter group have a strong potential for being mapped in relation to distinct geologic characteristics. These known characteristics can be used to produce accurate maps of areas with potential for occurrence, even though probabilities cannot be estimated reliably.

Identifying Man-Made Hazards

This section deals briefly with three sources of man-made hazards in urban areas and the means for identifying them at the initial planning stage of the comprehensive planning process: (1) the handling, storage, and processing of hazardous industrial chemicals; (2) the storage, transportation, treatment, and disposal of hazardous industrial wastes; and (3) high-pressure natural gas transmission pipelines.

Hazardous industrial chemicals. Low-income family housing in urban areas tends to be concentrated in undesirable locations, among which are land parcels adjacent to industrial facilities which handle, store, and process hazardous chemicals. These chemicals include flammable petroleum products such as liquified natural gas and liquified petroleum gas; typical industrial fossil fuels like gasoline, kerosene, and naphtha; and toxic vapors or gases which can accidentally be released into the air, such as ammonia, hydrogen chloride, and chlorine. The planner's concern is to locate hazardous industries away from existing or planned residential areas. Where residential and industrial uses must coexist, the task is to ensure minimum safe separation distances. Planners must be able to locate on a map and/or an aerial photograph the following information as baseline data:

Industries handling chemical products

Storage tanks and their surrounding dikes

Railroad tracks

Main highways and roads carrying industrial traffic

Barge docking areas

Tank truck and railroad car terminals

Fire stations

For each industry so identified, planners should prepare a list of chemicals brought in, stored, and shipped out, obtaining for each chemical its:

Relative potential for fire and explosion

Pertinent physical and chemical properties

Quantity stored or transported

Frequency of transport, by each mode

Transportation and storage pressure/temperature

Also important for each facility are past accident records, protection systems, emergency plans, and expansion plans. Public sources of data include the state fire marshal, state public utilities commission, local fire departments, and public health agencies. Visits to the facilities and in-person interviews with the plant engineer or safety director are also strongly recommended.

Hazardous wastes. A hazardous waste is "any waste or combination of wastes which pose a substantial present or potential hazard to human health or living organisms because such wastes are non-degradable or persistent in nature, or because they can be lethal, or because they may otherwise cause or tend to cause detrimental cumulative effects."[72] The EPA has estimated that approximately ten million tons of nonradioactive hazardous wastes are generated annually and that their generation will continue to increase at an annual rate of from 5% to 10%.[73] As a first step in managing this ever-increasing hazard, EPA has recommended that each state conduct a comprehensive survey whose results would be available to regional and local comprehensive planners. This survey would identify facilities that generate hazardous wastes; facilities that receive hazardous wastes for storage, treatment, and final disposal; and the collectors and haulers who transport the wastes. Storage and transportation information is directly relevant to anticipating the potential for accidents and other emergencies. Information on disposal methodology (landfill, dump, lagoon, incineration) is important for determining potential for media pollution. EPA has issued guidance materials on the content and conduct of hazardous wastes surveys which local planners can easily obtain.[74]

Natural gas pipelines. HUD has a special interest in natural gas pipeline safety, particularly in housing projects and mobile home parks that it assists or insures. The Office of Pipeline Safety in DOT has the responsibility to develop and enforce minimum safety standards for transporting gasses by pipeline, but since the responsibility of the gas utility usually stops at the master meter, it is incumbent upon the owners of housing projects and mobile home parks to comply with applicable local and federal standards. A gas leak in a densely populated housing project could result in a disastrous fire or explosion with many casualties. Accidental gas release can take place at a number of points in the system: in high-pressure transmission lines, in mains and sewers, and at various gas appliance and gas piping system components within or near the individual home. Although the problem is basically one of regulation and enforcement, planners should be aware at the outset of where the major high-pressure gas transmission pipelines are located; what the applicable federal and local codes require of new residential construction regarding pipeline safety; and what the roles of the various federal, state, and local agencies are in monitoring and emergency planning.

HISTORIC PRESERVATION

Residents of urban areas are increasingly recognizing the need for a sense of history and place. This need has been reflected in the evolution over the past forty years, of federal legislation relating to historic preservation. The Historic Sites Act of 1935 established a federal policy for preserving sites, buildings, and objects having national significance, and it authorized the National Park Service to maintain a National Register as an authoritative guide to properties that should be considered for protection. In 1949 Congress chartered the National Trust for Historic Preservation as a private, nonprofit organization to lead the preservation movement, particularly to foster public participation through educational, technical, and advisory programs. The National Historic Preservation Act of 1966 expanded the scope of the National Register to include sites which, although lacking national importance, still possess regional, state, or local significance. This act also established a program of matching grants to the states for historic resource surveys and preservation planning. The program is administered by State Historic Preservation Officers in conjunction with a state review board. The historic preservation officers in turn may allocate grant funds in accordance with a federally approved State Historic Preservation Plan to local governments, private organizations, and individuals for financing local surveys and for acquiring and developing National Register properties. Passage of the National Environmental Policy Act of 1969 provided the basis for additional consideration of historic preservation within the full range of environmental-planning concerns. Executive Order 11592, issued in 1971, required federal agencies to take steps to preserve federally owned historic properties and to conduct all of their programs so as to facilitate the preservaton of eligible nonfederal properties. The Historic and Archeological Preservation Data Act amendments of 1974 direct the Secretary of the Interior to recover and preserve any significant scientific, prehistorical, historical, or archeological data in danger of being irrevocably lost or destroyed by any federal or federally assisted program or activity.

Most important for integrating these considerations into comprehensive planning are the provisions of the Housing and Community Development Act of 1974. First, the act requires that all planning funded under Section 701 be carried out in accord with Section 106 of the National Historic Preservation Act of 1966. Specifically, the act requires that historic preservation planning be made an integral part of comprehensive planning and that each Section 701 grantee prepare an historic preservation assessment when federally assisted activities include preparation of plans or policies that may affect National Register properties. Planning activities eligible under Section 701 include survey and evaluation of historic properties, determination of preliminary cost estimates for restoration, development of local historic preservation plans, and conduct of historic preservation assessments as needed. Second, the act provides for Community Development Block Grants and grant-eligible activities to include acquisition, restoration, and preservation of historic properties, as well as local preservation planning and surveys. Block grant funds can serve as the local match for grant monies from the National Park Service. Under the environmental review procedures established for the CDBG program, local grantees are delegated the federal agency's responsibility for satisfying all federal laws and procedures relating to historic preservation. The obligation to comply with the historic preservation requirements of the National Historic Preservation Act of 1966 and Executive Order 11593 is mandatory, irrespective of the requirement for environmental assessments under NEPA. However, local efforts to satisfy these separate requirements should be coordinated, as appropriate. Third, the act authorizes HUD to insure lending institutions against losses they may sustain as a result of loans or credit advances for the preservation of historic structures listed in or eligible for listing in the National Register.

The National Register is not a complete inventory of cultural resources in each state at this time, and it is likely that only a small part of the potentially eligible properties in any given locality have been listed. At the planning studies stage, when communities take stock of existing buildings, sites, districts, and areas in formulating plans for future development, useful data on available cultural resources is clearly needed. The foundation for an effective local historic preservation program is a thorough survey identifying and evaluating such resources. The survey provides the working inventory of acceptable sites to be used throughout the rest of the planning process.

Historic Preservation Surveys

An important initial consideration is coordination with the State Historic Preservation Officer. State historic preservation officers can assist communities in one or more of the following activities:

Advising on what resources have already been surveyed by the state

Developing high-quality local surveys

Coordinating the local survey with that of the state

Nominating properties to the National Register

Applying for National Park Service matching grants

Obtaining information on other available sources of funding and preservation assistance [75]

Since the State HPO participates in environmental reviews conducted at the state level, coordination of the local survey with the state survey and the inclusion of local sites in the state inventory will ensure that such sites are considered in federal and statewide development plans. Ultimately, any HUD-funded planning should be integrated directly into the comprehensive statewide historic preservation plan.

Required documentation for Register-eligible sites includes: (1) a complete description of the physical appearance of the resource, (2) a statement of its significance, (3) clear photographs which show its major features, and (4) maps showing its precise location within the community. Specific National Register requirements regarding description of the resource vary according to whether it is in a building, structure, or object; an archeological site; an architectural or historic district; a commercial or industrial district; or a special engineering feature such as a bridge, canal, or lighthouse.[76] In assessing the significance of a property, the following information typically should be included: period of construction or use; the architect or builder, if known; historically important events or persons associated with the property; and information which the property has yielded or may be likely to yield (especially for archeological sites). Photographs provide the necessary visual documentation of sites and structures surveyed. The number of photographs necessary for complete documentation will, of course, vary according to the nature and complexity of the property. Maps provide a clear visual reference to the geographic location and size of the resource. Usually, the maps need not be elaborate; but when the resource is an entire district, a more detailed "sketch map" should be prepared.

The criteria for evaluating potential entries to the National Register are intentionally flexible, allowing for the diversity of the nation's resources:

> The quality of significance in American history, architecture, archeology, and culture is present in districts, sites, buildings, structures, and objects of state or local importance that possess integrity of location, design, setting, materials, workmanship, feeling and association and:

>> That are associated with events that have made a significant contribution to the broad patterns of our history; or

>> That are associated with the lives of persons significant in our past; or

>> That embody the distinctive characteristics of a type, period, or method of construction, or that represent the work of a master, or that possess high artistic values, or that represent a significant and distinguishable entity whose components may lack individual distinction; or

>> That have yielded, or may likely yield, information important in prehistory or history.[77]

These criteria offer a good standard for judging architectural, archeological, and historic significance. An important advantage of using the National Register criteria is that they are also used in the environmental review procedures for CDBG recipients.

The output of the survey and evaluation process is a cultural resources inventory which identifies properties significant to the community. It is a selective list, chosen from the survey on the basis of professional evaluation against established criteria. To ensure an adequate and balanced consideration of all the resources in the survey area, it is important that the professionals involved in the evaluation include representatives from the disciplines of architecture or architectural history, history, archeology, and related fields. The inventory itself should be "open," allowing other properties to be added as further survey work is done, as properties initially placed on the inventory are secured, or as other properties surveyed but not placed on the inventory are threatened by development.

DOT Historic and Cultural Resources Inventory

Federally assisted transportation planners operate under an additional legislative requirement to make a "special effort . . . to preserve . . . historic sites" and to refrain from approving any program or project "which requires the use of . . . any land from an historic site of national, state, or local significance . . . unless (1) there is no feasible and prudent alternative to the use of such land; and (2) such program includes all possible planning to minimize harm to such . . . historic sites."[78] Although the main thrust of this requirement was directed at highway planning, it also applies to other DOT-assisted activities as well, including location of airports and rail and rapid transit lines and facilities. Transportation officials throughout the country must consider the protection (and potential for rehabilitation and restoration) or historic sites in the earliest stages of the design and planning of transport facilities.

To this end, DOT has developed a planning study procedure called the Historic and Cultural Resources Inventory (HCRI).[79] Focused mainly on highways, the purpose of the HCRI is twofold: first, to identify potential conflicts between the goals of the highway department and those of preservation; and second, to point out alternative highway routes that enhance preservation objectives and community values without sacrificing the highway's usefulness. The HCRI relies on four basic techniques to catalog and rank a community's historic and cultural resources:

A review of previously published materials

Field surveys

Selected local interviews

Evaluation of current and past trends affecting preservation

DOT procedures recognize that valuable data may already exist in a particular area, so they call for obtaining from the State Historic Preservation Officer a listing of all properties currently included or nominated for inclusion in the National Register, as well as other known historic and cultural sites. However, much of the DOT's inventory work is in response to specific proposals for new highway construction. Therefore, in many instances, that work may not overlap with previous surveys. The HCRI is applied mainly to existing interstate highways, U.S. and state primary routes, and certain secondary routes, especially segments that serve expanding areas or are likely to be upgraded in the near future. These types of highways are subject to the greatest amount of change through federally aided projects — widenings, straightenings, improved interchanges, and traffic separation. These projects typically follow established travel patterns in corridors connecting existing and developing urban areas.

The inventory itself is completed in two stages: the precorridor selection stage and the preliminary route selection. The first stage is regarded as a broad survey relying primarily on published sources and official records. Its goal is to define the overall visual character and historic significance of the study area. Boundaries for the study area are set to include all potential highway corridors. At the preliminary route selection stage, the HCRI is concerned with a more detailed, comprehensive survey of the approved route location or corridor. Greater emphasis is then placed on identifying individual properties, establishing their historic and cultural significance, and assessing the potential effect of the proposed projects upon them.

The HCRI is essentially a tool for promoting environmental quality within a specific functional planning process: transportation. However, comprehensive planners must be aware of the HCRI process in order to (1) avoid duplication of effort, (2) benefit from the special perspective of the transportation planner, and (3) integrate functional planning considerations into a broader framework of the community's historic preservation goals.

SOCIAL EQUITY

The Housing and Community Development Act of 1974 commits HUD programs to achieving a number of important objectives regarding the built environment in urban areas: elimination of slums and blight; elimination of related conditions detrimental to health, safety, and public welfare; conservation and expansion of housing stock; and more rational use of land. Equally important for comprehensive planning are the social goals underlying these objectives. First, housing and community development programs seek to provide a decent home and a suitable living environment for all persons, but "principally those of low and moderate income."[80]

Within this target group there is a special obligation to deal with the problems of minorities, women, and the elderly. Second, HUD programs must seek "reduction of the isolation of income groups within communities . . . and the promotion of an increase in the diversity and vitality of neighborhoods through the spatial deconcentration of housing opportunities for persons of lower income."[81] Housing plans must reflect regional housing needs, especially those of the inner city. Third, the 1974 act contains a nondiscrimination clause similar in wording to Title VI of the Civil Rights Act of 1964 but which is a separate provision requiring that its own specific procedures be applied to Community Development Block Grants. Discrimination is banned in the offering of services or facilities, treatment of individuals, criteria and methods of administration, and determination of site locations for new housing or facilities. Furthermore, grantees who have discriminated in the past are required to take affirmative action to help overcome the effects of that discrimination.[82]

Comprehensive planning can play an important role in furthering these goals of social equity. At the planning studies stage, comprehensive planners should make special efforts to:

Provide accurate data on social and economic conditions in the community, especially on the problems and needs of low- and moderate-income households

Help communities formulate realistic Housing Assistance Plans (HAP's) consistent with regional housing needs

Develop a framework for integrating available data on socioeconomic and physical conditions, to serve as the basis for nondiscriminatory allocation of CDBG funds

The following sections take up each of these social-planning considerations in turn.

Socioeconomic Baseline Data

Comprehensive planners are usually the best source of data on socioeconomic conditions relevant to housing and community development. Drawing on census information, comprehensive planning agencies should be able quickly and easily to supply accurate data on these location-specific problem indicators:

Income. Median family income per census tract

Poverty. Percentage of families per census tract with incomes below the federal definition of poverty

Population density. Average number of people per residential acre per census tract

Overcrowded housing. Percentage of occupied units of housing per census tract which contain more than one person per room

Educational attainment. Median education attainment of persons aged 25 and over per census tract

Family organization. Percentage of families headed by females (no male head present) with children under 18 years of age

Drawing on other federal and local data as well as special studies, planners should also be able to characterize these other important social aggregates:

Substandard housing. Percentage of occupied units classified as substandard

Unemployment. Percentage of males 14 years and over unemployed

Welfare status. Percentage under age 21 receiving Aid to Families with Dependent Children

Health. Infant deaths per 1,000 live births

Crime and delinquency. Current arrests as a percentage of persons 18 years and over. Juvenile arrests as a percentage of persons under 18 years

To comply with the legislative requirement that housing and community-development programs consider whether the needs of minorities are more severe than those of the low-income population as a whole, comprehensive planners should also examine:

Whether the effects of past discrimination in housing have resulted in minority overconcentration, overcrowding, greater likelihood of living in substandard housing, or inaccessibility to new employment centers

Whether there is greater minority reliance on public transportation for the journey to work

Whether minority levels of unemployment and under-employment are higher

Whether there is a higher percentage of female-headed households among minorities

Whether there exist greater minority needs of bilingual education, information, and services

Whether minority neighborhoods lack municipal facilities and services commonly available in nonminority neighbor-hoods, including facilities for health care, education, recreation, convenience shopping, and services

Finally, to adequately address the needs of women, planners should examine whether women evidence:

Significantly lower income and earning potential

Higher levels of unemployment and underemployment

Higher incidence of discrimination in housing, both rental and sales

Greater need for supportive services at the neighborhood level, such as child care, counseling, health care, education-al and training opportunities, and convenience shopping and service facilities

These checklists are provided only as a guide to planners. They are not exhaustive, nor can they serve as a substitute for a genuine local effort to identify special needs of low-income persons.

Support to Housing Assistance Plans

All communities seeking Community Development Block Grants must submit a Housing Assistance Plan (HAP) for HUD approval. Among other things, the HAP is supposed to (1) accurately survey the condition of the housing stock in the community, (2) assess the housing assistance needs of lower income persons "re-siding or expected to reside" in the community, (3) specify a realis-tic annual goal for such housing assistance, and (4) indicate the general location of planned construction. The required housing element in Section 701 comprehensive plans should represent a significant source of data to local planners assessing housing needs and formulating housing goals. Furthermore, HUD regards it as an important input to the A-95 review process, which is intended to assure the consistency of areawide CDBG proposals.

An important social goal of HAP's is to "promote greater choice of housing opportunities and avoid undue concentration of assisted persons in areas containing a high proportion of lower income persons." Critical to meeting this goal is an accurate assessment of the housing assistance needs of low-income persons "expected to reside" in the community. The "expected to reside" language was intended by Congress to be the entry wedge for using Title I funds (block grants) to encourage regional distribution of low-income housing. As a result of employment generated by new or expected development in the community, a certain number of new workers from lower-income households located elsewhere within the region could be expected to seek housing in that community. Also falling within the "expected to reside" category would be those low-income workers already employed in the community but living elsewhere; they would seek to reside in the community if affordable housing were available. Local failure to assess adequately the housing needs of such workers can lead to possible legal challenges of CDBG approvals, as shown by the suit brought by the City of Hartford, Connecticut, against grant approvals for seven neighboring suburban communities.[83] Revised HUD guidelines for Housing Assistance Plans now require separate estimates of each of these two types of "expected" residents.[84] HUD expects that the housing elements of Section 701 comprehensive plans should contribute substantially to formulating this and other aspects of local HAP's and that HUD evaluation of future 701 planning grant proposals will take this contribution into account when reaching funding approval decisions. As an example of what a 701 agency can do, the Miami Valley Regional Planning Commission in Dayton, Ohio, drafts the individual housing assistance plans for each of its member communities with their concurrence. The local HAP's are sure to be in accord with regional housing needs.

To assist Section 701 planners, HUD has recently entered into an agreement with the Bureau of the Census to develop an entirely new computer program for analyzing 1970 Census data. The program will provide, for small areas, selected characteristics of households with wage earners by place of work and by place of residence.

Characteristics will include race, family income, age, family size, and type of tenure. When available, the data will provide the basis for estimating the housing assistance needs of lower-income persons working but not residing in the community. Also available from the Bureau of Economic Analysis will be updated census information reflecting the characteristics of commuters in 1975.[85]

HUD is also encouraging comprehensive-planning agencies to adopt areawide housing allocation systems, such as the "fair share" plan which underlies the HAP efforts of the Miami Valley Regional Planning Commission. Member jurisdictions would agree to develop a housing data base, which the 701 agency would keep current and which would be used to identify existing housing needs and the needs of the "expected to reside" group. The system would generate local housing assistance plans consistent with regional needs, and it would include an effective implementation program involving the private sector (for example, affirmative marketing plans). To induce development of such areawide housing allocation systems, HUD proposes to favor participating communities with supplemental Section 8 housing funds.[86]

Land-Based Planning Systems and Nondiscrimination

One approach to rationally targeting housing and community-development funds to the areas of greatest need — and thus for ensuring nondiscriminatory allocation — is to find ways to combine data on environmental and housing conditions with basic socioeconomic information on potential project beneficiaries. The object is to identify the areas of greatest physical and social need. To do this requires keying both sets of data to a common geographic reference, typically street segments, blocks, or census tracts. This integration of planning data can be accomplished at varying levels of technical sophistication, depending on user needs and characteristics.

As part of their planning for allocation of CDBG funds, comprehensive planners in Memphis, Tennessee, have developed a Geographic Priority Area Identification System. It is made up of four separate indices: (1) an environmental services index, (2) a structural rating scale, (3) a cross-impact matrix combining the environmental services and structural data, and (4) a socioeconomic index. The environmental services and structural conditions data were drawn from on-site surveys of some 12,000 street segments within the city limits. The socioeconomic data were drawn largely from the 1970 census. The combined data were then displayed by groupings of census tracts. Environmental services data used by the system included the condition of street surfaces and sidewalks, the extent of curb and gutter completion, the presence of litter, and the condition of open drainage facilities. Physical structures on each street segment were classified as good, fair, poor, or substantially deteriorated, based on estimates of the relative amount of time and effort that would be required to rehabilitate or redevelop the building. Socioeconomic data used in the system included poverty, overcrowding, population density, educational attainment, income, and family organization. Employing a series of screening criteria, Memphis planners ultimately identified fourteen priority areas which would receive 87% of the funds budgeted for their three-year community-development program. The land-based nature of the targeting process and the data integration it permits helped foster significant participation by elected officials and citizen and neighborhood groups in reviewing planning assumptions and outputs. Resulting plans could be reviewed for distributional equity and nondiscrimination.

Dayton, Ohio, has also attempted to concentrate its limited CDBG funds into selected neighborhoods based on an assessment of physical and social needs. However, its planners employed a different data base and selection logic for identifying priority areas than did those in Memphis. In Dayton, a commercially available data package developed and updated annually for some 2,000 cities and towns was used. The census tract is the basic geographic organizing unit for this system. Dayton planners used census tract data on housing occupancy and ownership rates, housing abandonment rates, income levels, and joblessness to divide the city into three types of neighborhoods: "transitional," "stable," and "strategic." Strategic areas, which will receive the bulk of Dayton's block grant funds, are neighborhoods with increasing problems which should yet be able to show dramatic improvement with limited but concentrated assistance.[87]

Land-based planning systems have been receiving much greater attention from comprehensive planners. Los Angeles, California; Lane County, Oregon; and the Houston-Galveston metropolitan region in Texas are just three areas where sophisticated efforts have been mounted to geocode nongeographic planning data with computers. Such systems, although designed to accomplish much greater data integration than the limited attempts of Memphis and Dayton, can have great utility in identifying distributional priorities for housing and community-development projects based on nondiscriminatory measures of physical and social need.

REFERENCES

1. See Carl Steinitz et al., *Honey Hill: A Systems Analysis for Planning the Multiple Use of Controlled Water Areas* (Cambridge, Mass.: Harvard University Graduate School of Design, Department of Landscape Architecture, Research Office, IWR Report 71-9, October 1971), especially Appendix D. Prepared for the U.S. Army Corps of Engineers Institute for Water Resources.

2. Southeastern Wisconsin in Regional Planning Commission, *Soils Development Guide* (Waukesha, Wisconsin: 1969).

3. R. Burton Litton, Jr., *Forest Landscape Description and Inventories — A Basis for Planning and Design* (Washington, D.C.: U.S. Department of Agriculture, Forest Service Research Paper PS V-49, 1968).

4. Association of Bay Area Governments, *Land Capability Analysis* (December 1975), p. 3.

5. Philip H. Lewis, *Study of Recreation and Open Space in Illinois* (Urbana, Illinois: University of Illinois, Department of Landscape Architecture and Bureau of Community Planning, 1964).

6. City of Dallas Department of Planning and Urban Development, *The Dallas Ecological Study* (1973), p. 20.

7. University of Pennsylvania Center for Ecological Research in Planning and Design, *Medford: Performance Requirements for the Maintenance of Social Values Represented by the Natural Environment of Medford Township, New Jersey* (Philadelphia: 1974).

8. Ibid., p. 5.

9. *Michigan Outdoor Recreation Study* (East Lansing, Michigan, 1966).

10. Carl Steinitz, Peter Rogers et al., *Urbanization and Change* (Cambridge, Mass.: Harvard University Department of Landscape Architecture, 1971).

11. Council on Environmental Quality, *Sixth Annual Report* (Washington, D.C., 1975), p. 161.

12. San Francisco Bay Conservation and Development Commission, *San Francisco Bay Plan* (San Francisco: 1969).

13. U.S. Environmental Protection Agency, *Measuring External Effects of Solid Waste Management* (Washington, D.C.: EPA-600/5-75-010, March 1975), p. 276.

14. Ibid.

15. David H. Marks et al., *Evaluation of Policy-Related Research in the Field of Municipal Solid Waste Management* (Massachusetts Institute of Technology, Department of Civil Engineering, 1974).

16. Thermo-Electron Corporation, *Potential for Effective Use of Fuel in Industry* (Waltham, Mass.: Thermo-Electron Corporation, 1974). Also S.G. Dukelow, "Energy Conservation in Current Power Plants," in *Energy Conservation Policy Options for Illinois: Proceedings of the Second Annual Illinois Energy Conference, June 24-25, 1974* (NTIS PB 240 548).

17. See S.E. Beall and M.M. Yarosh, "Status of Waste Heat Utilization and Dual-Purpose Plant Projects," (Oak Ridge, Tenn.: Oak Ridge National Laboratory, 1973).

18. Arthur D. Little, Inc., *Residential and Commercial Energy Use Patterns 1970-1990* (Washington, D.C.: U.S. Government Printing Office, 1974), part of the FEA Task Force Reports for Project Independence; Hittman Associates, *Residential Energy Consumption: Multifamily Housing Final Report* (Washington, D.C.: U.S. Government Printing Office, 1974).

19. Technology and Economics, Inc., *An Overview and Critical Evaluation of the Relationship Between Land Use and Energy Conservation*, submitted to the Federal Energy Administration (March 1976), p. 108.

20. Margaret F. Fels and Michael J. Munson, "Energy Thrift in Urban Transportation: Options for the Future" in *The Energy Conservation Papers* (Cambridge, Mass.: Ballinger, 1975); Jerry L. Edwards and Joseph L. Schofer, "Relationships between Energy Consumption and Urban Spatial Structure," in *Energy Policy Options for Illinois: Proceedings of the Second Annual Illinois Energy Conference, June 24-25, 1974* (NTIS PB 240 548); James S. Roberts, *Energy, Land Use, and Growth Policy: Implications for Metropolitan Washington* (Chicago: Real Estate Research Corporation, 1975).

21. Fels and Munson, op. cit., p. 57.

22. J.D. DeForest, *State Energy Information Systems*, prepared by the National Governors' Conference for the Economic Development Administration, U.S. Department of Commerce (July 1975, NTIS PB 247 457), p. 4.

23. Associated Universities, *Reference Energy Systems and Resource Data for Use in the Assessment of Energy Technologies* (NTIS PB 221 422).

24. Technology and Economics, Inc., op. cit., p. 187.

25. Robert A. Herendeen, "Energy Cost of Goods and Services," (Oak Ridge, Tenn.: Oak Ridge National Laboratory, 1973).

26. Roberts, op. cit.

27. J.D. Deforest, op. cit., Appendix E.

28. Agreement for Coordination of Activities between Office of Community Planning and Development (701), Department of Housing and Urban Development and Federal Energy Administration, dated August 27, 1975.

29. U.S. Environmental Protection Agency, *Promoting Environmental Quality Through Urban Planning and Controls* (Washington, D.C.: EPA-600/5-73-015, February 1974). See Section IVC.

30. San Francisco Department of City Planning, *The Urban Design Plan of San Francisco* (San Francisco: May 1971).

31. Department of Community Development, *Seattle Urban Design Report No. 1: Determinants of City Form* (Seattle: January 1971).

32. Minneapolis Department of Planning, *Problems in Downtown Minneapolis and Options for Downtown Problems* (Minneapolis, Minnesota: 1972).

33. City of Dallas Department of Planning and Urban Development, Urban Design Division, *Dallas Ecological Study. Phase 1, Data Storage System* (Dallas: 1972).

34. U.S. Environmental Protection Agency, *Promoting Environmental Quality Through Urban Planning and Controls* (Washington, D.C., EPA-60015-73-015), p. 298.

35. M.R. Wolfe and R.D. Shinn, *Urban Design Within the Comprehensive Planning Process* (Seattle: 1970). See Chapter 4, especially the concluding footnote.

36. U.S. Environmental Protection Agency, *Promoting Environmental Quality Through Urban Planning and Controls,* P. 188.

37. U.S. Environmental Protection Agency, *Guidelines for Areawide Waste Treatment Management Planning* (Washington, D.C.: August 1975), pp. 2-6 and 3-4.

38. U.S. Environmental Protection Agency, *Land Use Implications and Requirements of EPA Programs,* 1974, p. 9.

39. Ibid., p. 4.

40. For more detail on important land-use/water-quality relationships, see U.S. Environmental Protection Agency, *Performance Standards for Sensitive Lands: A Practical Guide for Local Administrators* (Washington, D.C., EPA-600/5-75-005, March 1975).

41. Interagency Agreement between the Department of Housing and Urban Development and the Environmental Protection Agency dated March 24, 1975, pp. 1, 3.

42. U.S. Environmental Protection Agency, *Coordinating 208 Planning and Air Quality Maintenance Area Planning* (Program Guidance Memorandum AM-14, October 30, 1975), p. 10.

43. U.S. Environmental Protection Agency, *Guidelines for Areawide Waste Treatment Management Planning*, p. 4-3.

44. U.S. Environmental Protection Agency, Program Guidance Memorandum AM-14, p. 11.

45. Ann L. Strong et al., *The Plan and Program for the Brandywine* (Philadelphia: University of Pennsylvania Institute for Environmental Studies, 1968).

46. See U.S. Environmental Protection Agency, *Coordinating 208 Planning and Air Quality Maintenance Area Planning*, pp. 2-3.

47. 42USC1857c-4(b) (1), (2).

48. 42USC1857c-5(a) (2) (B).

49. 42USC1857c-5(a) (4).

50. Charles Szczepanski, "Air Quality Considerations in HUD Programs and the Relationship to EPA Activities," in John J. Roberts (ed.), *Proceedings of a Specialty Conference on Long-Term Maintenance of Clean Air Standards*, February 4-5, 1975, pp. 48, 50.

51. Elizabeth H. Haskell, *An Evaluation of Section 208 as a Model for Air Quality Planning and Management*, prepared for the Office of Transportation and Land Use Policy, U.S. Environmental Protection Agency (July 1975), p. 31.

52. Charles Szczepanski, *Comments* on "Air Quality Management Using Land Use and Transportation," Fred C. Hart, contained in *Proceedings of a Specialty Conference on Long-Term Maintenance of Clean Air Standards*, loc. cit.

53. Charles Szczepanski, Ibid., p. 77.

54. Interagency Agreement between the Department of Housing and Urban Development and the Environmental Protection Agency dated March 25, 1975, p. 2.

55. U.S. Environmental Protection Agency, Program Guidance Memorandum AM-14, p. 2.

56. Dale Keyes, *Land Development and the Natural Environment: Estimating Impacts* (Washington, D.C.: The Urban Institute, 1976). See especially Part IIB.

57. U.S. Department of Housing and Urban Development, *Noise Abatement and Control: Departmental Policy, Implementation Responsibilities, and Standards* (Washington, D.C., August 4, 1971), p. 1.

58. U.S. Department of Transportation, Federal Highway Administration, *Noise Standards and Procedures* (Policy and Procedure Memorandum 90-2, dated February 8, 1973), p. 1.

59. Ibid., in the Transmittal Letter.

60. Metropolitan Washington, Council of Governments, *Sound Cooperation: First Phase of an Areawide Environmental Noise Study* (Washington, D.C.: June 1975).

61. David N. Keast, "Some Pitfalls of Community Noise Measurement," *Journal of the Air Pollution Control Federation* 25:1 (January 1975), p. 37.

62. L.S. Goodfriend and Associates, *Urban Noise Survey Methodology* (New York: 1971).

63. Keast, op. cit. See References 11, 12, and 13 cited at the end of the article.

64. Paul Borsky, "The Use of Social Surveys for Measuring Community Response to Noise Environments," in James Chapulnik (ed.), *Transportation Noise* (University of Washington, 1970).

65. Keifer and Associates, Inc., *Nationally Recognized Safe Land Use and Construction Practices* (January 1976), p. I-7.

66. Earl J. Baker and Joe G. McPhee, *Land Use Management and Regulation in Hazardous Areas: A Research Assessment* (Boulder: University of Colorado, 1975). See especially Chapter 4.

67. PL 93-251, Section 73.

68. For an exhaustive survey of existing state and local authority for land-use controls in flood hazard areas, see Keifer and Associates, op. cit., Chapter 3.

69. Baker and McPhee, op. cit., p. 2.

70. CFR, Title 24, Chapter 10, Section 1910.23, April 1, 1973.

71. CFR, Title 24, Chapter 10, Section 1910.23(b), Proposed Criteria, March 26, 1975.

72. U.S. Environmental Protection Agency, *State Program Implementation Hazardous Waste Surveys* (Washington, D.C.: 1973).

73. U.S. Environmental Protection Agency, *Report to Congress: Disposal of Hazardous Wastes* (Washington, D.C.: 1974), p. ix.

74. U.S. Environmental Protection Agency, *State Program Implementation Hazardous Waste Surveys.*

75. National Park Service, *Guidelines for Local Surveys: A Basis for Preservation Planning* (Washington, D.C.: Office of Archeological and Historic Preservation, Draft Report, 1976), pp. 12-13.

76. Ibid., pp. 51-56.

77. Ibid., pp. 5-6.

78. Department of Transportation Act of 1966, Section 4(f).

79. U.S. Department of Transportation, *Techniques for Incorporating Historic Preservation Objectives into the Highway Planning Process* (Washington, D.C.: April 1974).

80. Housing and Community Development Act of 1974, Section 101(c).

81. Ibid., Section 101(c) (6).

82. Ibid., Section 109.

83. *City of Hartford* vs. *Carla Hills*, 408F. Supp. 889 (1976).

84. 24CFR 570.303.

85. "HUD Helps Localities with Expected to Reside Data," *Practicing Planner* 6:1 (February 1976), pp. 3-4.

86. Memorandum from the Secretary of Housing and Urban Development to HUD Regional Administrators and Area Office Directors, *Utilization of Regional Housing Planning in Department Programs*, dated March 5, 1976.

87. For more detail on the Memphis and Dayton approaches, see Dan Yurman, "Focused Investments in the City," *Practicing Planner*, loc. cit., pp. 16-23.

Chapter 3
Development and Evaluation
of Plan Alternatives

This chapter deals with the second of the four major steps in comprehensive planning, namely, the development and evaluation of alternative plans and policies. Because of the nature of this step, it is not particularly useful to structure the discussion around individual environmental-planning considerations, as in the previous chapter. Instead, this chapter is organized in terms of five component tasks which, if carried out in an environmentally sensitive fashion, can greatly enhance the quality of comprehensive planning. These five tasks concern:

Guidance framework plans. These general statements of planning goals and policies help delimit the range of available alternatives. They can be developed for any level of government, from multistate regions on down to individual municipalities.

Development of plan alternatives. Plan alternatives can be generated and elaborated in a systematic way, sensitive both to general land-use patterns and specific environmental-planning objectives.

Evaluation of plan alternatives. A wide range of environmental evaluation techniques is available, including trade-off analysis, assessment of project impact, cost-benefit analysis, and social and cultural assessment.

Environmental assessment. HUD regulations specifically require development of an environmental assessment of assisted comprehensive plans.

Plan selection. The formal adoption process must be able to take into account the views of related government agencies, the general public, and the appropriate executive and legislative branches.

For each of these tasks, emphasis is placed on how environmental-planning considerations can be integrated into the process. The manual includes specific methodologies and examples of their application.

GUIDANCE FRAMEWORK PLANS

An essential intermediate step between the conduct of planning studies and formulation of planning alternatives is development of a planning framework or guidance document that defines the general lines that subsequent planning and policy-making activities should follow. The role of the guidance document is to frame the range of choices that are open to planners by setting forth, in explicit terms, information of the following kind:

> The goals and objectives that specific plans, policies, and programs are to achieve, the selection of which is based on a combination of preferences expressed by community interest groups and of the planning objectives derived from technical studies
>
> Planning principles and assumptions applied by planners in projecting trends and formulating basic policies for the planning area
>
> General policies, decision rules, and criteria that should guide the design of alternative solutions for achieving the goals and objectives

The degree of detail and range of policy topics addressed in a framework plan vary considerably according to the level of government from which the plan originates and the scope of planning concerns it covers. A framework plan may, as in the case of the California Environmental Goals and Policies Report, be developed specifically to deal with only particular aspects of the natural environment. The Goals for Dallas program and the Metropolitan Twin Cities Area's Development Guide, on the other hand, illustrate guidance frameworks that set forth goals and policies for the entire range of comprehensive-planning and management concerns, the former for a single municipality, the latter for a multijurisdictional metropolitan region.

Use of a framework plan to establish the rationale and parameters for subsequent, more detailed planning and policy making is not new, although it has not always been formalized in the past. In some cases the framework has existed simply as a consensus among planning staff. More typically, a land-use map, perhaps with some accompanying text, has served this function; but all too often the policies represented by the traditional land-use map have not been implemented. Partially to overcome this problem, guidance framework plans of recent years have emphasized, in addition to maps, more explicit documentation of the philosophic basis and assumptions underlying the policy rules; when these are made explicit, they can be more readily reviewed and revised in light of changing circumstances.

Articulation of basic goals, assumptions, and decision rules in a framework document serves several other useful purposes. First, when these things are spelled out clearly, the specific planning alternatives based on them have a far greater likelihood of being valid options, designed with the criteria for their assessment in mind. Second, agencies and departments engaged in functional planning are in a better position to coordinate their individual actions in a planning area when an overall framework is available as a central point of reference. Third, the information provided by the guidance framework gives private citizens and public officials a basis for making informed choices among alternatives put before them by planners. Arbitrariness in decision making is thereby reduced. Such a framework thus offers a solution to the familiar dilemma described by Burns: "While people demand that public participation should be an integral part of the process of planning, the information and analysis on which decisions need to be taken becomes more complex and the process more difficult to understand. Unless technicians can make their work comprehensible, the danger is that much valuable work on techniques will simply be ignored, for at the end of the day the public, in one form or another, makes the decision." [1]

This section will briefly describe five examples of framework plans developed recently to guide comprehensive-planning and management decision making along environmentally sensitive lines. These examples have been selected to highlight common themes as well as differences in purpose and approach taken at five different levels of government: interstate regional, statewide, county, metropolitan, and municipal.

Interstate Regional: The NAR Water Resources Study

At the interstate regional level, guidance planning obviously involves less specific detail than at other levels because of the sheer size of the geographic area and the institutional complexities to be addressed. The utility of a framework plan at this level lies in the consideration that can be given to environmental media, notably air and water, that do not obey jurisdictional boundaries or even those of their own natural "sheds." Interbasin transfers, for instance, whether intended or not, are an important environmental issue which does not lend itself to resolution at state or local levels of planning; it must be dealt with regionally.

One variety of guidance planning for an interstate region is "Level A" Water Resources Planning, and an excellent recent example of it is the North Atlantic Regional Water Resources Study.[2] This study, completed in 1972, constitutes a "comprehensive framework plan" with a fifty-year horizon to guide the management of water and related land and environmental resources in the North Atlantic Region (NAR). The NAR encompasses all or portions of thirteen northeastern states and the District of Columbia and twenty-one hydrologically defined areas ranging from large river basins to small coastal drainage areas. The study's coordinating committee included representatives of each state and river basin commission in the NAR and eight federal agencies.

The guidance framework that the study produced consists of recommendations concerning (1) regional and subregional management programs, including institutional needs for water, land, and environmental resources; (2) priorities for more detailed studies at the basin and project levels; (3) research needs; and (4) procedures for updating the plan. The report emphasized that:

> The Recommended Programs of the NAR [Study] are not meant to present "the" answer nor the "plan" for development of water and related land resources in the NAR. The programs provide a set of guidelines to which water resources planners may refer, and an organized body of fact and opinion on which they may rely in making subsequent decisions in water and related resources development.[3]

Statewide: California Environmental Goals and Policies Report

A policy framework for protecting land and water resources of statewide significance is proposed in California's First Environmental

Goals and Policies Report,[4] prepared in accordance with a 1970 state law. The "environment" that is the subject of this framework was limited to "natural or physical factors of the environment, including archeological and historical sites as well as air, water, native flora and fauna, and scenic vistas."[5] The goals and policies put forth in the report are to serve as:

A definition of the state role regarding the environment

A foundation for a more comprehensive state land-use policy protecting resources of statewide significance

A framework to guide local governments and the private sector in their individual priority-setting and decision-making processes

The recommended environmental goals and policies are presented under three suggested courses of action to promote environmental quality in the state: (1) abatement and control of environmental pollution, (2) protection of environmental resources of statewide "significance" and "critical concern," and (3) establishment of a continuing, multidisciplinary environmental-planning process.

Recommended goals and policies for action on environmental pollution emphasize analysis of cause-effect relations, establishment of standards and criteria, state provision of guidance to localities, and monitoring programs. The list of pollution problems for which goals and policies are suggested includes water, air, land use, noise, pesticides and solid waste.

Environmental resource goals and policies are set forth for eight categories of resources identified as potentially having statewide significance:

Scientific, scenic, and educational resources

Wildlife habitats

Forest and agriculture

Open space surrounding metropolitan areas

Beaches, lakes, and riverbank access

Connecting lands for recreation

Historic, archeological, and cultural resources

Lands of hazardous concern

Under each category of resource, particular geographic areas are recommended as candidates for designation by the governor as potential areas of "statewide significance" or "statewide critical concern," according to criteria spelled out in the policies. Use of such designation is recommended as a mechanism "to pull together the State's role and interest in significant resources and build upon existing statutes for enforcement."[6] It is intended that adoption of criteria and policies for significant and critical areas will assist localities in defining what is meant by "suitability for development" and will set the stage for formulation of a more comprehensive state land-use policy.

As for environmental planning, the goals and policies describe the characteristics of a recommended environmental-planning process and the institutions for implementing it, and they outline a proposed environmental resources protection plan for the state. A "reference" or "partnership" planning approach, which emphasizes both vertical coordination (between levels of government) and horizontal coordination (among state functional departments), is recommended. The process should be a continuous one, and it should be multidisciplinary. The plan sets forth procedures for identifying and formally designating significant resources and resource areas and for preparing development guidelines for these resources to assist localities.

County Level: Bucks County, Pennsylvania

An example of how one county is carrying out guidance planning is Bucks County's "development sector" framework concept for individual town plans.[7] This framework divides county lands into four categories: urban areas (largely developed), development areas (where there is pressure for growth), rural holding areas (largely agricultural and forest areas), and resource protection areas (natural, recreational, and historic areas that would be jeopardized by development). The major policy aims of the county framework are to channel growth at the urban fringe to designated development areas and so "prevent scattered development and urban sprawl"; to discourage growth in rural holding areas; and to prohibit development in resource protection areas.

The provision and withholding of public investments is to be a key tool for implementing the development sector concept, although rezoning and use of an official map showing the various area designations are also contemplated. Under this guidance framework, municipalities within the county prepare their own detailed land-use and zoning plans to guide local development, but zoning must not contradict the county's sector designations.

Metropolitan Level: The Twin Cities Metropolitan Development Guide

Development guidance planning in the Metropolitan Twin Cities Area grew out of the Minnesota State Legislature's acknowledgment of needs common to many metropolitan regions: to control and abate environmental degradation and to coordinate the development-related policies and actions of a multitude of governing units and functional agencies. In 1967, the legislature created a new agency, the Metropolitan Council of the Twin Cities Area, with statutory authority to "prepare and adopt a comprehensive development guide for the Metropolitan Area. It shall consist of a compilation of policy statements, goals, standards, programs, and maps prescribing guides for orderly and economic development, public and private, of the Metropolitan Area."[8] The area involved encompasses seven counties and 3,000 square miles.

The development framework portion of the *Guide*, adopted in March 1975, is intended to serve as:

A reference to be consulted by the council in its reviews of the long-range plans of municipalities, counties, and regional commissions

An aid in setting priorities and policies for metropolitan investments in public facilities and services that strongly influence the development of the region

A means to ensure that metropolitan systems and local support systems are designed to foster overall social, economic, and development objectives rather than single-purpose objectives

A basis for comments to federal agencies regarding the merits of local projects seeking federal funds, in the Council's A-95 Review capacity

A long-range policy guide for development decisions of governmental units and major private entities [9]

Preparation of the development framework chapter entailed extensive input from citizens and local government officials, as well as review of planning studies data and existing development policies. This needs analysis was the basis for setting the goals and policies of the development framework. The resulting framework is a set of goals which are then translated into policy statements for each of five geographic policy areas:

The metropolitan centers (central business districts of Minneapolis and St. Paul)

The fully developed areas (Minneapolis, St. Paul, and older, close-in suburbs)

The area of planned urbanization (the developing suburban communities that comprise the area of greatest current and future growth)

Freestanding growth centers (fourteen designated small cities in the rural area which have the public services and economic base to accommodate the major portion of rural growth. These centers were designated so that metropolitan investments might be concentrated in a limited number of suitable city centers.)

The rural service area (commercial agricultural regions and general rural-use regions which include rural centers)

All of these policy areas except for the rural service area are designated part of the Metropolitan Urban Service Area (MUSA). Development framework policy is generally to encourage growth — in a logical and systematic manner — in the MUSA where the infrastructure for development is basically in place, and specifically to discourage growth in the rural service area in the interest of holding down the costs of public services and protecting the agricultural economy and natural environment. This is essentially the same approach as that taken by Bucks County.

The implementation program for the development framework chapter employs five types of tools:

Development planning and regulation

Public facility planning and capital programming

Economic incentives

Tax policy

Education about metropolitan growth

The council is concentrating its initial efforts on developing the first three of these tools. They are given highest priority in response to the pressing need for a "required relationship between metropolitan investments and local investments" and between development decisions and public facilities investments, both metropolitan and local. The implementation effort is thus focused on coordination of overall development and redevelopment in the metropolitan area through "shared planning and implementation responsibilities based on metropolitan systems and investments and on local detailed land use and facility planning." An essential feature of the implementation program is that each governmental unit (county or municipality) responsible for providing facilities or regulating land use is required to adopt a comprehensive plan based on and consistent with metropolitan plans. Required elements of the comprehensive plan are: a metropolitan systems statement (supplied to the local governmental unit by the metropolitan council), a land-use plan, a public facilities plan, and an implementation program.

Municipal Level: Goals for Dallas

Goals for Dallas is the result of a broad-based citizen effort begun in 1965.[10] It was, and is, a means of guiding the growth of Dallas in ways desired by a consensus of its citizens. The program shows no evidence of a desire to arrest or dampen growth; its theme is that expected growth should be shaped to the design of the citizens. The guidance system conceived and put into action to accomplish this goal had three major elements: a citizen-oriented goal-setting and prioritizing process, formulation of plans and schedules for achieving the goals, and a system for monitoring progress towards the goals and revising them in light of changing circumstances.

The results of the initial goal-setting process, which involved the participation of some 100,000 citizens, were published in 1967. Recommended implementation actions likewise underwent extensive citizen review. The published set of proposals, entitled *Goals for Dallas: Achieving the Goals*, presented plans, schedules, and priorities. The goals fall under twelve headings of concern, each of which comprises several subgoals. For each subgoal, the document first states the goal, then presents an interpretation of the statement and the general approach to be taken for its attainment, documents progress already made, and finally lists the major steps yet to be taken.

Environmental concerns in this framework are expressed under the general goal category of "Design of the City." Subgoals include the following:

A continuous and coordinated city planning process

A dynamic, comprehensive plan for the city

District and neighborhood plans incorporating planning standards for facilities, services, and other factors

An open-space plan

A program to control signs and overhead utilities

An areawide drainage plan to assure effective flood control

A program to protect and enhance historic landmarks

A community renewal and rehabilitation program

A long-range housing plan

These plans and programs are intended, according to the General Goal Statement for Design of the City, to "provide guideposts for personal and business decisions, not only through codes and ordinances but by furnishing information which makes possible better-informed decisions, and by designs which influence change through force of ideas and example."[11]

The Goals for Dallas planning framework does not consist simply of published goals and strategies for their attainment. An ongoing planning-guidance process was initiated, and this process is considered by program sponsors to be the most significant result of the entire effort. A procedure for regular monitoring and follow-up of progress toward the goals is in operation, and the findings are reported periodically to the public.

DEVELOPMENT OF PLAN ALTERNATIVES

Guidance plans such as those discussed in the previous section provide the framework within which comprehensive plan alternatives can be developed. They translate the findings of planning studies into general statements of community goals and into development policies that then define the range of acceptable plan choices. This section briefly describes the process of developing plan and policy alternatives and the difficulties involved in adequately treating environmental considerations at this stage.

In this development, it is useful to distinguish between initial generation of alternative concepts and the subsequent elaboration of each into alternative plans.[12] Generation of concepts involves, as a prelude to elaboration, identifying key organizing principles and a set of basic attributes for each alternative. Elaboration itself consists of fitting a development concept to the geography of a particular planning area, delineating service system networks, and specifying supporting objectives and policies. Surprisingly, the literature on how to develop comprehensive plan alternatives is relatively thin.

Land-Use Alternatives

Perhaps the most illuminating discussion of the problem is found in a 1970 analysis of the experience of thirteen metropolitan planning efforts, restricted largely to development of land-use and transportation alternatives. This study recognized that "these programs were only part of a larger work program of the agencies involved; however, this type of activity was central to the agencies' efforts and was at the heart of the plan-making process."[13]

Two general approaches to structuring the development of alternatives were observed in the thirteen case studies. The first approach, which can be described as "linear," consists of generating, elaborating, and then evaluating one set of land-use and transportation alternatives. Finally, one alternative is selected as the final plan. The second approach is "cyclic." Each cycle consists of the generation, elaboration, and evaluation of alternatives, followed by a decision and reformulation stage as the basis for a new cycle. These two models of a plan-making process are shown as Figure 7.

Regardless of which planning logic was followed, the thirteen studies exhibited certain common approaches to the task of generating the organizing principles or concepts for the alternative plans. Organizing principles used to generate alternatives included:

Plan forms (linear city, radial corridors, spread city, multiple outlying centers)

Structural characteristics (low vs. high density, concentration vs. dispersal)

Transportation systems (modal emphasis, relative balance between freeways and arterials, specific freeway network configurations, different facility staging)

Development planning process (controlled vs. uncontrolled development, composite of local plans vs. centralized regional plan)

FIGURE 7
Approaches to Preparing and Evaluating Plan Alternatives

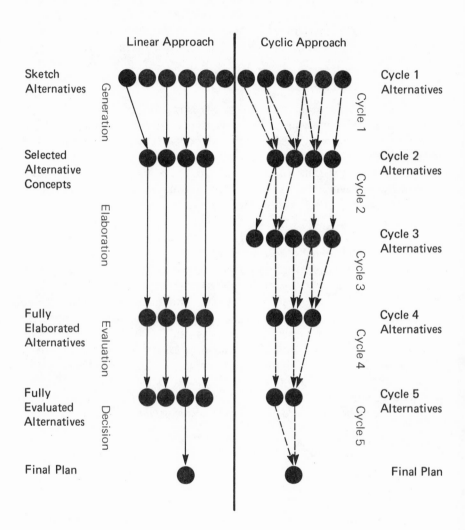

Source: David Boyce et al., *Metropolitan Plan Making,* p. 33.

> Objectives and standards (variations in residential density, neighborhood organization, spacing and level of service of transportation facilities, size and spacing of major commercial facilities)

It is clear that selection of the organizing concept of each alternative is a key decision point in making plans. With the linear approach, selection is critical because the limits set on the range of solutions considered may have a direct bearing on the effectiveness of the entire exercise. In the cyclic approach, selection is perhaps less critical because it can recur at the beginning of each cycle.

Elaboration of the land-use and transportation alternatives after the initial selection of generative concepts also exhibited certain common approaches. Among the similarities were the following techniques:

> Use of models for forecasting regional population, employment, and economic activity

> Use of models for spatially allocating regional growth and private investment

> Use of models for simulating system performance, such as flows on a transportation network

Generally, these three approaches were found to correspond to three differing levels of sensitivity to the process of urban growth.[14] The first approach is the least sensitive, essentially involving the construction of alternative physical patterns of end-state development. Little or no attention is paid to the staging of facilities, the development process, or statements of policy paralleling and supporting the physical development patterns. The second approach introduces simple concepts of an urban development process for spatially allocating households and employment. Staging of facilities is considered, mainly to facilitate operation of the procedure or model, and some attention is paid to the complexity of development decisions and to the need for policies guiding regional development. The third approach, which includes a wider range of policy specifications, devotes more systematic attention to the staging question and to the nature of the development process, and less attention to the end-state arrangement of facilities and activities.

The findings and conclusions of this 1970 study highlight the problems of integrating environmental-planning considerations into the process of identifying and developing comprehensive plan alternatives. First, all thirteen of the metropolitan planning efforts studied focused almost exclusively on physical development. There was only a cursory examination of potential social effects of the alternative plans. Second, typically short planning horizons (twenty to twenty-five years) combined with a marked tendency toward conservatism regarding the feasibility of planning options to produce far less variation among alternative plans than might have been anticipated or desired. Third, plans tended to concentrate on a single metropolitan scale and at a single level of detail; with few exceptions, they ignored significant questions of submetropolitan organization. This is a particularly important deficiency when it comes to identifying and assessing the differential effects of alternatives on the natural environment, where localized factors usually prevail. Natural environmental considerations tended to be overwhelmed by macro-level physical, demographic, and economic calculations.

Since the 1970 study of thirteen metropolitan areas, study techniques for developing and evaluating plan alternatives have been substantially improved, especially in regard to potential natural environment problems. Computer-assisted techniques, including grid-mapping, have been developed to enable planners to store and analyze natural environment data at the small-area level. However, these newer techniques have not been significantly more successful in incorporating social and cultural concerns, except as they relate to specific land uses (for example, for recreation or open space).

An excellent recent example of the use of computer graphics techniques for generating and comparing alternative regional land-use plans is provided by the work of Steinitz Rogers Associates in the Santa Ana River Basin of southern California.[15] The Santa Ana Basin above Prado Dam is an area of rapid growth, having experienced a five-fold increase in population since 1940. Most of the population now resides in the urbanized areas of Pomona, Riverside, and San Bernadino. The Steinitz Rogers approach calls for initial creation of a data base of regional land-use elements and site resources, with the data coded and analyzed on the one-kilometer-square UTM grid coordinate system. The data analysis package consists of two basic programs: (1) locational attractiveness models for thirteen discrete land-use types, where the outputs are weighted attractiveness indices; and (2) resource system vulnerability models in the form of matrices that evaluate the effects of potential future land uses on natural resources. The attractiveness models define the major land uses and activities which occur in the basin, as well as the criteria (largely economic) which will likely determine where and how these activities occur in the future. The vulnerability models define the degree of impact on resource systems resulting from the construction, operation and maintenance of the projected uses. Once the analysis models for locational attractiveness and resource system vulnerability have been prepared, the process is able to evaluate alternative development proposals in these terms.

The modeling framework stores, for any cell, the attractiveness of such land use and the effect each would have on each resource system. Any land-use plan can then be expressed as the decision to locate the various land uses in specific cells. When these land-use locations are entered into the computer, the evaluation framework sorts the entries against the previously stored attractiveness and vulnerability evaluations and produces a map and a table showing which plan locations have cumulative consequences for the resource systems. The only constraint on the description of an alternative land-use plan is that the uses which comprise that plan be defined in the same way as those which comprise the attractiveness and vulnerability models.

The ultimate objective of this approach is the capability to evaluate the multiple effects of particular uses in a given location. This evaluation depends upon a weighting scheme to identify the relative severity of effects. Steinitz Rogers used the simplest possible scheme for their Santa Ana work: a point rating system which scores one point for a compatible evaluation, two for a moderate, three for a severe, and four for a "threshold" (no recovery feasible via natural processes) evaluation. The rating scheme also considers each of the seven separate vulnerability analyses to be of equal weight. However, the evaluation output and format is flexible to the needs of the users; many different configurations are possible, including addition of any relative evaluation weightings the user wants to incorporate.

Alternatives for Other Environmental Considerations

Alternative plans and policies for environmental-planning considerations other than land use are difficult to discuss in the abstract. However, the remainder of this section is devoted to identifying environmentally sensitive *general* alternatives available to planners formulating either comprehensive or specific functional plans.

Energy Conservation

A prime consideration of transportation planning, for example, is encouragement of land-use patterns that minimize energy consumption. Alternatives to urban sprawl development include various forms of cluster development, which bring residences closer to centers of employment, shopping, and recreation opportunity. Technological alternatives exist in the form of replacing automobile travel with such innovative modes as Dial-A-Ride and personal rapid transit (PRT). Restricting automobile use in central cities is also possible. Finally, changes in life-style and attitudes are promising long-run alternatives. Consider people living close to both work and their friends, the substitution of walking and mass transit for much routine auto use, and the use of lightweight, energy-efficient autos for all other travel.

Water Quality

For management of point sources, the major alternatives revolve around the extent of regionalization of treatment; location and staging of treatment facilities and interceptors; the degree of industrial tie-in; and relative reliance upon water vs. land disposal of effluents. Also important are the potential for flow and waste reduction, for wastewater reuse, and for such management options as combined and storm sewer discharges and the disposal of residual sludges. For nonpoint source management, important options are open to planners regarding nonstructural regulatory solutions such as land acquisition, capital investment programming, designation of sensitive water-related lands for restricted development, performance standards for land management, requirements for a local EIS, and controls over land disposal of wastes and in-place or accumulated sources.

Air Quality

The two major classes of alternatives for air-quality maintenance planning are emission reduction and controls on transportation and land use. Emission-oriented alternatives include new source performance standards, fuel conversion, combination of emission sources, stack height regulations, and control of fugitive dust sources. Alternatives oriented to land use consist of emission density zoning, emission charges, transfer of source location, and indirect source review.

Noise Abatement and Control

To prevent future noise conflicts, comprehensive noise management can help by locating new noise sources away from existing or planned noise-sensitive areas, by regulating the intensity and pattern of development in noise-impacted areas, by evaluating whether there are quieter means of meeting the need that existing and planned noise sources are intended to serve, and by formulating measures to address and ameliorate existing noise conflicts.

Reduction of noise generation at the source can be accomplished by performance standards for the location, design, and construction of noise generators (airports, highways, industrial plants), limitations on the use of construction equipment that exceeds designated maximum noise levels, and restriction of noise-producing activities during certain times. Strategies that modify the path of noise transmission include special development concepts such as cluster- and planned-unit developments that maximize the distance between noise sources and sensitive receptors and which place noisy buildings so as to shield noise-sensitive areas; acoustical site planning and building design that insures that noise standards are met within buildings containing noise-sensitive activities and outside areas where noise-sensitive activities take place; and berms and barriers to separate noise generators from receptors.

To protect noise-sensitive receptors, alternative planning and land-use strategies include zoning and subdivision regulations which prohibit noise-sensitive uses in existing and planned noise-impacted areas; restrictions on subdividing land in noise-impacted areas; establishment of local interior and exterior standards; restrictions on noise-producing activities during certain times; relocation of noise-sensitive uses or noise generators to areas outside noise-impacted areas; public land acquisition ensuring compatible use through land-use controls; capital investments for community services to promote compatible development; and incentives for land assembly designated to promote noise-compatible activities in noise-exposed locations.

Flood and Other Hazards

Floodplain management strategies for reducing flood hazards include regulation of floodplain land use, construction of protective works, floodproofing of new and existing structures, information and warning systems, flood insurance, and relief and rehabilitation

FIGURE 8

Examples of Adjustments to Natural Hazards in the United States

Types of Hazards	Modify Event	Types of Adjustment Modify Vulnerability	Distribute Losses
Avalanche	Artificial release	Snow shields	Emergency relief
Coastal Erosion	Beach nourish-ment	Beach groines	Flood insurance
Drought	Cloud seeding	Cropping pattern	Crop insurance
Earthquake	Earthquake re-duction (theoretical)	Earthquake-resis-tant buildings	Emergency relief
Flood	Upstream water control	Flood-proofing	SBA loans
Frost	Orchard heating	Warning network	Crop insurance
Hail	Cloud seeding	Plant selection	Hail insurance
Hurricane	Cloud seeding	Land-use pattern	Emergency relief
Landslide	—	Land-use regulation	—
Lightning	Cloud seeding	Lightning con-ductors	Homeowners in-surance
Tornado	—	Warning network	Emergency relief
Tsunami	—	Warning network	Emergency relief
Urban Snow	—	Snow-removal preparations	Taxation for snow removal
Volcano	—	Land-use regulations	Emergency relief
Windstorm	—	Mobile home design	Property insurance

Source: White and Haas, *Assessment of Research on Natural Hazards,* p. 58.

expenditures. Regarding natural hazards as a whole, there are essentially three types of adjustment measures available to planners: (1) modifying the causes of the hazard, (2) modifying vulnerability to the natural event, and (3) distributing the losses. Figure 8 provides some examples of common adjustment measures available for certain natural hazards. As for man-made hazards, the basic planning alternatives available relate to industrial site selection, safe separation distances between industrial and residential/commercial uses; and regulation of industrial handling, storage, processing, and disposal of hazardous materials.

Historic Preservation

Strategies for historic preservation include maintenance of the architectural and physical integrity of significant individual resources; maintenance of groups or concentrations of resources while allowing promotion of future growth and development; maintenance and enhancement of environmental amenities such as riverbanks, pedestrian pathways, and vistas; and strengthening neighborhood identity and cohesion. Specific legal and financial tools to be considered include Historic District and Landmarks Commission ordinances; open space, facade, and interior performance standards and easements; covenants and reverter clauses; favorable tax provisions, such as those for credits, deductions, and abatement; incentives for adaptive uses of historic resources that are oriented to tourists as well as to the needs of the local population; use of Community Development Block Grant funding; and use of Section 312 rehabilitation loans which are available for code enforcement, and urban redevelopment.

Social Equity

The widest possible range of options should be considered for furthering social equity in housing and employment, including regional fair-share housing allocation plans; close scrutiny of individual municipal Housing Assistance Plans to ensure that they fulfill the "expected-to-reside" requirement for low- and moderate-income housing; provision of assisted housing and community facilities with an eye to deconcentration of low- and moderate-income households; regional or state review of local zoning ordinances; and provision of public transportation options to suburban centers of employment.

EVALUATION OF PLAN ALTERNATIVES

This section concentrates on techniques for evaluating comprehensive plan alternatives, and it includes examples of their successful local application. The evaluation problem is discussed under four major headings, reflecting important separate lines of methodological development:

Plan and policy tradeoff analysis, where regional comprehensive plans are evaluated for their ecological and economic effects and for the relevant tradeoffs therein

Project impact analysis, where specific project plans are evaluated for their consequences for the comprehensive plan

Benefit-Cost analysis, applied to determine the relative cost of achieving specific environmental objectives

Analysis of social and cultural concerns, which involves evaluating the effect of plans and policies on social well-being and on the general quality of life

The need to distinguish among these types of evaluation suggests the difficulty of integrating environmental considerations into the evaluation of alternatives. Depending upon the type of methodology applied, the evaluative focus can be an entire comprehensive plan, the relation between a specific component project and that plan, the benefits and costs of achieving a desired (or required) environmental-quality standard, or a general characterization of human well-being. Wherever possible, an attempt will be made to assess the applicability of each methodology to the seven environmental-planning considerations identified in the previous chapter.

Plan and Policy Tradeoff Analysis

There have been two principal approaches to the problem of incorporating the environment into the regional planning process, one of which focuses on the ecosystem as a determinant of regional development, and the other which focuses mainly on the economic activities of humans. The work of Ian McHarg[16] which exemplifies the ecologic approach, deals with the capacity of an area's ecosystem to absorb development. His approach provides a spatially disaggregated analysis of the compatibility of various ecosystems in the region with broad categories of development, usually expressed as general categories of land used for residential, commercial, industrial, and recreational purposes. The "carrying capacity" of the ecosystem expressed through the factors of geology, hydrology, wildlife, and vegetation is viewed as constraining the locational choices for development. The evaluation of the tightness of the constraints is subjective and usually expressed as binding or nonbinding for a certain class of land use. On the other hand, the economic activity approach, typified by the work of Walter Isard and James Hite,[17] is a "region-wide" evaluation of the gross tradeoff between the level of regional economic activity (without regard to the spatial distribution by sector) and the levels of waste load and physical requirements (such as land needs) generated by this level of economic activity. The focus is on the "macro" level, the tradeoff for the region as a whole between waste loads and the level of economic activity as a whole or by sectors.

Both the carrying capacity and economic activity approaches will be discussed in detail here. In recent work there has also been an attempt to synthesize these two approaches. The effort is based on the obvious fact that neither economic activity nor environmental capacity are homogeneous across regions. Two examples of such attempts at synthesis will also be discussed: the Environmental Decision Assistance System (EDAS) developed by the Houston-Galveston Area Council, and the Arizona Tradeoff Model (ATOM) developed for the State of Arizona by Battelle Memorial Institute.

Carrying Capacity Analysis

The seminal concepts in the natural ecologic approach stem from the work of Ian McHarg and are most forcefully presented in *Design with Nature.*[18] Very briefly, McHarg's procedure relies on making overlay maps of a set of natural environmental parameters bearing some relation to land use. For each environmental parameter, judgments are made as to the capability of various areas to support land development. These maps are then overlaid, and an area is selected for development according to the degree of opportunity offered across all the parameters. Such procedures have certain intrinsic defects. If an area were unsuitable for development across a single parameter, the overlaying procedures would automatically eliminate it although, with certain precautions, a single unsuitable characteristic might be accommodated. In this procedure, each parameter has equal weight. If one wishes to develop a land-management program for a particular area across all parameters, the procedure is cumbersome.

The procedure can be most easily understood through an example taken from McHarg's Staten Island study and recorded in *Design with Nature.* The categories of land use selected for evaluation were conservation, commercial-industrial, residential, and recreational. Many natural data sets were compiled and mapped; from these natural data sets, considering the four uses in question, over thirty factors were selected for use in the evaluation. Selection of evaluation factors was based on the knowledge and experience of the analyst, and these factors were in turn ranked as being of high, medium, or low importance.

The next step was evaluation of the suitability of the entire island for each particular use. For each use, McHarg chose the salient evaluation factors to reveal the areas most suitable for that use. For instance, for conservation the factors selected were:

Features of historic value

High-quality forests

High-quality marshes

Bay beaches

Streams

Water-associated wildlife habitats

Intertidal wildlife habitats

Unique geological features

Unique physiographic features

Scenic land features

Scenic water features

Scarce ecological associations

A map of each of the factors was created in color tones corresponding to the ranking scheme.

The next step in the process was to combine these factor maps to indicate areas of intrinsic suitability. For conservation, all twelve factor maps were made into transparent negatives which were then superimposed and photographed. The resulting photograph represented the summation of all the values employed and was therefore indicative of the areas most to least suitable for conservation. This photograph was then reconstituted as a single map. The determination of the areas most suitable for the other three uses (commercial-industrial, residential, recreation) was carried out in exactly the same fashion.

Economic Activity Approach

The economic activity approach focuses on region-wide evaluation of the tradeoffs between levels of economic activity (output, employment) and the levels of "residuals," or wastes, generated. The approach is inherently general, meaning that the effects, waste loads, and measures of economic activity cannot be spatially disaggregated within the region. The theoretical basis for this approach stems from the early work of Pigou and others, but it was given its most detailed presentation in an article by Ayres and Kneese.[19] Applications of the approach follow from the path-breaking work of Isard[20] and rely on relating the economy and the environment through an input-output approach. (This is a special case of the general model outlined by Kneese and Ayres.)

An *input-output model* is an economic model in which economic activity is grouped into sectors and is based on a transactions table. The *transactions table* is a matrix that gives the output of any given sector in terms of the inputs to that sector from each and every other sector in the economy. Total inputs to the economy must equal total outputs, and all quantities are expressed in dollars. One or more sectors are identified as final demands, typically households and government, and the model takes the form:

(1) $X = A \cdot X + Y$

or

(2) $X = (I - A)^{-1} Y$

where

X = vector of sectoral outputs

A = input-output transactions matrix

Y = vector of final demands

The transactions matrix is usually estimated empirically through surveys of the purchases and sales of a sample of firms in the region. It should be noted that the input-output model does not take into account any possible constraints imposed by lack of resources, labor, or other factors. Theoretically, it will specify by sector the levels of output needed to satisfy any level of final demand, given the direct linear relation between inputs and outputs specified by the transactions matrix. The Leontief inverse, $(I - A)^{-1}$, can be interpreted as specifying the direct and indirect requirements for supplying one dollar's worth of output to final demand. That is, for a sector to produce one dollar's worth of output it must directly purchase inputs from a variety of sectors in the economy, as expressed in the transactions table, A. However, these sectors must purchase inputs from a variety of sectors to produce the input needed for the first sector to expand, and so on and on. The expansion of one sector, then, has a "ripple" effect throughout the whole economy. The Leontief inverse, the expression of the total effect of all these ripples in the economy, can be derived algebraically.

This strictly economic model is easily modified to reflect the environmental load caused by economic growth in the region:

> There are two essential elements of the model . . . (1) the Leontief inverse of an input-output matrix of the local economy; and (2) a matrix showing the inflow from the environment and the residual outflow to the environment associated with one dollar of gross output of each sector of the input-output matrix. Inflows from the environment are given a positive sign, and residual outflows are given negative signs. The basic operation involves postmultiplying the environmental linkages matrix by the Leontief inverse:
>
> $$(E) (I-A)^{-1} = (R)$$
>
> where E is a matrix of inflows to and outflows from the economy to the environment, $(I-A)^{-1}$ is the Leontief inverse of an area input-output matrix, and R is a matrix of the direct and indirect environmental impact of each economic sector.[21]

The E matrix is usually estimated sector by sector from EPA industry studies, but it can be estimated from survey data of the firms in the region once an appropriate classification system for inflows and outflows (residuals) is chosen.

Discussing the uses of such a model estimated for the Charleston, South Carolina, area, Hite and Laurent explain that:

> The model allows a comparison of the direct and indirect linkage between the economic and ecologic systems for selected economic sectors and environmental goods. The direct emissions involve an economic sector exporting residuals directly to the environment. The direct and in-

direct linkages result from the economic interdependence between sectors in the local economy. A given sector's activities may have little or no direct effect on the environment; however, it must purchase inputs from other sectors, some of which do draw directly upon environmental resources. In this sense the given sector, by increasing the production of supplying sectors, may indirectly require use of environmental resources. For example, the Furniture and Fixtures sector emits no hydrocarbons directly into the air, but indirectly results in 0.0455 pounds of hydrocarbons being emitted per additional dollar of sales outside the region; on the other hand, Petroleum and Coal Products, which directly emits 5.0265 pounds of hydrocarbons per dollar of external sales directly and indirectly emits even more (5.0433 pounds). The importance of this point is that *all* economic sectors in the Charleston study area — either directly or indirectly — have ecologic linkages and are responsible for some level of natural environmental degradation.[22]

The direct and indirect environmental effects matrix R is an exact environmental corollary of our "ripple" effect in the strictly economic use of the model.

Proceeding in this fashion, it is then possible to evaluate some "region-wide" tradeoffs between economic growth and wasteloads and, thus, environmental effects. To do this it must be assumed that the production relations embodied in the A and E matrices remain the same for some future time or, put another way, no technological change or change in relative prices is assumed. Given this assumption, it is possible to project the levels of economic activity of the significant sectors of the regional economy and to examine their environmental loadings. For the South Carolina case, Hite and Laurent found that some sectors such as textiles and apparels accounted for over 70% of the expected growth in income, but that the wasteloads and therefore the environmental repercussions resulting from this growth would be relatively small for the region as a whole. Other sectors, however, such as chemical manufacturing, were found to generate far more environmental consequences per unit increase in income. Guided by this kind of information at the regional level, it is possible to evaluate gross tradeoffs between growth and environment. Many variations and extensions of this basic technique have been suggested and formulated, including the derivation of environmental/income multipliers and environmental/ employment multipliers. This approach has also been formulated in a linear programming framework so that the tradeoffs between economic growth and wasteloads can be examined in more detail.

The greatest drawback of the economic activity approach is that it fails to take into account the effects that may result from differing spatial distributions of economic activity. As seen in the work of McHarg, there are likely to be large variations in the ecosystem of a region. Thus, the actual level of environmental effect should vary with the distribution of the activity and waste disposal within that region even if the total amount of wastes discharged in the region remained constant.

There have been many recent attempts to combine the best features of the carrying capacity and economic activity approaches and formulate a methodology that evaluates the tradeoffs between different levels and types of economic activity by examining impacts on a small scale. Two such attempts to take the differential response of regional ecosystems to development into account are briefly discussed below.

Environmental Decision Assistance System

One approach to economic/ecologic modeling that combines improvements in technical modeling of complex environmental systems and allocation of economic activity is the Environmental Decision Assistance System (EDAS) of the Houston-Galveston Area Council.[23] This system combines an input/output model for the region, a regional land-use simulation model, and many "technical" models such as for water supply, Galveston Bay water quality, and solid waste. The input/output model is one of the eight estimated for regions of Texas that are combined to form the statewide input/output model. In EDAS, the regional input/output model drives the overall model in terms of expected region-wide levels of economic growth and allows detailed breakdowns of projected economic activity in each of seventy-four sectors. These detailed forecasts of economic activity, along with population projections for the region, are used as input to the Regional Simulation and Systems Control model (ReSiSCM), which allocates population and economic activity to 189 zones within the HGAC region.

Through various environmental-quality submodels, the EDAS approach enables planners to translate alternative allocations of future population and economic growth into specific sets of impacts, thus highlighting those areas of potential conflict. EDAS does not necessarily resolve these conflicts, but it performs a valuable function in identifying them and characterizing them in quantitative and spatial terms. The water-supply model is a fairly standard one from the literature, except that it allows for groundwater mining. The model computes water-use requirements for certain preselected zones within the region based on the allocations of residential population and industrial activity to the zone by ReSiSCM and compares this to estimates of the available groundwater and surface water in the zone. The Galveston Bay water-quality model is a two-dimensional simulation of levels of selected conservative and non-conservative substances in the Galveston Bay Estuary, mainly focusing on BOD and thermal properties. Given varying point-source inputs of wastes, tide, and current information on streamflow and quality data for the Trinity River, which flows into the bay, the model computes water quality for square-mile sections of the bay. The solid-waste model predicts the level and composition of solid waste loads for a zone given levels of economic activity and population. It is now being modified to optimize the location of sanitary landfill sites.

Arizona Tradeoff Model (ATOM)

Another approach to the synthesis of economic and ecologic techniques led to the development of the Arizona Tradeoff Model (ATOM) by Battelle Memorial Institute.[24] In contrast to EDAS, ATOM focuses on evaluating the tradeoff between economic growth for subregions (6 X 10 miles) of the state and a generalized index of environmental quality for the entire subregion. However, by dealing with such large subunits, ATOM sacrifices detail in the allocation process and in the evaluation of environmental effect. Once the allocation of economic activity/land use is final for a simulation period and physical, chemical, and land-use constraints are known, the decision-maker compares the composite index of environmental quality for each of the sixty-square-mile areas to the level of employment and other economic measures for the area.

Project Impact Analysis

This manual deals with assessing the environmental consequences of comprehensive plans, not those of individual projects. HUD has prepared a separate document for this latter purpose, the *Interim Guide for Environmental Assessment*. In at least three important situations, however, the useful distinction between plan- and project-level assessment breaks down in practice. First, although the effects of any one project taken alone may not be significant, the collective consequences of a number of related developments undertaken in the same area may prove to be very significant. Their total effects may not be simply additive; rather, they may be something more than and different from the sum of their parts. Second, many large developments have "spillover effects:" environmental consequences beyond the boundaries of their immediate jurisdiction. Third, new developments frequently induce associated investments and changed patterns of social and economic activity off-site in the wider community, leading to what the planning literature refers to as "secondary impacts." In all three of these situations, it becomes very important that individual projects be evaluated within the context of the area's comprehensive plan.

This section takes up the problem of relating project-level impacts to the environmental goals and objectives of the comprehensive plan. It briefly discusses available impact measures and their use, then provides a more detailed treatment of two existing approaches to bringing together plan- and project-level impact considerations: the Land Use Tradeoff Model developed by Battelle and the concept of Impact Zoning first put forward by Rahenkamp, Sachs, Wells and Associates.

Effects of Land Development

Attempts to evaluate the environmental consequences of proposed development characteristically share a number of important shortcomings. Often they are not sufficiently comprehensive. They leave out significant social and economic considerations and tend to concentrate on technical criteria and intermediate effects rather than on results for people. They also frequently employ vague qualitative criteria where quantification could help sharpen evaluative judgments. Recently HUD funded the Urban Institute to develop measures and techniques designed to overcome these deficiencies, "to describe impacts on citizens more explicitly, systematically, comprehensively, and in reasonably nontechnical terms."[25] The product of this effort, now available to comprehensive planners, provides information on key issues and considerations in evaluating the changes associated with proposed land development and on the relative merits of alternative techniques for estimating impacts in light of the costs, skills, and data required and of the validity of their results.[26] Individual studies are available for estimating development effects on the natural environment, income and employment, municipal costs and revenues, and social values.

An important conclusion of the Urban Institute's work is that "comprehensive" land use planning and the impact review of individual projects can and should be coordinated. "Where a few large or many small developments are community-wide in scale, the impacts can be related to development output (emissions or effluents) or even to design criteria (impervious ground cover) and targets established. Individual reviews in many cases can be reduced to comparing the target . . . value with the output from or characteristics of the proposed development (added to the current levels)."[27] The resulting recommendation was that communities consider incorporating target or "budget" values for such things as air emissions, water effluents, and impervious cover in their comprehensive plans. In this way, planners can begin to take into account the larger environmental implications of the incremental effects of individual development approaches. Clearly, such a framework could be used to account for not only the direct results of the development itself, but also for cumulative, spillover, and secondary effects.

Land Use Tradeoff Model

The Land Use Tradeoff Model (LUTOM), developed originally by Battelle for the South Carolina State Port Authority, is a particularly interesting example of a technique for evaluating the effects of proposed developments.[28] It is "comprehensive" in the sense that it considers economic and social as well as natural environment factors for each location decision made. LUTOM was designed specifically for use in Beaufort and Jasper Counties, South Carolina, but it can have broader application for comprehensive planning wherever and at whatever level it is practiced.

The basic LUTOM model consists of the following five elements:

Map overlays showing how uses of the land will change in the region because of particular policies. These map overlays illustrate planning concepts based on hypothetical development proposals. The concept plans illustrate likely new land uses. When superimposed over the existing land use map, the Concept Plan overlays show how land use changes are projected to occur.

Map overlays showing the physical, economic, and social features of the land that will affect or be affected by change. These three map overlays are aggregates of the various features being considered in the evaluation of land suitability. Suitability is defined as the degree to which the land is acceptable for particular types of land use. The factors being considered in preparing the economic, environmental, and social suitability overlays are as follows:

(a) Economic suitability considers existing land use and development costs of the land.

(b) Environmental suitability considers soil, topography, salt water intrusion, and vegetative cover.

(c) Social suitability considers unique ecological and historical features of the land, population density, and type of residential development.

Tables showing aggregate scores that diagnose the effects of the physical, economic, and social features of the land and predict the "suitability" of the land for supporting development. These tables provide ratings on the suitability of all land for development. Ratings are based on a numerical scale of 1 to 7, where 7 is most suitable. Development is categorized into 20 different types of land use. The land uses include various types of residential, commercial, industrial, extractive resources, institutional, and recreation/open space. One table is developed for each of the three broad categories of analysis: environmental, economic, and social.

Tables of compatibility scores that provide planners with guidance on how sensitive the total environment is to land use changes. These tables provide ratings on how compatible one land use is with another. Ratings are based on a numerical scale of 1 to 5, where 5 is most compatible. The same land use categories are used as above. However, in this case the scores represent pair-wise comparisons between every possible combination of land-use categories. Once again, one table is developed for each of the three broad categories: environmental, economic, and social.

> *Assessment indicators to show the environmental, economic, and social impacts of all the land use changes predicted from land use policies.* These indicators are used to measure the overall regional impact from the proposed Concept Plan. The indicators are quantitative.[29]

The evaluative criteria used to assess individual proposed developments under the LUTOM approach include:

Economic criteria
— Personal income, property taxes, land values
— Expenditures for highways, police, fire, education
— Direct and secondary employment
— Unemployment
— Direct salaries and wages, indirect income
— Retail sales
— Housing starts

Environmental criteria
— Ecology of aquatic and terrestrial communities
— Water supply and demand
— Salt water intrusion
— Water quality
— Air quality
— Aesthetic variety of land use

Social criteria
— Unique historical and cultural features
— Sewered population
— Recreational accessibility
— Regional health services
— Interest-group changes

In LUTOM's initial application in South Carolina, Battelle identified several important shortcomings of the model. First, it is not built to assess complex urban systems but is, rather, a simplified planning tool most useful for relating project plans to their effects on general development policies. Second, this first application leaves serious questions as to the capacity of any simplified model to deal effectively with economic and social issues, whether by a matrix technique or otherwise. Third, the model needs to be expanded to include other important natural environment considerations, including noise pollution and natural and man-made hazards. However, despite these shortcomings, LUTOM is still a valuable conceptual framework for generally linking the EIS and comprehensive-planning processes.

Impact Zoning

A second recent attempt to relate comprehensive development plans and policies to the evaluation of project-level impacts is the impact zoning approach developed and elaborated by Rahenkamp, Sachs, Wells and Associates. One of its originators has supplied an excellent working definition of this approach: "Impact Zoning is a process of land use analysis that measures the capacities of the natural, physical, market, and fiscal systems. As an instrument of land use management, a legally defensible implementation of impact zoning requires definitive performance standards related to public health, safety, and welfare as well as a proper legislative and administrative framework for negotiation between town and public or private developer."[30]

The relation between land-use capacities and land-use demands is addressed within the framework of four basic systems: (1) the natural environment, including drainage patterns, water sources, and significant features of the landscape; (2) the man-made systems, including road networks, public water systems, and existing neighborhoods; (3) the market system, that is, the growth rate of the community as it relates to present population, available land, and the growth rate of the surrounding region; and (4) the fiscal situation of the community. Each proposed development is assessed for its consequences for these four systems. Therefore, implementation of an impact zoning approach requires a sound data base in order to provide a valid and uniformly applied assessment of proposed alternatives to the community's land-use structure. It is also necessary to develop defensible standards defining the allowable limits of such effects. Impact zoning requires objective performance standards which specify the minimum and/or maximum permissible effects of an activity based on quantifiable measures.

Impact zoning is a process, not a product. "It does [not] and cannot exist in the form of a model ordinance, because to be effective it must be specifically adapted to an individual community."[31] The community's legitimate police powers constitute its legal base, or "minimum position." The community's "maximum position" is its policy base, which is embodied in the goals and objectives of its comprehensive plan. The means of proceeding from the minimum to the maximum position entails a negotiation process, as shown in Figure 9. Negotiated impact zoning recognizes that, in exchange for higher densities, the developer agrees to conform to the established standards of the community regarding economic and natural environmental factors. Performance standards provide a uniform measure of the effect proposed development will have on the capacities of the community, and they enable the community to determine the extent of its ability to accommodate the developer's proposal. The results of impact analysis regarding natural, physical, market, and fiscal factors provide the community with specific data on the potential effects of the development. On this basis, the community can proceed to negotiate optimum alternatives to the legal minimum. Innovative design is stifled if the community is then unable or unwilling to make logical tradeoffs. As long as certain performance criteria are met, there is a wide range of possibilities for negotiation.

A recent example of a community where the impact zoning approach has been implemented is Duxbury, Massachusetts, a suburban town south of Boston that is experiencing strong development pressures. Rahenkamp, Sachs, Wells and Associates embodied this negotiation process in the comprehensive plan and the revised zoning ordinance it developed for the town.[32] It is still too early to assess the results of the Duxbury experience with impact zoning. However, impact zoning would seem to meet the basic test of integrating environmental-planning considerations, including social and economic factors, into an ongoing process of formulating and implementing a comprehensive plan for development.

Cost-Benefit Analysis of Environmental-Management Plans

Cost-benefit analysis has been developed and refined in response to the need for a broad view in evaluating public expenditures. Since the range of factors to be considered in decision making is wider for the public sector than for the private, the public sector has sought an evaluation technique that would be compatible with the decision-making mechanism in the private sector but which would be more exhaustive. Cost-benefit analysis takes the objective of the private sector, which attempts to maximize the difference between revenue and cost (profit) and defines both revenue (benefits) and costs more broadly. Cost-benefit analysis is an attempt to

FIGURE 9
Impact Zoning Negotiation Process

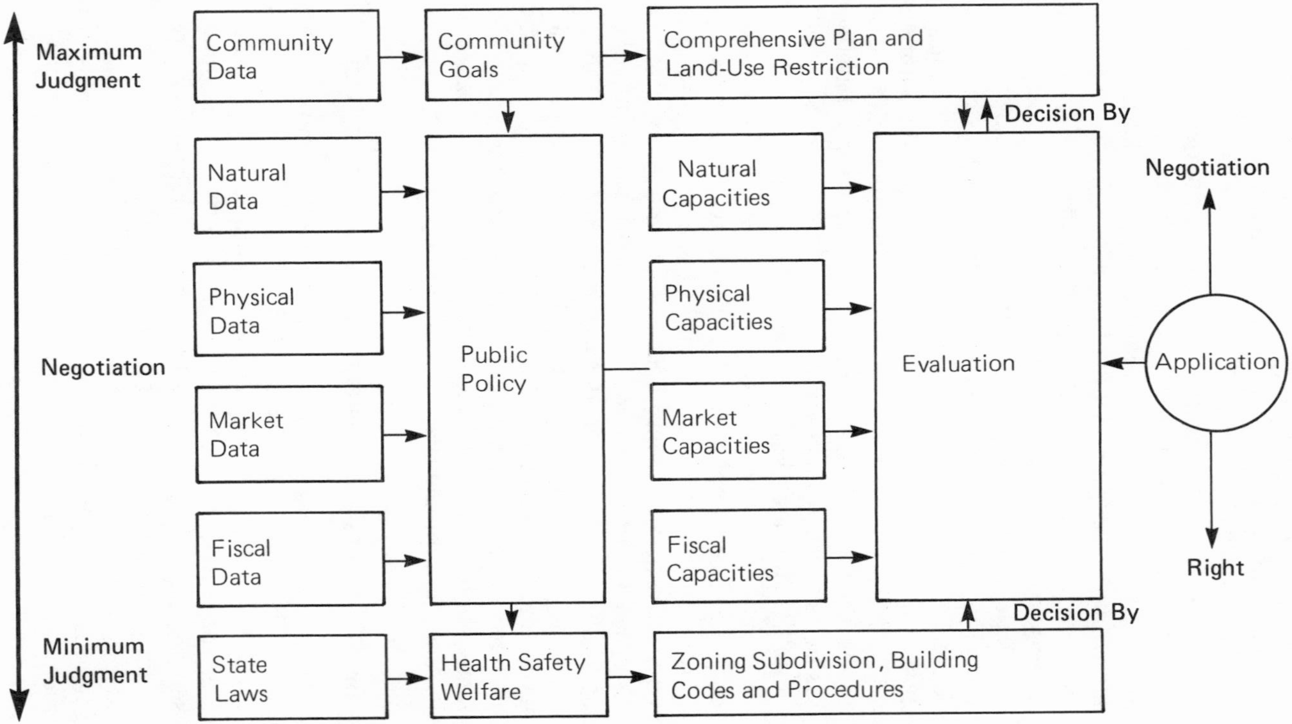

Source: Rahenkamp, Sachs, Wells, *Duxbury Comprehensive Master Plan Statement*, 1973, p. 34.

achieve allocative efficiency within the public sector.[33] Benefits include direct revenue, which may or may not be earned by a particular project, as well as other tangible and intangible items which contribute to public welfare. Costs include both direct and indirect costs. Indirect costs may be tangible, such as a reduction in the level of employment, or intangible, such as a reduction in the aesthetic quality of life.

Cost-benefit analysis provides a framework within which to evaluate projects when it is desirable to take a broad and long view. The application of cost-benefit analysis requires that the following questions be addressed:

Which costs and which benefits are to be included?

How are they to be valued?

What interest rate(s) should be used to discount future costs and benefits?

The particular costs and benefits to be included identify the scope of the analysis. Projects are site-specific, but their effects may be transmitted because of regional interdependencies to other areas. Generally, the scope of a cost-benefit analysis depends upon the sphere of concern of the agency or organization undertaking the study. For example, a community that undertakes a cost-benefit study will generally not consider costs (benefits) which are borne (received) by groups or individuals outside the community. In addition, although we have stated that cost-benefit analysis takes a broader view of both costs and benefits, the degree to which all or only some of the costs and benefits are considered is a matter of judgment.

The valuation of benefits and, to a lesser extent, costs is probably the most difficult problem in cost-benefit analysis. The valuation of benefits requires, first, that the benefit be measurable in physical units and, second, that the physical unit can be assigned an appropriate price. Although most benefits having physical units are measurable in principle, varying degrees of difficulty are encountered in practice. The question of the appropriate price to use once having measured the physical benefits is complex if the particular item is one which is not traded in a market. Market prices do not exist for items such as aesthetics, freedom from disease, human life, and elimination of stress. The methods which have most often been used to value these types of items are to:

Consider what people are willing to pay to eliminate or protect themselves from undesirable effects such as disease (or what they are willing to pay to acquire desirable effects);[34] and

Look for products whose price may reflect these desirable or undesirable effects, such as land prices.[35]

A third technique sometimes considered is the "option demand." Basically, the option demand is measured either by the price an individual is willing to pay in order to preserve his option to use something in the future, or by the price at which the individual is willing to sell that option.[36] This technique has been frequently proposed for valuing recreational land.

The question of the appropriate discount rate is particularly important when evaluating projects incurring costs early in their life and resulting in benefits which accrue far into the future. For instance, activities involving floodplain regulation may warrant a lower rate of discount for one or more reasons. First, such projects preserve flexibility for future use and hence the decisions are more easily reversed. A project that does not produce an irreversible effect is less risky; therefore, its benefits should be discounted at a lower rate. Second, benefits which are received by individuals (rather than by corporations) should carry a lower discount rate, since individuals have historically earned a lower rate of return on assets. Finally, the value which society, acting collectively, places upon future rather than present consumption may differ from that assigned by an individual. Society may be willing to take a longer view of projects with payoffs far in the future than private individuals. This tolerance may arise from the fact that society views itself as having a longer life than any one of its members. The social time preference rate, in other words, is different from the private time preference rate.

This section will discuss the utility of cost-benefit analysis to the task at hand, namely, integrating environmental considerations into the evaluation of alternative comprehensive plans and policies. It will deal with the problems of determining the appropriate geographic scope and range of environmental objectives to which the type of analysis can be applied. It will then provide specific examples of how cost-benefit analysis has been applied to problems of coastal zone management, water quality, air quality, noise abatement and control, and flood hazards.

Project-Level vs. Regional Analysis

Theoretically, cost-benefit analysis can be applied to every "project" having potential environmental effects — even, for instance, to each discharge permit application under Section 402 of the 1972 Federal Water Pollution Control Act Amendments. But a number of practical problems would result if such a project-by-project approach were taken. First, the large number of projects (sources) would quickly make the task of cost-benefit analysis unmanageable. More important, methodological difficulties would make such an approach unproductive, even if it were administratively feasible. For one thing, it would be nearly impossible to determine the marginal benefits of control in all but the simplest case. In any complex case, the marginal benefit of control in any one firm would depend upon the level of control from all other sources, including natural sources. A marginal benefit function for any single source in a complex situation can be obtained only by making arbitrary assumptions about the level of control of other sources and about the share of benefits from control of all sources (a joint product) that should be assigned to any one source. The same methodological problem applies to determining costs; again, there may be a joint secondary cost when one firm's going out of business or reducing employment causes other firms to do the same, and the question would be how to allocate it.

Analysis and planning on a regional level simplify some of the problems with project analysis. In particular, the problems of assigning costs and benefits that are essentially joint products to individual projects can be avoided. From the regional cost-benefit standpoint, for instance, the desired levels of ambient water quality can be determined, assuming one has a single damage function and a least-cost cost function for the area. The distribution of discharge permits consistent with the water-quality goal can then be determined by the least-cost or economic efficiency model. Assuming that cost curves for the individual firms and the economic effect of each firm's response are known, this procedure would solve the problem of determining how damage, a joint product, is assigned to firms. It also takes account of the external economic consequences of the response of individual firms.

There are also problems in applying cost-benefit analysis at this wider, regional level. Although ideally, as one economist has argued, "the kind and size of area used for environmental planning should be small enough for manageable planning but large enough to encompass the entire area for which significant economic, political, and social interactions exist,"[37] these conditions turn out to be very difficult to meet. The reality is that there are different natural geographic entities for different planning needs; the airshed does not correspond with the river basin, and neither corresponds with areas of high economic and social interdependence. Again, analytic boundaries should correspond with political boundaries, since plans and permits must be implemented by political jurisdictions, but this is not typically the case. Regardless of how analytic boundaries are drawn, not all of the effects of environmental control actions will be contained within them. The effects of a control program that are not contained within the area of analysis are known as "spillover" effects. They can be extensive, and their consideration is relevant because part of the optimum strategy — politically as well as economically — to reduce damage in any given area may well be to convince neighboring areas to reduce the residual flows coming across the border.

For the most part, the federal government has opted to plan and perform cost-benefit analysis of environmental-management programs at the regional level. Furthermore, despite the problems involved, federal environmental agencies have tended to favor social-political area boundaries (such as COG's and A-95 Review Areas) over problem-shed boundaries for planning and analysis. "It is easier to plan on the basis of social-political areas because it is easier to track environmental residuals across political boundaries than to track economic effects of political [implementation] actions across natural boundaries."[38] This preference is reflected in EPA's designation of Section 208 areawide water-quality management areas and in its stated intention to vest AQMA planning responsibility with these same regional agencies. HUD's emphasis on the land-use and housing elements of Section 701 comprehensive plans has also been regional.

Single-Purpose vs. Comprehensive Analysis

The appropriate substantive as well as geographic scope importantly affects the utility of cost-benefit analysis for comprehensive planners. One issue is whether cost-benefit analysis should focus on just one pollutant or on a set of pollutants. "In principle, analysis should be done for each pollutant, but this is not always adequate for correct control decisions. When there are synergistic effects with other pollutants, damage estimates for a single pollutant have to be conditional upon the level of other pollutants.

When control technology is 'lumpy' and controls several pollutants simultaneously, the joint cost has to be allocated to each pollutant."[39] Thus the decision to undertake cost-benefit analysis on a one-pollutant or multipollutant basis depends on the individual situation, that is, on the interactions among pollutants and on the extent of joint control technology. The same considerations apply to the issue of whether to concentrate cost-benefit analysis on just one environmental medium or to take a more comprehensive multimedia approach. Pollution control actions and plans can and should be judged on the basis of multiple objectives, including economic development, transportation, and scarce resource preemption as well as on goals for specific media like water, air, and land.

Once analysis involves multiple objectives, the results need not be a single cost-benefit ratio. "There is no reason to believe that a decision-maker's job is made easier or more correct by having all the benefits and costs aggregated into a single cost-benefit ratio. Indeed there is good reason to believe that a more useful and meaningful approach is to prepare simple matrices showing the different objectives, the major kinds of costs and benefits [not ratios], and the distribution of costs and benefits to population subgroups."[40] Perhaps the most important issue as far as comprehensive planning is concerned is this latter choice between cost-benefit analysis, narrowly defined, and a broader process of "policy evaluation." Cost-benefit analysis is a formal procedure built upon fairly restrictive definitions of "cost," "benefit," and "efficiency" and upon specialized analytic techniques largely derived from economic theory. Here the term "policy evaluation" describes a more general process of comparing all the favorable and unfavorable aspects of a proposed public program. A complete policy evaluation would not be limited to a cost-benefit analysis; in addition, it would include consideration of distributional effects, political feasibility, legality, and so on. Even when not all of the formal techniques of cost-benefit analysis are brought to bear on the problem, the effort to compare costs and benefits forces the analyst to clarify program objectives, assemble relevant technical data, and identify tangible and intangible program effects — all activities critical to environmentally sensitive comprehensive planning.

A considerable amount of work has been done on policy evaluation applied to environmental considerations in planning. The following sections briefly describe applications of policy-analysis techniques to coastal-zone, water-quality, air-quality, noise-abatement, and flood-hazard management.

Coastal-zone management. Although not explicitly called for in the Coastal Zone Management Act of 1972, the need to examine the economic as well as environmental effects of CZM programs is clearly recognized by concerned federal, state, and local officials. The Office of Coastal Zone Management and the Council on Environmental Quality are currently sponsoring research to develop a "policy evaluation" methodology to aid government officials and program managers attempting to implement, monitor, and evaluate coastal management plans. The methodology is also to be designed to meet the information needs of affected economic interests, such as the real estate, construction, and oil and gas industries.

Recently, using this general analytic framework, two separate evaluations of the California Coastal Plan concluded that implementation of the plan would result in an overall net benefit. One cautioned that "these are potential benefits. Their attainment depends on the specific nature of state and local conditions . . . but given the magnitude of the potential benefit it is reasonable to predict that programs can be designed to yield a net economic and social benefit, if sufficient care is given to the inclusion of fair and equitable means to allocate both the benefits and associated costs."[41] The second study less cautiously concluded that "overall, the economic benefits of coastal zone management in California will, at a minimum, offset noncompensated losses in land values or business opportunity. The positive effects of a more attractive, secure physical environment combined with greater efficiencies attained from elimination from urban sprawl will outweigh these losses overall."[42]

Water quality. The cost-benefit literature on water-quality management is probably more highly developed than for any other environmental-planning consideration.[43] However, the specific application of cost-benefit methodology to evaluation of alternative water-quality management plans, such as those called for under Section 208 of the 1972 FWPCA amendments, is still in its infancy. The EPA *Guidelines* for implementing Section 208 planning do provide a general policy evaluation framework which comprehensive planners can usefully examine. EPA's position, reflected in the *Guidelines*, is that "no rigorous analytical method exists which will readily identify the best plan for the area. . . . Many factors should be considered in comparing the alternatives. While some of the factors, in particular cost assessment, can be quantified, others can only be qualitatively assessed . . . . Plan assessment involves the comparison of all key factors deemed pertinent for reliable decision-making."[44] It should be noted that there have been promising attempts to make policy evaluation analysis of water-quality management problems more formal, in effect by expanding the scope of cost-benefit analysis. The most recent of such efforts is the work of Dorfman and Jacoby.[45] But the utility of these attempts to evaluate alternative water-quality plans is still quite limited.

Air quality. Most of the cost-benefit research done to date in the field of air pollution has been directed to aggregate analyses of the national costs and benefits of various emission-reduction strategies. A recent review of this research by the National Academy of Sciences found widespread discrepancies in attempts to quantify and compare costs and benefits. They arise chiefly from: "(1) significant deficiencies in the available scientific data base which make even qualitative descriptions of some costs and benefits difficult; (2) differences of opinion among investigators with respect to the most valid techniques or methodologies for evaluating the effects of air pollution; and (3) an apparent tendency on the part of investigators to ignore effects which appear difficult to quantify."[46] Regarding a specific attempt to evaluate the costs and benefits of compliance with the automobile emission standards established by the Clean Air amendments of 1970, the National Academy concluded that "in fact such large uncertainties in data and methodology exist that no simple calculation of a benefit/cost ratio is warranted."[47] Much less effort has been devoted to cost-benefit analysis of nonemission reduction strategies, such as land-use and transportation controls, although the same methodological difficulties could be expected to obtain.

As with water-quality management, the existing EPA *Guidelines for AWMA Planning and Analysis* stop short of requiring cost-benefit analysis of alternative plans and settle for a more limited policy evaluation approach.[48] They divide economic cost considerations into direct and indirect costs. The *Guidelines* recognize that "while it is highly desirable that social effects of maintenance measures be quantified, their complexity and current state-of-the-art make such quantification infeasible."[49] Instead of direct quantification, EPA recommends use of the weighted ranking approach developed by Klee.[50]

EPA has funded at least one effort to develop a regional air-pollution cost-benefit model specifically for use by planners.[51] The Regional Air Pollution Analysis model is actually a chain of computer-based models combining economic, cost-benefit, and systems analysis procedures to evaluate regional air resource problems. It is a cross-sectional model; that is, air-pollution control strategies are evaluated at one instantaneous moment. This means that the model must be applied in annual intervals over the length of the project life, and the results must be discounted back to the present if conventional cost-benefit analysis is to be conducted. Other limitations of the RAPA model are that (1) it treats pollutants individually, neglecting effects that levels and control measures for other pollutants may have on the benefits and control costs for the specific pollutant under consideration; and (2) it is limited to only two pollutants — sulfur dioxide and particulates — primarily because of the use of a long-term average diffusion segment.

Noise abatement and control. Noise pollution has generally not received as much attention in the cost-benefit literature as water and air pollution. In the absence of explicit environmental noise damage functions, most analyses in this area have been of the more limited cost-effectiveness type. They identify noise-abatement alternatives that minimize the total costs of meeting standards that specify the maximum allowable duration-frequency weighted noise levels at various types of receptor sites.[52] Since the objective of attaining standards is taken as given, it is not necessary to compare it with the other policy objectives; thus, a crucial aspect of cost-benefit analysis — the need to measure the value of the objective (benefit) in commensurate dollar units — is avoided. Typically, these procedures require the identification of all significant noise sources and receptors in an area and of the alternative means and costs of reducing the noise at each source, at each receptor, and in the paths between each source and receptor. They require estimates of the costs and effectiveness of various noise-reduction alternatives in terms of the total decrease in the intensity or duration of noise experienced at various locations within the affected area. A knowledge of the effects of the remaining noise on each receptor is also required. The model itself is specified by sets of equations designed to be solved on high-speed computers using both mathematical-optimization and simulation techniques.

Use of such models for developing and evaluating regional noise-management alternatives involves substantial effort, and considerable research is required before they can be used with confidence by comprehensive planners. However, fairly simple paper-and-pencil calculations may also be attempted. Particularly necessary are improved techniques for predicting and verifying noise attenuation in urban areas, for estimating costs of noise abatement as a function of the reduction achieved, and for defining and evaluating noise-management alternatives based on various economic and social criteria.[53]

Flood-hazard management. Numerous studies have attempted to assess the costs and benefits of alternative floodplain-management strategies. Perhaps of greatest interest to comprehensive planners are those cost-benefit models directed specifically toward regulation of land use in the floodplain.[54] Typically, such models attempt to deal with the following benefit and cost items:

Reduction of flood losses to private property and public facilities

Reduction of population and investment at-risk, in terms of deaths, injury, and illness

Reduction of private and public expenditures for evacuation, relief, rehabilitation, and reconstruction

Reduction of economic disruption, including interruption of the production of goods, services, and employment; secondary effects on financial institutions, public utilities and airports; and inflation of building and contruction costs after the disaster

Reduction of economic and social vulnerability and uncertainty

Reduction of social and psychological consequences

Reduction of adverse effects on those groups within the affected population least capable of sustaining them

Diversion of resources from other economic uses for reconstruction

Costs of foregone economic uses of the floodplain

Additional construction costs to meet regulatory requirements

Costs of land acquisition for floodways and plan space use

Costs of hazard delineation and the administration and enforcement of ordinances and regulations

A recent paper by Baker has shown how the existing cost-benefit methodologies for evaluating land-use regulation in riverine floodplains can be extended to a more general model for determining the type and level of land-use management that should be applied as an adjustment to any natural hazard.[55] The example used by Baker to illustrate the model is that of the hurricane storm-surge hazard for a hypothetical community in Florida.

Social and Cultural Considerations

Previous sections have dealt with evaluation methodologies generally directed toward land use, media quality, and hazard reduction. Although the approaches discussed have attempted to incorporate selected measures of social and cultural effect, none have done so in any systematic or sustained way. This final section on evaluation methodologies is devoted to experimental approaches currently being developed to integrate social and cultural considerations into comprehensive planning and management. Although their integrative power is still somewhat limited, two particularly promising approaches will be discussed: (1) the Quality of Life concept; and (2) the Social Well-Being Account of the Water Resources Council's *Principles and Standards*.

Quality of Life

A 1972 symposium sponsored by the Environmental Protection Agency concluded that "Quality of Life means different things to different people . . . . At present no concensus exists as to what it is or what it means . . . yet a consensus does exist regarding the importance of the QOL concept, the need to define it, and its significance as a potential new management tool."[56] The emergence of the QOL concept reflects the desire among planners and citizens alike to go beyond consideration of merely economic criteria in decision making and to include concerns about pollution, health, overcrowding, cultural opportunities, and political influence. The first order of QOL research has been to develop a sufficiently rigorous and precise definition of the concept; the attempts to date, although extensive, have not led to agreement on any single formulation.[57] In addition to definitional efforts, much research has been devoted to selection of appropriate QOL factors and of objective and subjective indicators for quantification and measurement of these factors. Again, although there is some convergence, the differences in approach are substantial. Even if measurement problems could be resolved satisfactorily, the need to devise a suitable composite measure or index of QOL for individuals, groups, and areas would still remain. The EPA-sponsored symposium concluded somewhat guardedly that "the difficulty, of course, is that the science of QOL measurement is so new that it is not yet possible to say . . . whether a particular measurement is meaningful in the sense that it relates to how individuals (and groups) perceive their quality of life . . . . Obviously there are serious and difficult research problems to be solved before we can introduce into the planning and decision-making process a QOL index that can be used with confidence."[58]

Available to comprehensive planners as baseline data for a description of social conditions and trends at the national level is *Social Indicators 1973*, published by the Office of Management and Budget.[59] It contains a collection of statistical measures of individual and family well-being and of social system outputs organized into eight major social areas: health, public safety, education, employment, income, housing, leisure and recreation, and population growth and distribution. National totals for each of the 176 indicators are disaggregated by age, sex, and race, although the degree of detail varies across indicators. Aside from a few regional breakdowns, disaggregation was not carried out.

Using the Social Indicators data base, a 1975 study done by the Midwest Research Institute for EPA developed a comprehensive, static cross-section analysis of the quality of life in 1970 for 243 large, medium, and small SMSA's.[60] Three-fourths of the U.S. population live in metropolitan areas, so a metropolitan QOL assessment is more appropriate and useful for comprehensive planning. The MRI study, based on a quality of life production model, developed a systematic methodology for constructing economic, political, environmental, health and education, and social indicators to reflect the overall "health" of the nation and its citizens' well-being. Census data for the 243 SMSA's were collected, and standardized values were computed for all the indicators. Using the standardized values within each size class, SMSA's were divided into five categories and assigned points of five, four, three, two, or one, respectively, for outstanding, excellent, good, adequate, and substandard. Subcomponent, component, and overall scores were then developed for each of the three size classes using a scheme of assigning equal weights. Clearly, equal weightings accurately reflect some individual's tastes and are inappropriate for others who place greater value on one component index than another. However, these composite indices do serve as a rough QOL comparison across SMSA's. If updated periodically, planners can use them to measure at least the direction of social trends in their area.

The basic problem with QOL formulations is to find ways to integrate them into a formal planning process. One approach which has successfully combined natural, physical, social, and cultural aspects of QOL within a planning process framework is the Environmental Evaluation System (EES).[61] The EES, designed by Battelle for the Bureau of Reclamation, provides a means for measuring or estimating selected environmental effects of large-scale water resource development projects. The EES can be used both in the evaluation of project consequences and in the planning process to minimize potential adverse effects in future projects. There is no difference, however, in the way EES is used for these different purposes, only in how the results are applied.

"Environment," as used in the EES, is defined to include four categories: ecology, environmental pollution, aesthetics, and human interest. These four categories are further broken down into eighteen components and, eventually, seventy-eight parameters, each reflecting a unit or an aspect of environmental significance worthy of separate consideration. This is essentially a definition of QOL by category listing. Aesthetics includes the indirect visual effect of natural settings and the direct visual of man-made structures. Human interest relates to effects on elements of the environment that influence people's cultural or emotional behavior or overall life patterns.

In order to evaluate the net environmental effects of a project and to make tradeoffs in selecting among alternatives, the EES transforms all parameters into commensurate units. The technique used to accomplish this consists of the following three steps: (1) transforming all parameter estimates into corresponding environmental-quality values, using specially developed value functions; (2) weighting all parameters in proportion to their relative importance by means of ranked pair-wise comparison and Delphi procedures; and (3) multiplying the environmental quality of the parameters by their relative weights to obtain commensurate units, or "Environmental Impact Units" (EIU's). The system is used to evaluate the expected future condition of environmental quality, first without and then with the project. A loss of EIU's represents an adverse effect, and a gain in EIU's signals a beneficial effect.

The Social Well-Being Account

Closely related to the QOL concept, although defined strictly for water resources development planning, is the Social Well-Being Account of the Water Resources Council's *Principles and Standards*.[62] The *Standards* require that the beneficial and adverse effects of proposed federal water-resource developments be evaluated, as part of ongoing planning, in terms of four "accounts" — national economic development, environmental quality, regional development, and social well-being. The Battelle EES is, in effect, an attempt to operationalize the environmental quality account. In a related study for the Bureau of Reclamation, Abt Associates developed an assessment procedure for preparing the social well-being account.[63] The SWB account is organized into five major components (individual effects, community effects, area effects, national effects, and aggregate social effects); in turn, each component is composed of a number of evaluation categories. The components are the basic units of analysis for assessing the social effects of various water-development plans. The evaluation categories provide the actual data on forecasted impacts upon which effects are then assessed. Completion of the SWB account requires five steps:

Description of the history of water resources of the area, and of the functions, activities, impact area, and schedule of alternative water plans

Description of the planning area to be affected in terms of its history, present-day social profile, and life-style

Identification of the future social impacts attributable to each alternative plan for each of the components and their evaluation categories

Comparison of the future beneficial and adverse social effects of the alternative plans

Recommendation of the plan with optimal future social well-being effects on the planning area

Ultimately, of course, the choice of a water resource development plan will be some function of the combined social, economic, environmental, and regional effects.

The process followed in preparing the SWB account is shown in Figure 10. Effects can be summarized for each alternative plan or for the same evaluation category across all the alternative plans. Based on analysis of individual evaluation categories, three aggregate measures of social effect are then developed:

Quality of Life deals with the physical and mental well-being of the individual and family and with their perceptions of the opportunities for further development of individual and family life in the future.

FIGURE 10

An Overview of the Social Well-Being Account, Its Components, and Their Evaluation Categories

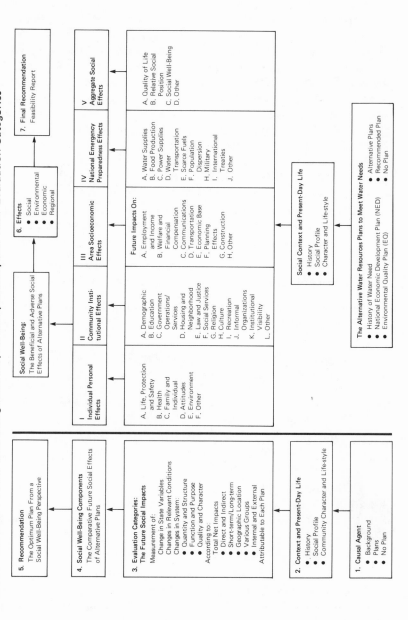

Relative social position concerns the extent to which the various social benefits and adverse effects of plan implementation would be equitably distributed among various individuals or groups in the community and the capacity of individuals and groups to bear social costs.

Social well-being refers to the overall effects of the alternative on the character and capacities of the community and its formal and informal institutions.

These aggregate social consequences are then compared to present-day social conditions, and to each other, across plan alternatives. Four potential sets of tradeoffs are also considered at this point: (1) short-term vs. long-term effects, (2) direct vs. indirect effects, (3) geographical distribution of effects, and (4) specific groups affected. A summary of effects across plans is prepared, and the best plan as far as social well-being is concerned is recommended to the rest of the planning team.

Water resource development projects can take place in built-up urban areas, although much Bureau of Reclamation work is done in less heavily developed locations. The importance of the SWB account approach, for the purposes of this manual, is mainly that it is a social assessment procedure that is an integral component of an ongoing environmental planning process.

ENVIRONMENTAL ASSESSMENT

Preparation of an environmental assessment of the consequences of the selected plan is another essential step in integrating environmental considerations into comprehensive planning and management. Analyzing the environmental effects of the plan is particularly important for two reasons. First, projects to carry out the plan may enjoy quicker EIS processing if they are consistent with the general environmental analysis performed at the comprehensive plan level. Second, identifying environmental effects before projects are proposed may encourage their development with greater concern for environmental considerations, thereby reducing the logjam of projects requiring redesign.

Many activities funded under federal or federally assisted programs such as the Comprehensive Planning Assistance Program (701) and the Community Development Block Grant Program are required by law and administrative regulation to be conducted in accordance with the provisions of the National Environmental Policy Act of 1969 (NEPA), which requires the preparation of an EIS under

Section 102(2)(c). Although the Council on Environmental Quality established guidelines for the preparation of environmental impact statements in 1973,[64] each federal agency has promulgated its own regulations to describe how and when impact statements are to be prepared. The Department of Housing and Urban Development regulations, published in the *Federal Register*, Wednesday, July 18, 1973 (amended November 4, 1974, and June 11, 1976), contain the environmental-assessment and clearance policy for HUD actions. The procedure includes a three-level environmental clearance review: a normal environmental clearance to check for consistency with policies; a special environmental clearance for those actions that require deeper evaluation; and an environmental impact statement clearance where comprehensive environmental investigation is required. "Planning assistance projects are exempted from the procedural requirements, [although] . . . an environmental assessment of the final planning product [is] required as part of the proposed planning program."[65] Under Section 600.60(b) of the regulations for the Comprehensive Planning Assistance Program, each applicant for the program grant is charged with preparing the environmental assessment, as distinct from an environmental impact statement. The assessment is required of the work resulting from the grant when it includes developmental policies and plans affecting the protection of natural areas, land-use development, major community facilities, or utility or transportation systems.

Environmental assessments may be required for planning activities under state law. As of April 1975, twenty-four states required an environmental impact statement process based on the federal model. Some had specific requirements for such statements.[66]

EIS Preparation Responsibilities

Under Section 102(2)(c) of NEPA, all agencies of the federal government shall include in every major federal action significantly affecting the quality of the human environment a statement of the environmental effects of proposed actions and of reasonable alternatives to such actions. Various court cases have interpreted this regulation to explicitly require the agency's own detailed environmental impact statement.[67]

However, in response to court rulings holding that federal agencies must prepare the EIS's for projects to be undertaken by states with grants under the Federal-Aid Highway Program, Congress amended NEPA in 1975 (PL 94-83).[68] The amendment allows the state agency to prepare the EIS, provided that ultimate responsibility remains with the responsible federal official. That official must furnish guidance, participate in the statement's preparation, and independently evaluate any state-prepared statement prior to its approval and adoption. To fall within the scope of the amendment, an impact statement project must be a part of a federal grant program and the recipient must be a statewide agency with statewide jurisdiction.

Responsibility for EIS preparation has also been delegated under provisions of Section 104(h) of the Housing and Community Development Act of 1974. That section allows HUD to delegate its NEPA responsibilities for the Community Development Block Grant program to the grant applicants, principally to local cities and towns. For all practical purposes, the regulations promulgated relieve the department of responsibility for preparing EIS's on the local projects funded by the grants. Local applicants are required to certify that they have complied with the NEPA procedural requirements and to assume the role of the "responsible federal official" under NEPA.[69] Section 58.21 under those regulations, it should be noted, exempts from the requirements of the environmental review, environmental studies and certain planning and capacity-building activities eligible for assistance under Title I.

The Nature and Content of an Environmental Assessment

Although the environmental assessment required for Section 701 comprehensive plans is not a formal EIS, it parallels the study required under Section 102(2)(c) of the National Environmental Policy Act. The text of the assessment is to be appended to the plan and used in the public deliberations leading to its approval or rejection. The major intention of the environmental assessment is to underscore the plan's environmental consequences and make them more liable to public consideration before the plan becomes public policy.[70] The environmental assessment should highlight the conflicts between development proposals and the environment.

HUD stresses that the assessment "shall not be written as justification for any proposed project, program, task, or policy." Instead, the environmental assessment should clearly state the environmental basis for, and the tradeoffs involved in, the proposal's formulation. The environmental assessment should describe specific policy recommendations and the underlying environmental philosophy contained in the overall planning program. The criteria used in considering the environmental aspects involved in the planning and policy proposals should be spelled out, particularly where the plan or policy proposals would have a deleterious effect on the environment. The statement must demonstrate that during the decision-making process there was knowledge of the environmental implications of the proposals.[71]

Impact statements and assessments should be based on and reflect a process of sound scientific analysis, including sufficient documentation. The level and extent of analysis in the statement should be commensurate with the information needs of the decision-makers and the public, and analysis should also be commensurate with the importance of the environmental issues involved.[72]

To a great degree, the environmental information included in the formulation of the plan itself will provide the building blocks for the environmental impact statement or assessment.[73] Comprehensive plans include such elements as land-use plans and controls; plans and policies prepared under the Clean Air Act or the Federal Water Pollution Control Act Amendments of 1972; plans for the location of infrastructure systems, such as water, sewer, utility lines, and highways; and policies or plans for the abatement of residual wastes (noise, radiation, solid waste). The immediate consequences of these plans, as well as the secondary or indirect effects of their implementation, are legitimately the subject of the impact statement or assessment and have been recognized as such in CEQ guidelines (Section 1500.8) and in HUD guidelines (Section 600.65).

Although the majority of EIS's have been concerned with the localized environmental effects of such major federal projects as building highway segments and dams, and of specific federal loans, grants, permits, and licenses, an environmental impact statement may encompass more than a single project. When impact statements are prepared for comprehensive plans, they are in effect program impact statements. It is therefore important to understand recent developments regarding the program impact statement.

According to CEQ guidelines, program statements may be necessary to assess the effects of individual actions on a given geographical area; to assess environmental impacts that are generic or common to a series of agency actions; or to assess the overall effect of a large-scale program or chain of projects.[74] According to subsequent judicial interpretation, even if the agency has not defined its actions as a comprehensive agency program, a program EIS is required.[75] Four factors were identified to determine when a program statement is required:

How likely is the program to come to fruition, and how soon will that occur?

To what extent is meaningful information presently available on the effects of implementation of the program and on alternatives and their effects?

To what extent are irretrievable commitments being made and options precluded as refinement of the proposal progresses?

How severe will the environmental effects be if the program is implemented?

Requirements of the Environmental Assessment

According to the HUD requirements governing Section 701 comprehensive-planning activities, specifically those in Section 600.65(b), environmental assessments are to contain six standard elements, roughly parallel to those required for environmental impact statements. The following sections analyze in more detail the scope and content of each of the elements. The discussion is based upon material contained in *Environmental Assessment Requirements: A Guidance Document for 701 Participants*, prepared by the State of New Jersey, Department of Community Affairs.

(1) *A summary or abstract of the proposed plan(s).* A summary statement should be prepared outlining each of the major proposals or policies that will result in development and will involve environmental alternatives and consequences. Summaries might be prepared by functional categories including, but not limited to, land use, transportation systems, community facilities, utility systems, protection of natural areas or critical environmental areas, air and water quality, historic preservation, and fish and wildlife management.

(2) *The potential environmental effect — beneficial as well as adverse — of the proposed plan(s) and any adverse environmental effects which could not be avoided should the proposed plan(s) or policies be implemented.* The analyst should identify the beneficial effects of the major elements of the proposed plans, including adverse conditions and trends likely to occur if the proposed plans

and policies are not implemented. For example, "The plans propose land uses, types of development, and development measures compatible with the surrounding community in terms of density, architectural design, and the natural setting; they will recreate or preserve the community's sense of place and its desirability as a place to live." Another example is the identification of areas or components critical to environmental quality, of natural hazard areas, and of ways to avoid incompatible development proposals in these areas.

The adverse environmental effects that could not be avoided should the proposed development plans or policies be implemented should be identified. This section should point out where development plans or policies will result in hazards to human life and property (development in flood-prone areas); loss of environmental opportunities and amenities (scenic values or historic properties); destruction of environmental resources or creation of ecological imbalances (destruction of wildlife habitats; development on prime agricultural land; destruction of groundwater recharge areas; negative effects on streams, lakes, shorelands, wetlands; destruction of unique geologic or archeologic features); inefficient use of resources (large scale developments, excessive water requirements); and the effect on areas of critical environmental concern.

The results of implementing the plan or policy on all public facilities should be identified. The effect of the location of key facilities, such as airports, highway interchanges, shopping centers, and ports, on surrounding areas should be identified, and consideration should be given to the secondary growth and development likely to occur as a result of their location. Consideration should also be given to the consequences of the plan on schools, employment, shopping, parks and open space, police, fire, health and social services, transportation lines, water supplies, sanitary and storm sewers, solid waste disposal, energy, and utilities.

Consideration should also be given to questions of equity arising from the plan's implementation. This requirement involves an examination of the plan's effect on the social fabric of the community; the segment of the population displaced, if any; aesthetics and urban design considerations; and the distribution of developmental consequences within the community. Also, provisions contemplated for providing access to the amenities of the manmade environment should be examined, including access to jobs, housing, and recreational opportunities.

(3) *Alternatives to the proposed plan(s) and an analysis of those alternatives.* This section would describe the alternative plans

or policies considered in the formulation of the recommended plan. The adverse effects or the enhancement of environmental quality which would have resulted from the reasonable alternative plans should be identified. An analysis of each of the alternatives and their environmental benefits, costs, and risks that is sufficient for comparative evaluation should also be included. Examples of such alternatives include no action or postponed action pending further study; actions of a significantly different nature providing similar benefits with different effects (for example, nonstructural alternatives to flood control programs); other approaches related to different perspectives of the proposed plan or policies (a predominantly economic plan, a predominantly environmental plan, or a composite plan); and different measures by which the plan is to be carried out.

This section of the assessment should also be used to document the problems and objections raised by other federal, state, and local agencies and by the private sector during the plan's review and to explain the disposition of the issues involved. It should also set forth the activities proposed to minimize or ameliorate the adverse environmental effects identified earlier.

(4) *The relation under the proposed plan(s) between local short-term uses of the environment and the maintenance and enhancement of long-term productivity.* This section should evaluate and assess the plan and its policies from the perspective of its cumulative, long-term effects. It should contain a discussion of the extent to which the proposed plan, if implemented, would foreclose future options; and it should point out short-term localized gains versus long-term widespread losses (or vice-versa), and tradeoffs for each. For example, construction disruptions and temporary relocation of populations should be balanced against induced growth, development and community renewal. Likewise, development of an area for a much-needed tax ratable should be balanced against the destruction of a unique historic site or natural area or by the prolonged disruption of a cohesive community.

(5) *Any irreversible and irretrievable commitments of resources resulting from the proposed plan's implementation.* Here, the assessment should determine where proposed plans or policies will encourage any development trends which would result in the loss of irreplaceable ecosystems, natural areas, or unique areas or properties.

(6) *A statement setting forth applicable federal, state, and local environmental controls.* This section should identify existing

federal, state, and local environmental controls and explain how the plan is compatible and in conformance with them. State laws regarding air, water, noise, wetlands, floodplains, fish and wildlife, and other aspects of the environment as well as local land-use controls, subdivision controls, building codes, noise ordinances, and other relevant factors should be set forth. When federal, state, or local approvals are required, that fact should be stated.

PLAN AND POLICY SELECTION

If the plan is an instrument to be used by leaders of the community to establish policies and to make decisions regarding community development, it must be officially adopted by a duly authorized body. The process by which the plan is adopted depends as much on the form of government of the planning jurisdiction as it does on the role of the planning agency in that government.

Because planning does not fall neatly into either a "line" or a "staff" activity in government, various concepts of the planning role have emerged. Planning has been seen as an independent activity of the planning commission, to whom technical staff is responsible. It has also been viewed as a staff aid reporting directly to the chief executive. Finally, planning has been seen as a policy-making activity of the legislative body, giving political flair to the process. No matter what form of government, both the legislative and the executive arms will be responsible for carrying out the plan, so both must be directly involved in its development and selection.

Regardless of the specific forms of the adoption process and the planning function, the environmental considerations weighed in the evaluation of plan alternatives must be clearly identified and concisely stated so that they may be understood by review agencies and the general public.

Review and Comment Procedures

After the responsible planning agency has prepared the comprehensive plan prior to official action, the plan is usually sent to other interested parties, including related public agencies, agencies of adjacent governmental jurisdictions, private organizations, and citizen groups, for their review and comment. Along with public hearings held on the plan, this process provides the means by which issues or disagreements regarding the plan may surface. It is the responsibility of the planning agency to reconcile these comments with the plan, incorporate changes to respond to them, and revise the plan as necessary.

One official review and comment process has been established under OMB's Circular A-95. Circular A-95 establishes procedures for the review and coordination of many federal activities which concern state and local government. Particularly for applications for federal assistance and, to a lesser degree, for program outputs such as the comprehensive plan itself, reviews are conducted by state and areawide "planning and development clearinghouses" under the overall administration of the Federal Regional Councils. Clearinghouse agencies are usually state planning offices or regional planning agencies. Through their review, conflicts with plans of other jurisdictions and with other programs can be identified and reconciled.

In order to fully meet their review and comment responsibilities under A-95 and other similar processes, public agencies and interested private organizations must be able to take account of the potential environmental consequences of implementing the recommended plan. The plan document must clearly identify what aspects of the national economic and social environment are likely to be affected should the preferred plan be implemented. In each case the nature, extent, and significance of its likely effect should be characterized and its importance for ultimate plan selection established. Particularly important for effective review and comment is a clear presentation of any existing conflicts among environmental considerations and the values involved in making tradeoff decisions. This same level of analysis should also be available for each of the major alternatives considered prior to recommendation of the preferred plan. Reviewers must be able to judge whether all reasonable alternatives to the proposed plan were fully and fairly evaluated and to understand the basis for the final plan selection.

Evaluating Community Preferences

Early and continuing involvement by interested citizens is an integral part of the development and selection of the comprehensive plan. Not only does citizen participation place the elements of decision making on public view, it allows agreement to be established on public policy as expressed in the comprehensive plan.

Citizen involvement came of age in the 1960's with the urban renewal program and especially under the Model Cities Act, which institutionalized mandatory citizen participation in all aspects of program planning and management. Under the Housing and Community Development Act of 1974, not only are meetings to discuss housing and community-development projects to be announced and a minimum of two hearings to be held, but communities qualifying for Community Development funding are required to develop a plan for citizen participation. Requirements for citizen involvement are also provided under the Comprehensive Planning Program (701) in Section § 600.800 of the regulations published in the *Federal Register*, August 22, 1975. Recipients of the Section 701 funds are required to develop a procedure for ongoing comprehensive planning that permits citizen involvement where major plans, policies, priorities, or objectives are being determined. The criteria used to measure compliance with the citizen involvement requirement include: (1) extent of interaction and involvement, including the opportunity to help initiate as well as to react to proposals; (2) access to the decision-making process; (3) communication techniques, including providing technical data and professional material to citizens so that they understand the effects of the public programs, options, and alternative decisions; and (4) a statement of citizen involvement, including the identification of activities undertaken to meet these requirements.

The involvement of citizens is often based in the neighborhoods and supplemented by citywide public hearings and broad-based advisory committees. Areawide organizations tend to have governmentally based citizen participation programs reflecting the internal structure of the organizations themselves, commonly an advisory committee consisting of representatives from the private sector and various levels of government. Areawide organizations also make use of newsletters and task forces. A few state governments have used television, mail surveys, and public hearings to ascertain public views. Using locally based processes in conjunction with a statewide advisory group or technical task force has also met with some success. Although it is important for citizens to be involved in the substantive aspects of the comprehensive planning process, citizens should also assist recipient governments in determining what form of involvement is best for their state, region, or community. In any event, the program requirements for comprehensive planning are, in effect, performance standards designed to ensure citizen involvement rather than requirements for a specific mechanism.[76]

A particularly innovative example of citizen involvement took place in the New York metropolitan area.[77] Through CHOICES FOR '76, a series of televised town meetings in the spring of 1973, some 10% of the twenty million residents of the area were confronted with fifty-one critical issues on the region's living conditions and were given a chance to choose among the alternatives. The Regional Plan Association sponsored the project and developed the background for five films, each shown on every television channel covering New York City, Newark, New Haven, Bridgeport, Paterson, Trenton, Hartford, and Long Island. Ballots to register responses to the issues were made available, and background information was provided in a paperback book, in newspapers, and by private companies. The project was financed by HUD, eighty corporations, and twenty-two foundations.[78]

Citizen involvement is an important vehicle for soliciting and expressing legitimate concerns about the environmental consequences of proposed policies and plans. Many citizen groups are organized around environmental concerns and play a valuable role in ensuring that public officials take environmental values into account when making planning decisions. Their staffs, occasionally paid but more often volunteer, frequently contribute useful data and analyses to the comprehensive planning process. Ideally, their input is sought and obtained early in the process, during problem analysis and the formulation and evaluation of alternatives. In this way they have a chance to influence planning outcomes well in advance of the plan selection hearings, when their involvement may have to assume an adversary nature. The key to effective citizen involvement regarding environmental considerations is an accessible planning process which, as a matter of course, fully analyzes the environmental consequences of all reasonable plan alternatives and presents a clear statement of all the issues and tradeoffs involved.

REFERENCES

1. Nathaniel Lichfield, Michael Whitbread, and Peter Kettle, *Evaluation in the Planning Process* (Oxford, England: Pergamon Press, 1975), p. xi.

2. U.S. Army Corps of Engineers, North Atlantic Division, *North Atlantic Regional Water Resources Study: Report*, prepared for the North Atlantic Regional Water Resources Study Coordinating Committee (June 1972).

3. Ibid., p. 4.

4. State of California, Governor's Office, *Environmental Goals and Policies* (March 1, 1972).

5. Ibid., p. 9.

6. Ibid., p. 25.

7. See discussion in Edward J. Kaiser et al., *Promoting Environmental Quality Through Urban Planning and Controls* (Washington, D.C.: Environmental Protection Agency, EPA-600/5-73-015).

8. Metropolitan Council of the Twin Cities Area, *Development Framework: Policy, Plan Program* (St. Paul, Minnesota: 1975), p. iii.

9. Ibid., p. 50.

10. The Goals for Dallas program is documented in a series of four volumes published by Goals for Dallas and available from Cokesbury, Dallas, Texas:

    Goals for Dallas: Submitted for Consideration by Dallas Citizens (1966).

    Goals for Dallas: Mutual Aims of its Citizens (1967).

    Goals for Dallas: Proposals for Achieving the Goals (1969).

    Goals for Dallas: Achieving the Goals (1970).

11. *Goals for Dallas: Achieving the Goals* (1970), p. 12.

12. David Boyce et al., *Metropolitan Plan Making: An Analysis of Experience with the Preparation and Evaluation of Alternative Land Use and Transportation Plans* (Philadelphia: Regional Science Research Institute, Monograph Series No. 4, 1970), pp. 26-27.

13. Ibid. The thirteen planning studies analyzed were conducted in Philadelphia, Minneapolis-St. Paul, Boston, Baltimore, Milwaukee, the San Francisco Bay Area, Chicago, Detroit, New York, Pittsburgh, Washington, D.C., Los Angeles, and New York State.

14. Ibid., p. 43.

15. Steinitz Rogers Associates, *The Santa Ana River Basin: An Example of the Use of Computer Graphics in Regional Plan Evaluation* (Cambridge, Mass.: NTIS No. AD/A-013 404, June, 1975).

16. Ian McHarg, *Design with Nature*, (New York: The Natural Science Press, 1969).

17. James C. Hite, *Environmental Planning: An Economic Analysis* (New York: Praeger Publishers, 1972).

    Walter Isard et al., "On the Linkage of Socioeconomic and Ecologic Systems," *Proceedings of the Regional Science Association* 21 (1968), p. 79.

Walter Isard and Tze Hsiung Tung, "Selected Noneconomic Commodities, Definitions, and Speculations on Supply and Demand, Measurement and Utility," *Proceedings of the Regional Science Association Papers* 13 (1964), p. 71.

Thomas V. Langford, *Regional Input-Output Study: Recollections, Reflections, and Diverse Notes on the Philadelphia Experience* (Cambridge, Mass.: The MIT Press, 1971).

See also W. Leontief and W. Ford, "Air Pollution and the Economic Structure: The Empirical Results of Input-Output Computations," (mimeo, Harvard University, January 1971).

18. McHarg, op. cit.

19. Robert V. Ayers and Allen Kneese, "Production, Consumption, and Externalities," *American Economic Review* 59:4 (June 1969).

20. See Reference 18 above.

21. E. A. Laurent and J. C. Hite, "Economic-Ecologic Linkages and Regional Growth: A Case Study," *Land Economics* 48 (Fall 1972), p. 71.

22. Laurent and Hite, op. cit., p. 72.

23. Houston-Galveston Area Council, ReSiSCM, Houston, 1971.

24. *Development of the Arizona Environmental and Economic Tradeoff Model* (Planning Division, Department of Economic Planning and Development, Office of the Governor, State of Arizona, March 1973).

25. Philip Schaenman and Thomas Muller, *Measuring Impacts of Land Development: An Initial Approach* (Washington, D.C.: The Urban Institute, 1974), p. 6.

26. See Dale Keyes, *Land Development and the Natural Environment: Estimating Impacts*, and Thomas Muller, *Fiscal Impacts of Land Development: A Critique of Methods and Review of Issues*, both published by the Urban Institute, 1975.

27. Keyes, op. cit., pp. 4-5.

28. Gerald Nehman et al., *Application of the Land Use Tradeoff Model to Assess Land Use Capabilities of the Beaufort-Jasper County Area*, two vols. (Columbus, Ohio: Battelle Columbus Laboratories, 1974).

29. Ibid., Volume I, pp. 2-3.

30. John Rahenkamp, from a speech before the Pennsylvania Planning Association, Bethlehem, Pennsylvania, October 2, 1975.

31. Eric Kelly, "Impact Zoning: Concept for Growth Management," *Colorado Municipalities* 51:5 (September/October 1975), p. 142.

32. See Rahenkamp, Sachs, Wells, and Associates, "Duxbury Comprehensive Master Plan Statement," RSWA Planning Library Report Z-6, 1973, and "Revised Impact Zoning Ordinances for Duxbury, Massachusetts," RSWA Planning Library Report Z-7, 1974.

33. The analogy must be qualified. The private sector does not necessarily choose the combination of projects that maximizes net benefits. The reason is that the economic objective is only one of a number considered in evaluating a project. For example, society may wish to use certain projects to redistribute income or provide a more stable institutional structure within an area.

34. H.E. Klarman, "Syphilis Control Programs," in Robert Dorfman (ed.), *Measuring Benefits of Government Investment* (Washington, D.C.: The Brookings Institution, 1965).

35. L.D. James, "The Role of Economics in Planning Flood Plain Land Use," *Journal of the Hydraulics Divison,* Proceedings of the ASCE, 98 (HY5, No. 8935).

36. See B. Weisbrod, "Collective Consumption Services of Individual Consumption Goods," *Quarterly Journal of Economics* 78.

37. Fred Abel, "Project-by-Project Analysis vs. Comprehensive Planning," in *Evaluation of Techniques for Cost-Benefit Analysis of Water Pollution Control Programs and Policies,* Report of the Administration of the Environmental Protection Agency to the Congress of the United States (December 1974), p. 666.

38. Ibid., p. 668.

39. Ibid., p. 671.

40. Ibid.

41. *The Economic Benefits of Coastal Zone Management: An Overview* (Washington, D.C.: Urban Land Institute, March 1976), p. 26.

42. *Business Prospects Under Coastal Zone Management* (Chicago: Real Estate Research Corporation, March 1976), p. 11.

43. For an excellent summary volume and bibliography see *Evaluation of Techniques for Cost-Benefit Analysis of Water Pollution Control Programs and Policies* (Reference #38).

44. U.S. Environmental Protection Agency, *Guidelines for Areawide Waste Treatment Management Planning* (Washington, D.C., August 1975), pp. 32-1.

45. See Robert Dorfman and Henry Jacoby, "A Model of Public Decisions Illustrated by a Water Pollution Policy Problem" in *The Analysis and Evaluation of Public Expenditures: The PPB System,* Volume I, (Washington, D.C.: Government Printing Office, 1969), pp. 226-274. Also see their later volume, *Models for Managing Regional Water Quality Management* (Cambridge, Mass.: Harvard University Press, 1973).

46. *The Social and Economic Costs and Benefits of Compliance with the Auto Emission Standards Established by the Clean Air Amendments of 1970,* an Interim Report prepared for the Committee on Public Works, United States Senate, by the Environmental Studies Board, Commission on Natural Resources, National Research Council, National Academy of Sciences (December, 1973), p. 5.

47. Ibid., p. 8.

48. U.S. Environmental Protection Agency, *Guidelines for Air Quality Maintenance Planning and Analysis, Volume 2: Plan Preparation* (Washington, D.C., EPA-450/4-74-002, July 1974). See Section V and Appendix B.

49. Ibid., p. V-12.

50. A. J. Klee, "The Role of Decision Models in the Evaluation of Competing Environmental Health Alternatives," *Management Science, Journal of the Institute of Management Sciences* 18:2 (October 1971).

51. K. Woodcock, *Model for Regional Air Pollution Cost/Benefit Analysis* (McLean, Virginia: TRW Systems Group, May 1971), prepared for the Environmental Protection Agency, Contract No. PH 22-68-60.

52. For example, see Daniel Loucks, Blair Bower, and Walter O. Spofford, Jr., "Environmental Noise Management," *Journal of the Environmental Engineering Division, Proceedings of the American Society of Civil Engineers* 99:EE6 (December 1973).

53. Ibid., p. 8209.

54. Four recent approaches to evaluating riverine land-use regulation alternatives are (1) William Whipple, "Optimizing Investment in Flood Control and Floodplain Zoning, *Water Resources Research*, Volume 5, pp. 761-766; (2) TRW Systems Group, *A Methodology for Floodplain Development and Management*, Institute for Water Resources Report 69-3, 1969; (3) J. Day, "A Recursive Model for Nonstructural Flood Damage Control," *Water Resources Research* 6, pp. 1262-1271; and (4) L. D. James, "The Role of Economics in Planning Floodplain Land Use, *Journal of the Hydraulics Division, Proceedings of the American Society of Civil Engineers* 98 (HY 5, # 8935), pp. 981-992.

55. Earl J. Baker, *Toward an Evaluation of Policy Alternatives Governing Hazard Zone Land Use* (Boulder, Colorado: University of Colorado, Institute for Behavioral Studies, 1976).

56. *The Quality of Life Concept, A Potential New Tool for Decision-Makers* (Washington, D.C.: U.S. Environmental Protection Agency, March 1973), p. I-1.

57. For two excellent reviews of the literature on the development of the QOL concept, see Angus Campbell and Phillip Converse, *The Human Measuring of Social Change* (New York: Russell Sage Foundation, 1972); and Norman C. Dalkey, Ralph Lewis, and David Snyder, "Measurement and Analysis of the Quality of Life" (Santa Monica: The RAND Corporation, August 1970), prepared for the U.S. Department of Transportation.

58. *The Quality of Life Concept*, pp. I-61-I-62.

59. Executive Office of the President, Office of Management and Budget, *Social Indicators 1973* (Washington, D.C.: U.S. Government Printing Office, 1973).

60. Ben Chieh Liu, *Quality of Life Indicators in the U.S. Metropolitan Area 1970* (Kansas City, Missouri: Midwest Research Institute, 1975).

61. Norbert Dee et al., *Environmental Evaluation System for Water Resource Planning* (Columbus, Ohio: Battelle Columbus Laboratories, 1972). Available from NTIS as PB 208 822.

62. U.S. Water Resources Council, *Principles and Standards for Planning Water and Related Land Resources*, effective October 25, 1973. See Section IIH.

63. Stephen Fitzsimmons, Lorrie Stuart, and Peter Wolff, *Social Assessment Manual: A Guide to the Preparation of the Social Well-Being Account for Planning Water Resource Projects* (Boulder, Colorado: Westview Press, 1977).

64. 40 CRF 1500.

65. 38 FR 137, Wednesday, July 19, 1975, Section 5(a)(1), p. 1985.

66. Council on Environmental Quality, *Sixth Annual Report* (1975), p. 653.

67. *Greene County Planning Board* vs. *FPC*, 455 F 2d. 412 (2nd Cir., 1972).

68. *Conservation Society of Southern Vermont* vs. *Brinegar*, 508 F 2d.927 (2nd Cir., 1974).

69. 40 FR 4, Tuesday, January 7, 1975, §58, 1(a)(2).

70. Local Planning Assistance Unit, New Jersey Department of Community Affairs, *The Environmental Assessment Requirement: A Guidance Document for 701 Participants*, revised January 13, 1975.

71. Ibid.

72. CEQ, *Sixth Annual Report*, p. 633.

73. See Harold Wise, "The Environmental Impact Statement and the Comprehensive Plan" in Robert N. Burchell and David Listokin (eds.), *Future Land Use* (Rochester, N.Y.: Rutgers University Press, 1975); and AIP, "The Comprehensive Plan and Environmental Quality," prepared for Environmental Statistics Division, ORD, EPA, February 1974.

74. CEQ guidelines on Preparation of Environmental Impact Statement, *Federal Register*, August 1, 1973.

75. *Scientists Institute for Public Information* vs. *AEC* 481 F 2d .1079 (D.C. Cir., 1973), 7 ERC 1986, 7 ERC 1988; *Sierra Club* vs. *Morton*, 5 ELR 20462 (D.C. Cir., June 16, 1975).

76. Claudia Pharis, "Citizen Involvement in Comprehensive Planning," in *HUD Challenge* (January 1976), p. 22.

77. Regional Planning Association, "The Metropolis Speaks," (New York: August 1974), no. 95.

78. See Regional Planning Association, *Listening to the Metropolis, An Evaluation of the New York Region's Choices for '76 Mass Media Town Meetings* (New York: 1974). Also see their *Handbook on Public Participation in Regional Planning* (New York: 1974).

Chapter 4
Plan Implementation

Preceding chapters describe steps by which environmental considerations are incorporated in a comprehensive plan. This chapter examines the methods by which a plan, once completed and adopted, is implemented. Thus, emphasis is placed on legal, administrative, and financial tools for implementation.

The implementation of a plan is really an attempt by the public to influence public and private activities in a way that is consistent with a plan's policies and recommendations for future community growth and development.

If there is any one measure of a plan's success, it is the degree to which it is put to use. Planners recognize this — their biggest professional fear is of producing a plan that "ends up on the shelf." One way to ensure that this doesn't happen is to bear in mind during the plan's formulation the laws, institutions, and financial arrangements available for implementing it. The process of recommending actions must include consideration of the means by which they are to be carried out.

It is also important to remember that methods of implementation are wide-ranging. Although this chapter will explore the traditional legislative, administrative, and regulatory implementation tools, other and sometimes more useful informal methods of implementation can also be used occasionally to achieve results. Often, quite a lot can be accomplished simply by persuasion or by providing the right information to the right person. Political and popular pressure can also be used effectively.

Usually, no single tool or method can "implement" a plan. The essence of implementation is the orchestration of a series of actions or the development of a strategy which, if carried out, will achieve desired objectives. The best results are likely to be achieved by some combination of two or more approaches because implementation is rarely a single-purpose affair — which is usually the case in the pursuit of multifaceted environmental, economic, and social objectives. It is therefore wise to consider, as specific circumstances warrant, the integrated use of various tools to achieve comprehensive objectives.

The aim of this chapter is to examine the implementation tools available for use by state and local governments and, to a lesser extent, by the federal government. Our goal cannot be to exhaust the subject but only to survey, with the aid of examples from around the country, the range of approaches that are open to state and local governments. The variations in legal authorities among the fifty states are numerous; therefore, do not assume that an approach adopted by one locality can readily be transferred to another. On the other hand, one or more of the approaches described below should be suitable, perhaps with modifications, to the needs of many localities.

DIRECT IMPLEMENTING ACTIONS

When government itself spends money for various purposes or projects, it implements plans directly. The forms of government spending range from outright grants to various forms of subsidization. This section will explore three major types of government expenditures: public acquisition of land, public construction of improvements, and public assistance to development.

Public Acquisition of Land

Acquisition of land by state and local agencies is an effective tool for implementing public development policies. Acquisition of private property is limited by the Fifth Amendment of the Constitution to situations where there is a public purpose for which the land is being acquired and where just compensation for property is paid to the owner. Government can acquire land by the power of eminent domain, which is the power of the sovereign to condemn or compulsorily "take" private property for specific, necessary public purposes. Land may also be acquired by the public through negotiated purchase from a willing seller or by gift from a landowner.

Although there are practical financial limitations on the ability of government to acquire land, acquisition is attractive because it can ensure the protection of critical natural areas or open space, allow urban areas to be redeveloped, and be used to encourage preferred development in particular areas in conformance with land-use plans.

There are a number of forms by which government can acquire and hold title to land. Purchase of the land outright (or, in legal terms, "buying the fee simple") assures the purchaser that he is acquiring all rights associated with the land. Less-than-fee-simple interests may also be acquired, and because they may be obtained at lower cost, this form of acquisition may be more widespread. Less-than-fee interests, usually called "easements," constitute specific rights acquired by one party to use the land of another for a special purpose. A positive easement secures for the buyer the right to actually use the land in question for specific purposes; negative easements are restrictions on the uses to which the landowner himself may put the land. In either case, the compensation due the landowner is the value of whatever property rights are relinquished, as measured by the difference in the market value of the land with and without the restriction. Typically, easements or conservation restrictions are acquired to restrict development in conservation areas.

Easements or restrictions also have the advantage of allowing the owner of the land to enjoy real estate taxes reduced by the value of the encumbrance; continuing to allow the landowner to use the property; providing the landowner with a tax deduction in the amount of the value of the gift of an easement, such as a view, which may be freely given.

The Massachusetts Conservation Restriction Law[1] is an example of enabling legislation for easements which is worth discussing in some detail. The law defines conservation restrictions as rights appropriate to keeping "land or water areas predominantly in their natural, scenic, or open condition or in agricultural, farming, or forest use." Activities that could jeopardize water quality may be expressly forbidden or limited by such restrictions, including: "(a) construction or placing of buildings . . . or other structures on or above the ground; (b) dumping or placing of soil or other substance or material as landfill, or dumping or placing of trash, waste, or unsightly or offensive materials; (c) removal or destruction of trees, shrubs or other vegetation; (d) excavation, dredging, or removal of loam, peat, gravel, soil, rock, or other mineral substance . . . ; (e) surface use except for agricultural, farming, forest, or outdoor recreational purposes or purposes permitting the land or water area to remain predominantly in its natural condition; (f) activities detrimental to drainage, flood control, water conservation, erosion control or soil conservation . . . ." These restrictions can be tailored to fit particular situations. Generally, the restrictions provide that all rights not expressly conveyed are reserved to the grantor, thus allowing the grantor a range of consistent uses. Occasionally, an easement allowing the grantee to enter the premises and inspect for violations is conveyed along with the restriction.

The acquiring party must be either a governmental or a charitable body whose purposes include conservation. Acquisitions may be by eminent domain, gift, or contractual agreement, and must be approved by the appropriate state and local agencies. When a restriction has been recorded so as to provide public notice that the land is encumbered, it becomes enforceable over time from one landowner to another, by means of an injunction or proceeding in equity, if necessary.[2] The landowner may be released from the restriction upon payment of such consideration as the holder may determine, but only after a public hearing on the matter following advance public notice. "The requirement that a public hearing be held before any action is taken will safeguard against the use of variance practices that have proved so dangerous and arbitrary in the administration of the zoning power."[3]

A similar example of the use of easements is found in New Jersey, where a law authorizes certain governmental bodies to acquire "interests or rights consisting, in whole or in part, of restrictions on the use of land by others."[4]

A Pennsylvania law enables counties to enter into a contract with landowners for the preservation of land in farm, forest, water-supply, or other open-space uses.[5] By such a covenant, the landowner commits himself to maintaining his land as open space for ten years, while the county promises in turn to assess the property at a value no greater than it is worth with the encumbrance of the restrictive covenant. This device gives the owner some relief from property and estate taxes as well as a charitable deduction from his income tax. It also enables him to retain title and to continue living on the land without intrusions from the public and to use the land in any manner he wishes so long as he preserves it consistently within the terms of the restriction.

Private conservation organizations can play a valuable role in the acquisition of conservation easements. Much of the success of state and local conservation programs is due to the assistance and information provided to landowners by the Nature Conservancy, The Conservation Foundation, and the Trust for Public Lands.

Government can also buy the land and then sell it back, subject to development restrictions, to the original owner or to a new owner. Similarly, it can buy land and lease it to another party for use consistent with the terms of the lease. Under the excess condemnation laws of some states, the state can buy more land than is needed for a particular purpose — such as a highway — and then lease back or sell back the land for uses that will make it serve as a buffer zone. The conditions of the lease not only determine the use, but allow a modest rent to provide the community with an appreciable return on its investment. In Canada, this device has been used in Saskatchewan and Ottawa to encourage the continuation of farming and to preserve greenbelt areas.

Another variation in acquiring land is the *negotiated life tenancy* agreement, in which property is purchased with the provision that the original owner shall be allowed to continue to use the land, subject to normal restrictions, for a stated period of years or for his lifetime. In return, the government is afforded a reduced purchase price. This arrangement has been used by the National Park Service in acquiring parcels of land for national parks.

Commonly, all levels of government acquire land, although at different times and for different purposes. Generally, however, only the federal government has had the funds for large general-purpose acquisition programs. For the past decade or so, the federal government has provided grants to states, counties, and cities for the acquisition of land for open space, parks, and related uses.[6] HUD's Community Development Block Grant Program consolidated some of these grants and provides monies for locally assisted programs, which may be used for the acquisition and development of open space for park and recreation purposes. Another source of federal funds is the Land and Water Conservation Fund Program administered by the Bureau of Outdoor Recreation of the Department of the Interior. The fund finances the cost of preparing and maintaining outdoor recreation plans and of acquiring land and water areas for outdoor recreation in accordance with the plan. Some state programs — Massachusetts' Self-Help program, for example — have also provided funds which match federal and local shares of land-acquisition costs.

Public Construction of Improvements

Another area of direct government authority which influences the implementation of plans is the authority to construct public improvements. Because they are essential services, certain types of improvements are necessary preconditions of further development of an area. Thus, decisions on the locations of sewers, highways, and other utilities often serve as powerful tools to guide development in accordance with planning policies. Other kinds of public facilities, such as airports, dams, dikes, and highways interchanges, induce additional development because of their extensive effects or their external benefits. Construction of these kinds of public developments, if consistant with public policy, can also help implement plans.

Location of Infrastructure

All public facilities affect the placement, type, and timing of residential, commercial, and industrial development. Although government is not generally required to provide public facilities, water, sewer lines, and highways, schools and other facilities are normally constructed by general-purpose local governments or in some cases by special districts. The federal government and the states exercise a considerable degree of control over local programs through grant programs and technical assistance, such as community development funds, sewer and sewage treatment plant grants, highway funds, and airport construction assistance. Moreover, states usually oversee the location of water and sewer service under regulatory authority exercised by such various functional departments as public health, public utility, and environmental affairs offices.

One of the most difficult problems in implementing plans is the extent of control over the timing of development. A recent ruling in New York, in *Golden* vs. *Planning Board of Ramapo*,[7] affirms the right of a municipality to regulate the phasing of its growth through the provision of public facilities. The court said that "where existing physical and financial resources of a community are inadequate to furnish the essential services and facilities which a substantial increase in population requires, there is a rational basis for phased growth." Faced with a growth rate of about 1,000 dwelling units per year prior to the adoption of the ordinance, Ramapo sought, by amending its zoning ordinance, to prevent the development and sale of land for new housing. Under this ordinance, the developer of such housing receives a special permit regardless of the existing residential zoning. The permit is granted for development in an area of town served by a minimum level of certain community facilities. Installation and location of new public facilities in the town is scheduled over time in accordance with the town's Capital Improvement Program (CIP), which includes provisions for capital expenditures for sewerage, drainage, parks and recreation areas, roads, and firehouses. Where a development is proposed for an area lacking a minimum level of such facilities, developers may obtain permits only if they are willing to bear the cost of providing the lacking services.

The CIP spans an eighteen-year period. Thus, land that will not be properly served by facilities for as long as eighteen years may not be developed for residential purposes. The tax on this land is reduced to reflect its diminished value. Development permits are granted only on the basis of a point system "that quantifies the proximity of land to planned capital improvements. The timing of development over 18 years is controlled under this scheme without altering the underlying spatial zoning patterns."

Developers who challenged the time-phased development program argued that it was invalid because: (1) the control or regulation of population growth through timing controls was not included in the zoning enabling act as an allowable purpose or method; (2) the program was exclusionary in that it raised barriers to people moving into the town; and (3) it constituted a public taking without just compensation. The Court of Appeals rejected those arguments and was particularly persuaded by the existence of a commitment by the town to low-income housing, tax relief for deferred development properties, and the existence of a capital budget to implement the plan.

A somewhat similar approach was upheld by a federal court in California in *Construction Industry Association of Sonoma County vs. City of Petaluma.*[8] Petaluma had limited construction of new dwelling units to five hundred per year, pursuant to announced policies of preserving its small-town character and surrounding open space, of keeping new development within the bounds of available municipal services, and of providing a permanent greenbelt around the city. The court held that the "public welfare" purpose of zoning was sufficiently broad to include these objectives. Although the Petaluma plan was deemed "a reasonable and legitimate exercise of the police power," the court observed that the plan did not freeze local population at present or near-present levels, did not restrict an individual's constitutional right to travel, and did not have the undesirable effect of excluding any particular income class or racial minority group. In fact, the plan contemplated that between 8 and 12% of the previous year's housing quota would be allocated to low- and moderate-income housing.

Major Public Facilities

Public facilities often affect both a narrow geographic area and a region or a state. In fact, interstate highways which link large urban centers have national consequences. Power facilities may serve more than one city or state. Large flood control structures on a single river may affect many states as well as provide multiple benefits. Because of such broad effects, which induce considerable associated development, implementation of major public-facility projects should be creatively used to serve other planning purposes. The damming of streams to create reservoirs for any purpose — flood control, recreation, water supply — involves not only changes to the water system, but also some land-development activities. Authority to construct improvements on rivers for flood control, (including channel and major drainage improvements) and other purposes is vested in the Army Corps of Engineers. Airports and other kinds of port facilities also stimulate economic activity and associated development and are typically constructed by and maintained under the jurisdiction of special-purpose districts or public authorities.

Although both publicly owned and private power facilities are generally subject to federal, state, and sometimes local regulations governing their location, enough flexibility exists in selecting actual sites to allow considerable variation in the influence of a plant on local, regional, and even state development patterns. The problem of utility siting may also involve air pollution, noise pollution, thermal pollution of water, and solid waste disposal problems. Selecting an optimum location in relation to power consumers should be seen from a planning perspective as a problem with consequences beyond those for the power grid.

Capital Improvements Programming

Capital improvements programming[9] is the preparation and updating of a proposed schedule of public works and related equipment to be built or purchased by local govenments during the next few years. To be effective it should cover the community's entire range of public facility and service requirements and be consistent with the community's development goals. All future projects should be listed in order of construction priority, together with cost estimates and the anticipated means of financing each project.

The capital improvements program is generally based on the locality's comprehensive plan, including physical planning and financial projections. In the absence of such a plan, however, it is based on community objectives as defined by the city or county government and on proposals submitted by various officials and departments. The land acquisition and construction activities of all neighboring and overlapping jurisdictions — municipalities, counties, special districts, authorities, and even the state — should also be included, or at least considered, wherever possible in the capital improvements program.

Where a comprehensive physical development plan exists, the basic facts and projections needed for sound capital improvements programming are readily available, and the plan should provide criteria to guide decisions on project selection and the assignment of priorities. Thus, a capital improvements program, like zoning and subdivision control, is a means of implementing certain aspects of the comprehensive plan.

One of the major benefits of capital improvements programming is that it affords a basis for bringing order out of the complex relations that exist among neighboring and overlapping units of local government. This is so because, in many cases, one unit of local government may have to work with authorities and special districts with independent power to finance their own activities. Although each city, county, or special district may develop its own capital improvements program, there is a growing recognition that, on such matters as streets, schools, parks, and water and sewer facilities, there is a need to coordinate planning among major agencies.

The major steps in this programming process are: (1) submission of proposed capital improvements projects by operating departments to the program coordinator, (2) financial analysis of the community's ability to pay for the projects and of the means to be used in financing them, (3) review and selection of projects for inclusion in the program in order of their priority, (4) preparation of a tentative six-year program, (5) consideration and final approval of the program by the governing body, (6) public approval of financing arrangements for individual projects, and (7) annual review and revision of the program. A realistic capital improvements program is inextricably related to fiscal capacity. Knowledge of past experience and an awareness of trends in taxation, assessment, and public expenditures for the local government and for other units of comparable size and fiscal capacity are essential for the development and evaluation of a capital improvements program. Consideration must be given to state-imposed debt limits, per-capita income and expenditures, and the long-term effect of the various capital projects on the local government's capital and operating budget.

Alternative methods by which the CIP is carried out and capital improvements financed include:

Pay-as-you-go. Pay-as-you-go is the financing of improvement projects from current revenues. Such revenues may come from general taxation, fees, charges for services, special funds, or special assessments. Advantages of this method include the saving of interest costs on borrowed money and providing for greater future budget flexibility. The major disadvantage is the need to have uncommitted cash available, a requirement which often precludes the financing of extensive capital improvements in a small community. Reserve-fund financing is a variation of the pay-as-you-go method. Accumulations may result from surplus or "earmarked" operational revenues that are set aside, from depreciation accounts, or from the sale of capital assets.

General obligation bonds. Projects providing community-wide benefits may be financed by general obligation bonds. Through this method, the taxing power of the jurisdiction is pledged to pay interest upon and retire the debt. General obligation bonds can be sold to finance permanent types of improvements such as schools, municipal buildings, parks, and recreation facilities. Such bonds may require the approval of the electorate and may be repaid out of the community's general revenues.

Revenue bonds. Revenue bonds are frequently sold for projects such as water and sewerage systems, stadiums, swimming pools, airports, and other revenue-producing facilities. Such bonds usually are not included in state-imposed debt limits, as are general obligation bonds, because they are not backed by the full faith and credit of the local jurisdiction. For this same reason, interest rates are almost always higher on these bonds than on general obligation bonds and voter approval is seldom required.

Lease-purchase. Local governments using the lease-purchase method prepare specifications for a needed public works project and take steps to have it constructed by a private company or authority. The facility is then leased by the municipality at an annual or monthly rental. At the end of the lease period, the title to the facility can be conveyed to the municipality without any future payments. The rental over the years will have paid the total original cost plus interest. Localities in some states have used this method to avoid the necessity of calling bond elections or to avoid debt limits. This type of financing has sometimes proved to be excessively costly. In addition, its legality has been questioned in some states; in others, the obligation is considered as part of the municipal debt.

Authorities and special districts. Authorities and special districts are usually created to manage facilities that are supported by user charges. (Toll roads and water and sewerage systems are examples of such facilities.) Special districts with power to tax are also created for the purpose of issuing bonds and constructing facilities that may not be self-supporting. Sometimes they are necessary to avoid restrictive debt limits. The authority device may offer a convenient method of financing interjurisdictional facilities; however, its use also creates many problems. Chief among these is the scattering of governmental responsibility. Moreover, the debt incurred by an authority or special district is still a part of a community's total financial obligation, even where it is not counted in the debt limit of a general-purpose government.

Special assessments. Public works programs financed most equitably by special assessments are those that benefit certain properties more than others. Local improvements financed by this method often include street paving, sanitary sewers, and water mains.

Joint financing. A proposed program may include certain projects which are equally beneficial to two or more governmental agencies, authorities, or special districts. If so, financing by both bodies acting together may be appropriate. Such cooperation may bring about projects that would otherwise have to be deferred for many years and thus can result in better service and lower costs for the area.

Tax base revenue sharing. In this method of raising revenue, each local government in a region contributes a percentage of its net growth of property tax valuations to a regional instrumentality for redistribution to various local governments according to specified criteria, such as population and need. This system avoids competition among communities for ratables and allows each community to share equitably in the economic development of the region. Such schemes have been instituted in the Twin Cities Metropolitan Area in Minnesota and in the Hackensack Meadowlands Area in New Jersey.

Public Assistance to Development

A final way government directly influences plan implementation is by providing assistance to private sector development. Examples of this type of activity include new towns, urban renewal, historic preservation, and rent subsidies.

New Towns

Large self-contained new communities have long been the planner's dream because balanced environments for living, working, and playing are created within an attractive and efficient physical framework. New towns range from systematic urbanization of isolated rural land to large subdivisions on the edge of urban areas, and they may spring up in areas subjected to relatively intense planning regardless of their location or present state of development.

Under Title VIII of the Urban Growth and Community Development Act of 1970, Congress provided federal financial assistance for new towns as a means of effectuating a national urban growth policy. Because the financing of new towns is complex and difficult, the act authorized the Department of Housing and Urban Development, acting on behalf of the United States, to guarantee the repayment of loans to approved new town developments. Three conditions that had to be met to obtain approval were: (1) a showing that the new town would preserve or enhance desirable aspects of the natural and urban environment; (2) the new town would be consistent with related state, local, and private plans for the area; and (3) the new town would include low- and moderate-income housing. Unfortunately, recent economic conditions have forced some of the communities approved under this program into difficult financial situations. HUD has severely curtailed and redefined the program so that future new towns will be constructed with limited federal assistance.

Urban Redevelopment

Urban redevelopment had its roots in the slum clearance and housing projects initiated by the federal government in the 1930's. In 1949, Congress enacted the Housing Act, Title I of which provided for federal cost-share assistance to local public agencies for assembly, clearance, site preparation, and sale or lease of land for urban redevelopment projects. The 1954 amendments to the act sought to place greater emphasis on rehabilitation and restoration of blighted areas, rather than on total demolition and redevelopment.

Provisions were also adopted to require a "workable program" intended to encourage the integration of urban redevelopment projects with plans for overall community development. In 1974, urban renewal as a specific categorical grant program was eliminated in favor of Community Development Block Grants, which consolidate funds for a number of redevelopment activities.

Historic Preservation

Preservation of historic landmarks is related closely to environmental planning. Under the National Historic Preservation Act of 1966 and the Demonstration Cities and Metropolitan Development Act of 1966, federal matching grants are provided to state and local government to acquire and develop historic landmarks.

Some states have their own historic preservation programs, such as Pennsylvania (Historical and Museum Commission) and Maryland (Historical Trust Law). Others have enabling legislation that permits local governments to devise their own programs of historic preservation. Usually, local governments attempt to preserve historic landmarks through the exercise of the police power, acquisition by eminent domain, or provision of technical or financial assistance to private developers. In addition to efforts to save isolated structures, many cities have attempted to preserve entire historic districts, such as the Vieux Carre of New Orleans and Beacon Hill in Boston.

Rent Subsidies

Final examples of government assistance to private development are the various subsidies given by government to activities which achieve public purposes.

Section 201(a) of the Housing and Community Development Act of 1974 authorizes a low-income housing assistance program. The program (administered by HUD and referred to as Section 8) directly assists eligible families occupying new, substantially rehabilitated, or existing rental units through assistance payment contracts with owners (including private owners, cooperatives, and public housing agencies). The amount of assistance provided for a given unit equals the difference between the established maximum rent for the unit and the occupant family's required contribution to rent, or not less than 15 or more than 25% of total family income.

In a real sense, this type of direct government action is the prime method by which housing assistance plans are implemented as required under the act as part of a community's eligibility for continued block grant funds.

REGULATORY APPROACHES

In order to understand how the police power, under which development regulations are administered, is used to implement plans, it is necessary to examine the legal framework for the regulatory authority.

The powers reserved to the states under the Tenth Amendment to the United States Constitution include the powers to tax and spend for the public welfare and for the maintenance of government itself; to acquire, manage, and dispose of property for public purposes; and to regulate private activity in the interest of the public health, safety, and general welfare. These sovereign powers of the states, particularly the regulatory ones, are generally known as "police powers." They are the ultimate source of authority for the regulatory approaches discussed below. Their exercise is limited by a number of constitutional restraints, of which the most important for our purposes are that government power be exercised in the public interest; that the means of government intervention be reasonably necessary for the accomplishment of a public purpose; that standards of procedural due process be observed in the regulation of private activity; that states refrain from discriminating unreasonably against any class of persons in the application of their laws; and that private property not be taken for public use without just compensation. Within these constitutional limitations, the states may avail themselves of a broad range of strategies for environmental protection.

In spite of this broad authority, most states have delegated a large measure of their police powers to local governments, either through "home rule" provisions of state law or, more commonly, through enabling statutes. State constitutions, municipal charters adopted in accordance with constitutional or statutory provisions, and enabling legislation are the fundamental sources of local government authority. It must be borne in mind that local governments have no inherent authority of their own, but only such powers as are granted to them by the constitution and statutes of the state in which they are located. Thus, there may be a question as to whether a local government has the authority to legislate in a particular manner to deal with a particular problem. For example, it may lie within the general police power of a municipality to regulate the disposal of waste, but not to impose a tax upon waste products released to the environment, even though the legislative goal might be the same in either case. In such an event, the municipality would have to obtain specific legislative authority to impose a tax.

Home rule provisions, which are designed to carve out a legislative jurisdiction in which local governments can operate free of state interference, typically authorize municipalities "to exercise all powers of local self-government and to adopt and enforce within their limits such local police, sanitary, and other regulations as are not in conflict with general laws." Such a clause may, for example, authorize a municipality to require of a subdivider that he dedicate land for public purposes, even in the absence of any statutory authority to exact such a condition. On the other hand, municipalities in home rule jurisdictions may not in fact have greater powers to control pollution than in states where home rule is not recognized. This is true for two reasons. First, state law may "preempt the field" in matters transcending local concern. State regulation, in other words, may be so pervasive or so comprehensive with respect to a particular activity that no room is left for local governments to adopt regulations of their own pertaining to the same subject matter. It is a question of legislative intent, commonly interpreted by the courts, as to whether state intervention is preemptive or whether state and local enactments can work concurrently in the same field. Where preemption does not exist, local regulations are commonly sustained if they require controls as strict as or stricter than state law. If conflict is otherwise found to exist between state and local enactments, the former will always prevail. These determinations are quite independent of whether home rule has been granted municipalities in matters of local concern.

Second, state enactments delegating police power to local governments may be so broad in scope as to approach constitutional home rule by legislative means. For example, municipalities may be authorized by statute to "take all action necessary or convenient for the government of their local affairs," or to "enact all ordinances, regulations, and by-laws for the well-ordering, managing, and directing of the prudential affairs and police of their respective towns." Thus, state legislatures may delegate broad powers to municipalities to provide for the safety, health, welfare, and convenience of their respective communities. So even in jurisdictions without constitutional home rule, municipalities may have extensive powers to regulate pollutant-generating activity.

The upshot of this brief discussion of a very complicated topic is that local governments may have greater powers than they realize, but they should still obtain the advice of legal counsel before attempting to extend the reach of their environmental controls beyond time-tested procedures.

Constitutional Questions

Takings. As already noted, private property may not be taken for public use without just compensation. The question whether a taking has occurred may arise in any case where the uses of private property are restricted for environmental objectives. The law on this subject is in a state of flux, and it varies considerably from state to state. It is therefore necessary to refer to the judicial precedents of a particular state before deciding where the line may be drawn between valid restrictions imposed in the exercise of the police power and restrictions that may be invalidated as takings of a particular piece of property.

The lessons to be learned from recent case law (discussed below) are that the risk of invalidation by the courts can be minimized if the regulatory scheme (1) is demonstrably based on avoidance of injury to the public at large from irresponsible uses of private property, and (2) consistent with that objective, still leaves the owner free to put his land to one or more reasonable uses that reasonably maintain its economic value. It will also help if the regulation can be justified in terms of public health and safety rather than aesthetics or other less tangible aspects of public welfare.[10] Moreover, as indicated in the Ramapo and Petaluma cases cited earlier, use restrictions are more likely to be upheld if they are of only temporary duration. In general, performance or specification standards precisely geared to environmental objectives will have the best chance of surviving constitutional challenge because they do not rule out most land uses (even though they may well increase the costs of development).

Substantive due process. A regulation may be declared unconstitutional if its provisions are arbitrary or unreasonable and bear no substantial relation to the public health, safety, or general welfare. In other words, regulations must be based on legitimate governmental purposes and be reasonably calculated to accomplish them. For example, large-lot zoning may be acceptable if its purpose truly is to avoid excessive concentrations of septic tanks on soils of limited absorptive capacity, but not if its underlying purpose is to halt town growth or to exclude lower-income groups.[11] Such measures should therefore be based on objective data which will tend to justify both the ends and the means. Assuring the constitutional validity of land-use restrictions and requirements is a major reason for local governments to incorporate natural resource inventories and ecological planning studies into their decision-making processes.

Equal protection. States and their political subdivisions are constitutionally prohibited from denying to any person the equal protection of the laws. Since environmental regulations frequently restrict some persons to a greater degree than others, they may run a risk of being invalidated because of unreasonable, arbitrary, or invidiously discriminatory classification for regulatory purposes. "The basic principles of the equal protection doctrine are well established: any state or municipal legislative classification must be a rational one, bearing a reasonable relationship to a proper legislative purpose."[12] Thus, for example, properties designated as critical water-related lands (riverbanks, wetlands, aquifers, steep slopes) could be made subject to special use restrictions without running afoul of this constitutional standard, so long as the restrictions are essential to sound environmental management in the public interest. Here, then, is another constitutional reason for gearing land-use controls to natural resource inventories or to ecological planning studies. It should be added that a municipality need not regulate simultaneously all instances of a particular problem. Regulation has to begin somewhere, and there is no constitutional infirmity in a piecemeal approach that is free of ulterior discriminatory motives.

Procedural due process. Local governments ordinarily derive their powers to act from enabling statutes of their state legislatures. Such delegated powers must be exercised not only for approved purposes but in accordance with prescribed statutory procedures. These regulations may require, for example, that a local agency give advance public notice of and opportunity for public hearing on proposed legislative or regulatory action; that it adhere to prescribed voting procedures; that it afford opportunity for adjudicatory hearing on proposed issuance or denial of permits; and that it base certain types of decisions on a judicially reviewable record. Even where state law does not require such procedures, it is a good idea to adopt them for the sake of clarity, fairness, and openness in decision making.

If an agency is to administer a permit system or to pass upon proposed development plans, its regulations should clearly indicate who must apply for approval, what information must be included on the application form, within what period it must be submitted and acted upon, and according to what criteria permission will be granted or denied. It is a fundamental tenet of due process that agencies structure the exercise of their own discretion in accordance with impartial rules.

Adherence to elementary concepts of procedural due process will avoid constitutional objections on this ground and will tend to maximize political support for — or at least public acquiescence in — whatever decisons are reached.

Land-Use Regulations

In most states, enabling legislation authorizes local government to adopt zoning ordinances, subdivision regulations, and building and health codes. These are the traditional regulatory vehicles by which governments take actions to implement plans, particularly for environmental purposes.

The object of the grant of zoning power is most often the legislative body or the municipal government, but that power may be conferred upon a planning commission, zoning board, or similar public agency. Enabling acts for local zoning vary suprisingly little in general outline, for most of them are based on the Standard State Zoning Enabling Act, published by the Department of Commerce in 1926. This model act, drafted prior to the Supreme Court's decision in *Euclid* vs. *Ambler Realty Co.*[13] which upheld the community's right to establish land-use districts — the power to zone — was a major reason for the rapid spread of zoning after that decision. The first three sections of the act outline its scope and intent and explain the nature of zoning.

Euclidean zoning, as it is called, became widespread after the decision in *Euclid*. Under this type of zoning, a municipality adopts an ordinance which divides the town into districts or zones with particular uses allowed in each. In its simplest form there are three types of use districts: industrial, commercial, and residential. The zones are cumulative in that in the industrial zone any use is allowed; in a commercial zone all but industrial uses are permissible. The residential portions are the only exclusive areas. Some uses, such as cemeteries, are not placed in any area. Rather, a determination as to their location is made on an ad hoc basis. In a modern community, many more zones are the rule, and the plans are characterized by greater flexibility. Commonly, zoning boards of adjustment, as authorized by the ordinances, interpret the ordinance when disputes arise. A dissatisfied landowner's ultimate recourse is to the court.

The traditional zoning ordinance includes detailed "dimensional" controls that specify building height and bulk, minimum depth of side, front, and backyards, minimum lot size and frontage, and percentage of the lot not to be built upon. The standards vary according to the use district. *Floor area ratio*, or the ratio between the total floor area of the building and the ground area of the site, is used to allow greater flexibility in density standards.

Some land uses require a degree of flexibility not provided by a rigid zoning scheme. Four devices available to deal with this need are the variance, the special-use zone, the special-use permit or conditional use, and the floating zone. The variance is a process by which hardship created by the ordinance can be mitigated by allowing specific exceptions to its application. The special-use zone provides a separate zone for one particular use within a larger zone. Most of the newer ordinances list the uses which are permitted "as of right" in each zone, and they also list "special" or "conditional" uses which may be permitted upon the approval of the zoning board of adjustment. The floating zone is a special-use district defined by standards but not applied to any particular area until a developer asks the board to rezone the land in that category.

All controls included in zoning regulations are really means of defining types and intensity of land use. Trends in the revision of the zoning system have been (1) to attempt to relate controls more closely to planning criteria and (2) to attempt to make controls more flexible without excluding the discretionary authority of the zoning board. One of the examples of this trend is to relate control not to use but to effect. Most zoning controls are in effect performance standards, or proposed ways of distinguishing among types of uses. Technical performance standards have been developed to deal with a number of types of potential nuisances and uses, such as noise, vibration, smoke, odor, dust, fire, and explosive hazards.

On larger sites, a greater density of development and better land use can be achieved by creative land-planning designs. Also, it is sometimes advisable to allow uses on large parcels of land which ordinarily are not desirable in a single specific zoning district. Limited commercial facilities in a large residential project is a good example. New kinds of zoning regulations such as planned unit developments and cluster zoning have been developed to meet these needs.

Essentially, Planned Unit-Development (PUD) ordinances establish a PUD district and provide that, before any development or use can occur, the owner must submit a PUD plan and obtain its approval from the local administering agency. There are no typical regulations, but each development is approved on its own merits. A variation is to adopt a provision permitting the board of appeals, which also grants variances and special permits, to approve planned unit-development projects anywhere in the community upon showing that the proposal is generally consistent with existing planning, in the best interests of the community, and consistent with appropriate development standards.

Cluster-zoning provisions permit landowners who plan to subdivide their parcels to build on a smaller portion of the subdivision or to cluster the houses, thus leaving the rest for open space. This design concept keeps the overall density the same but allows clustering within a given area. Where certain critical natural areas are located within a site, clustering allows them to be preserved. In addition to consolidating open spaces, cluster zoning's more efficient layout allows substantial savings in street and utility development.

With increasing sophistication, communities are making decisions as to where to locate land uses based on the effect of development. Each type of development has its own associated costs. Higher densities may mean fewer school-age children; lower density development requires longer sewer runs, longer roads, and more land. Also to be considered are the effects of covering the land and the consequent ability of the soil to absorb water runoff, sewage, and water supply. Large-lot zoning, cluster development, and planned unit development are all ways in which these considerations are built into the land-use control process.

Subdivision regulations are the controls governing the layout of streets and lots and the provision of necessary services. Subdivision control assures that development will meet accepted standards and that new homes will be properly provided with municipal services, adequate sewage disposal, roads, water, drainage, and so on. The subdivision review process can positively guide development and implement plans by conditioning permit approval on adequate compliance with elements of the subdivision regulations.

It is usually argued that registration of a subdivision is a "privilege" which the community confers on the developer, in return for which he must comply with the requirements of the regulations.

Therefore, these requirements can go further than zoning regulations, which confer no compensating advantage. Because both zoning and subdivision regulation are exercised under the police power, the distinction may be dubious. In any event, the policy behind subdivision requirements is that all necessary improvements should be provided by the developer rather than at public expense.

It is this rationale that towns have used to require the developer to dedicate a portion of the land to be developed for open space. This is known as "mandatory dedication" of open space. Some courts have found this requirement illegal. Consequently, a variation of the requirement has arisen; developers are required to contribute money for parks or schools to be located elsewhere in the community in an amount equal to the demands for those facilities created by this development.

Limits of Regulation

Because police power regulations are the primary instrument by which plans are carried out, it is important to understand the extent of permissible regulation. The Fifth Amendment requires that private property shall not be taken for public use without just compensation. Society's desires to protect certain resources and regulate environmentally critical features of land under the police power nearly always conflict with the desire of the private landowner to realize economic value from his land. The line distinguishing the exercise of that police power and constitutional "takings" which require compensation is not clear and is dependent upon facts in each particular case.

At least four theories for deciding when a "taking" occurs emerge from the court opinions: the "physical invasion" theory, the "nuisance abatement" theory, the "dimunition of value" theory, and the "balancing" of public good vs. individual loss theory.

The first theory holds that an appropriation of private property for public uses which requires compensation only occurs by actual transfer of title. Where invasions of property for a public purpose occur which effectively destroy or impair the property's usefulness, it is almost universally held that a taking occurs which requires compensation. There are limitations, however, insofar as compensation need not be made if property is taken in times of emergency such as fire, earthquake, flood, or war.

Where there is no direct physical intrusion but where private property is used in a manner which substantially harms the general

public, compensation is not required when the public reacts to protect itself. Particularly where health and safety are involved, regulations without compensation are well accepted to require individuals
to bear the expense of conforming to public standards. Thus, regulations that treat alterations of channel or floodway capacity to prevent waters flowing into other lands as analogous to nuisance uses
have been sustained. It is also generally accepted that a property
owner may not construct a dam, levee, or other obstruction in a
channel or floodway if it would substantially increase ordinary flood
heights and subsequently cause damage to other land. Some com-
mentators believe that since government is acting in an "arbitral
capacity" in resolving land-use conflicts among property owners,
the regulations are to be viewed as noncompensable.

Under the third theory, competing interests are weighed against
each other. On one side would be the extent of government interference measured by the economic or physical loss to the individual;
on the other side would be the public benefit derived from government action. Clearly, the issue is dependent upon particular facts
and circumstances. In upholding the authority of a town to enact
floodplain zoning, the court in *Turnpike Realty Co.* vs. *Town of
Dedham*[14] said that such restrictions must be balanced against the
potential harm to the community from overdevelopment of a floodplain area.

The most common and widely used theory is one which is
based on the extent of the economic loss that governmental action
has caused to the landowner. Mr. Justice Holmes, in *Pennsylvania
Coal Co.* vs. *Mahon*,[15] formulated the classic test for a taking when
he stated that in determining the limits of the police power

> one fact for consideration is the extent of the diminution.
> When it reaches a certain magnitude, in most if not all
> cases, there must be an exercise of eminent domain and
> compensation to sustain the act . . . . The general rule,
> at least, is that while property may be regulated to a
> certain extent, if regulation goes too far it will be recog-
> nized as a taking.[16]

Again, how far is too far is determined on the facts of each
case. Scholars have noted that with regulations which were found
invalid as a taking and which contained a cost analysis, the weighted
mean reduction in land value was 73%.

More recent and sophisticated cases resort to the formula that awards or denies compensation depending on whether "a reasonable use" of the property remains after the regulations. Reasonable use seems to refer to some economically profitable use rather than to any possible use; thus, the landowner need not be allowed to make the most profitable use of his land so long as some economic use is allowed. An otherwise valid regulation is not defective because it deprives property of its most beneficial use. In a New Jersey decision,[17] however, a large number of open-space uses could not save a zoning scheme where all of the permitted uses on lands in high-value areas were uneconomic. The decision suggests that if an ordinance prohibits or severely restricts fill, which is necessary for some economic use of the land, the regulation may be unconstitutional as depriving the land of all reasonable use.

The law, however, is changing on this point. Three recent cases illustrate that reasonable remaining uses are not to be measured solely in economic terms, especially where critical natural features are in question *(Candlestick; Just)*, and that a taking does not occur when a moratorium is placed on development pending completion of a comprehensive plan *(Steel Hill)*.

In the first situation, the argument is as follows:

As understanding of the interrelatedness of environmental concerns increases, so also does the identification of what might be called critical, 'natural' features of the land, the alteration of which will drastically affect areas of vital public concern. The wetlands cases provide a good example. Population and urban expansion pressures have presented developers with opportunities to realize profits through expensive fill or reclamation techniques designed to overcome natural limitations in land. Such land, in its undeveloped state, serves a number of important functions, including flood control and ecological balance. To assume that one has an inherent right to make such alterations ignores or distorts an obvious relationship between such activity and interest should not seem an undue restriction on the concept.[18]

For example, in *Candlestick Properties, Inc.*, vs. *San Francisco Bay Conservation and Development Commission,*[19] a case testing the powers of the BCDC, the court upheld a denial of a permit to fill bay lands. The land at issue, which was submerged at high tide by waters of the bay, had been acquired specifically as a place to deposit fill from construction projects. The land was thus of no value except as a place to deposit fill for filled land. The court nevertheless upheld the restrictions, noting the legislature's declaration of the strong public interest in the preservation of the bay and the threats thereto by filling. Thus, refusing to allow the filling did not amount to an undue restriction on private property in view of the necessity for controlling the filling of the bay. The court also found that the purpose of the regulations was to preserve the existing character of the bay while a determination was made as to how it should be developed in the future.

In *Just* vs. *Marionette County*,[20] a Wisconsin court explicitly refused to recognize as legitimate expectations of economic profit that were inconsistent with widely prevailing public standards. In upholding prohibitions to wetland filling, the court emphasized the vital function that such land served in its natural state, and said:

> In the instant case we have a restriction on the use of a citizen's property, not to secure a benefit for the public, but to prevent a harm from the change in the natural character of the citizen's property . . . . What makes this case different from most condemnation or police power zoning cases is the interrelationship of the wetlands, the swamps, and the natural environment of the shorelands to the purity of the water and to such natural resources as navigation, fishing, and scenic beauty . . . .
> Is the ownership of a parcel of land so absolute that man can change its nature to suit any of his purposes? An owner of land has no absolute and unlimited right to change the essential natural character of his land so as to use it for a purpose for which it was unsuited in its natural state and which injures the rights of others. The exercise of the police power in zoning must be reasonable and we think it is not an unreasonable exercise of that power to prevent harm to public rights by limiting the use of private property to its natural uses . . . . The Justs argue their property has been severely depreciated in value. But this depreciation of value is not based on the use of the land in its natural state but on what the land would be worth if it could be filled and used for the location of a dwelling. While loss of value is to be considered in determining whether a restriction is a constructive taking,

value based upon changing the character of land at the expense of harm to public rights is not an essential factor or controlling.[21]

A final exception to the idea that loss of value automatically constitutes a taking is found in the use of development moratoria pending a fuller understanding of the potential consequences of alterations to ecological systems. Protecting "opportunities foregone" and temporarily destroying economic value is not such a drastic invasion of private property, since the value may eventually be restored. *Candlestick* and *Steel Hill Development, Inc. vs. Sanbornton*[22] are illustrations of this point. The latter case upheld the validity of a New Hampshire town zoning amendment imposing a six-acre minimum lot requirement on 50% of the town's area and rezoning 70% of the company's land. The court recognized that:

> at this time of uncertainty as to the right balance between ecological and population pressures, we cannot help but feel that the town's ordinance, which severely restricts development, may properly stand for the present as a legitimate stopgap measure. In effect the town has bought time for its citizens not unlike the action taken in referendum by the City of Boulder, Colorado, to restrict growth on an emergency basis until adequate study can be made of future needs.[23]

Regulating Critical, Hazardous, or Sensitive Areas

Environmentally sensitive areas are those whose destruction or disturbance will immediately affect the life of a community by either (1) creating hazards such as flooding and landslides, (2) destroying important public resources such as water supplies and the water quality of lakes and rivers, or (3) wasting important productive lands and renewable resources. The necessity for governmental involvement in environmentally sensitive areas comes from the essentially public character of these resources. Loss of such areas not only means the destruction of some intrinsic environmental values but also a social and economic loss to the community. Therefore, government or the public may legitimately go to greater lengths under the police power to protect these areas.

It should be noted that water pollution plans, mandated under the Federal Water Pollution Control Act Amendments of 1972 (PL 92-500) rely on various forms of land-use controls for their implementation just as would other more comprehensive plans. Therefore, specific strategies for water-related land-use controls are discussed here as examples of controls for various environmentally sensitive areas.

Floodplains

Essentially, three theories justify the imposition of regulatory controls in the floodplains. First, if development is permitted in either a floodway (the normal stream channel plus that part of the floodplain which is flooded) or on a floodplain (the larger area which would be flooded during an extraordinary flood), floods may seriously threaten the people who live there. Second, during times of flood, structures or obstructions in the floodplain distort the flow of the stream to cause additional damage upstream, by backing up water, and downstream, by increasing the velocity of the water. Public intervention is needed to prevent one developer from imposing costs on his neighbor. Finally, preventing unwise floodplain development minimizes demands made on the government for disaster relief in times of flood.

Nonstructural controls for floods, such as regulations in the form of floodplain zoning, subdivision, building codes, and relocation programs contrasts sharply with traditional methods of dealing with floods. Since 1936, the federal government, through the Corps of Engineers, has been building dams and other channel and structural improvements to reduce flood losses. Because development in the floodplains has been allowed to continue, these structural controls have had limited success in reducing losses. In 1974, Congress enacted the Water Resources Development Act (PL 93-283), which for the first time provided federal cost-sharing for nonstructural controls and which, it is hoped, marks the beginning of new approaches to floodplain management.

Another factor in the increase of land-use controls for flood hazard areas by local governments is the National Flood Insurance Act of 1968, administered by the Department of Housing and Urban Development. The act provides subsidized flood insurance to homeowners, provided their community has adopted land-use controls that meet prescribed standards for flood hazards. Structures are required to be elevated above the level of the one hundred-year flood. The Flood Disaster Relief Act of 1974, as amended by the Housing and Community Development Act of 1977, requires banks and savings and loan associations insured by federal instrumentalities to notify recipients of mortgages that flood disaster relief may not be available if their land is located in a flood hazard area and if no flood-proofing measures are taken. These acts also make provisions for emergency preparedness plans and disaster relief.

A number of states have added the word "flood" to their standard zoning-enabling law in order to authorize municipal regulation of floodplain development. Several states, notably Connecticut and Iowa, have established state-level regulations of construction in the floodplain by establishing encroachment lines beyond which new development is to be approved by state permit. Local regulatory approaches include both land-use controls (regulatory development in the floodplain, or regulatory development more stringently in the floodway than in the floodplain) and building codes (governing the methods by which buildings are constructed to ensure that they are flood-proofed).

Wetlands

Wetland control cases are among early instances of the use of regulations to control land for ecological or environmental purposes. The importance of wetlands as recharge areas for aquifers, as absorption areas to minimize runoff, and as areas for fish and wildlife spawning areas has become well known.

The general method of controlling wetlands is by statutes and ordinances which either prohibit or require a permit for certain activities, usually the dredging or filling of wetlands. An alternative method is to map wetlands and issue "protective orders" for the areas that specify the uses to be permitted as of right, those permitted with conditions, and other uses requiring special permits.

Earlier cases regulating the use of wetlands did not fare well in the courts. Courts often found ordinances to be in excess of the legislative grant of authority because they promoted the preservation of natural resources and not the protection of property owners from threats to their safety. It seems, then, that courts are willing to go further in allowing the dimunition in value of private property where safety measures are involved. Two recent cases, *Candlestick Properties* and *Just*, which have approved regulations controlling private use of wetlands, indicate a change in the attitude of some courts to this issue.

In any case, where conservation regulations are concerned, courts will continue to rely heavily on the question of the difference in the value of the land with the restriction and without the restriction, and whether there are other uses for the land that will enable the owners to obtain a return on their investment. Probably necessary for adequate wetlands control laws is the authority to compensate owners when desired regulations would cause a substantial reduction in the value of property. The state could provide compensation by purchasing a limitation on the use of the land through a conservation easement or similar device.

Erosion and Sedimentation Controls

Techniques of direct regulation are being applied by a growing number of communities "to sensitize development to the erosion/sedimentation potential of the site."[24] Ordinances requiring erosion and sedimentation controls for development approval may be enacted under a separate enabling authority or by amendment to the community's basic zoning or subdivision ordinance. Where a community feels confident that a particular set of controls should be adopted for all developments of a designated class, or for all earth-moving activities that can be identified as having a high erosion potential, it will make sense to specify the necessary controls in the ordinance itself or in rules and regulations adopted by the appropriate state agency. Such regulations can be quite precise, despite the generality of their application. For example, regulations of the Pennsylvania Department of Environmental Resources require that:

> Diversion terraces shall be constructed up-grade of a project area to convey runoff around the . . . area. For temporary diversion the channel shall have the capacity to convey 2.75 cubic feet for each acre of project area tributary to it and shall be cleaned when the storage capacity of the basic is reduced to 5,000 cubic feet per acre . . . . Outlet structures shall be designed to pass a minimum flow of 2.0 cubic feet per second for each acre of project area tributary to the basin.[25]

More commonly, state and local regulations do not specify uniform controls for all development but provide instead a set of principles for evaluating development and concomitant controls on a case-by-case basis, according to variable site characteristics such as type of soils, degree and length of slope, size, and duration of exposed surfaces. Such principles may state, for example, that the smallest practicable area of land shall be exposed at any one time during development; that natural features shall be preserved whenever possible; that temporary vegetation or mulching shall be used to protect critical areas exposed during development and permanent final vegetation installed as soon as practical in the development process; and that development in general shall be fitted to topography and soils in such a way as to create the least erosion potential.[26] Accordingly, development proposed for steeper slopes or on soils of relatively high erodability will be subject to stricter standards than equivalent development in flat terrain or on more resistant soil. In this manner, flexibility in the administration of the ordinance can be assured, taking account of a wide variety of possible interactions between site characteristics and types of development.

The ordinance may also refer the developer to a manual on erosion and sedimentation control, in which are set forth detailed guidelines or standards for various types of controls that could be incorporated into site plans, construction practices, and ongoing maintenance procedures. Because the manual can be amended from time to time in light of experience and as new techniques are developed for controlling runoff and erosion, this arrangement eliminates the need to go through the formal process of amending the ordinance itself every time a change is made in the technical guidelines. This approach also has the advantage of furnishing detailed technical assistance to the developer while encouraging technical innovation. Assistance in preparing the manual can be obtained from the Soil Conservation Service of the United States Department of Agriculture and from a number of states (including Maryland and Pennsylvania) which have already developed detailed manuals for the use of their local governments.[27]

Typically, the ordinance provides that no land area may be disturbed until a plan for soil erosion and sedimentation control has been submitted to and approved by the relevant agency. This could be the planning department, the county soil district, the municipal building inspector, city engineer, planning commission, or even the town council, depending on "relevant state enabling legislation, the effectiveness and efficiency . . . and the capabilities of the evaluative body."[28]

Since the effectiveness of this type of regulation depends heavily upon the judgment of the reviewing body, "it is apparent that additional evaluative resources are required, such as a competent planning staff with some training in the soil sciences and soil conservation practices."[29] Soil conservation districts, where they exist, can assist in performing the necessary evaluations. Under some arrangements, "each application for development is required to have an erosion and sedimentation control plan in line with the standards established by the district. The district then evaluates the control plan and, in some cases, serves as the enforcement agent."[30]

A good example of an erosion and sedimentation control ordinance is the one adopted by Washington County, Maryland. It provides that "the surface of land in this County shall not be disturbed or changed for any nonagricultural purpose whatever . . . except in accordance with a plan for control of erosion and sedimentation approved by the Soil Conservation District and a grading permit approved by the Building Permit Department of Washington County." (In addition to agricultural practices and structures, the ordinance exempts from its provisions the construction of single-family residences and their accessory buildings on lots of two acres or more). With each application for a grading permit, the plan, specifications, and a time schedule must be submitted and accompanied by the applicant's certification that all land clearing, construction, and development will be done pursuant to that plan. The plan must be prepared or approved and signed by a professional engineer, land surveyor, or architect. It must show topography and soil types; vegetative practices; a grading plan; proposed improvements; and provisions for erosion control, both during construction and afterwards; and a schedule and sequence of operations. All grading plans and specifications must include provisions "in substantial accordance with" the Design Manual for Erosion and Sediment Control for Washington County.

If the application conforms to the foregoing requirements, the Soil Conservation District must approve it and forward one copy of its written approval to the County Engineer, one copy to the Planning and Zoning Commission, and two copies to the Building Permit Department of Washington County, which then issues the grading permit to the applicant.

The ordinance further provides that the developer and all subsequent owners of the property "shall maintain all permanent antierosion devices, retaining walls, structures, plantings, and other protective devices." To assure compliance with the ordinance and the permits issued under it, the County Engineer is to inspect the work done under approved plans and permits and to issue certificates of satisfactory completion to permittees.

The approach adopted by DeKalb County, Georgia, is to specify at length in the county code those standards to be observed with respect to erosion and sedimentation control, while leaving most of the details to the architect or engineer who prepares the control plans to accompany the development application. For example, the ordinance provides that "sedimentation facilities (debris basins, sedimentation traps) and other control measures such as hay bales, berms, interceptor ditches, and terraces shall be installed in conjunction with the initial grading operations and be maintained throughout the development and construction process to remove sediment from runoff waters draining land under development." Land that has been cleared for development must be protected "by appropriate vegetation and land-covering techniques such as seeding, sodding, [and] ground cover installation." No grading, cutting, or filling is allowed on any site under development if it will result in bringing unprotected land surfaces into contact with surface water, "unless erosion control and sedimentation control devices can be installed between the grading area and water surface."[31]

An ordinance can combine specifications for control measures with some degree of orientation toward natural performance standards. For example, the law could require that the erosion and sedimentation control plan result in runoff and erosion no greater than would occur if the land had remained in its natural state. To that end, the ordinance would direct that the developer use, to the maximum feasible extent, natural control features such as existing swamps and swales; employ cluster development where practical to reduce the total area of impervious surface and to preserve open spaces and topographical features that are critical to surface-water management; avoid concentrations of flow, take steps to dissipate runoff velocities, and reestablish vegetative cover as soon as possible after land disturbance; and adhere strictly to any applicable requirements for designated critical areas. While specifying certain design standards, the ordinance could at the same time allow innovative control devices to be employed if engineering analysis shows their performance capabilities would meet the objectives of the regulation.[32]

Erosion and sedimentation controls need not and should not be confined to districts of critical planning concern. Such controls may be needed throughout a community in order to prevent the migration of sediments from one location to another. Thus, controls of this sort can usefully supplement other types of land-use regulation.

Controls over Land Disposal of Waste

A growing number of states have adopted detailed regulations on the siting, operation, and maintenance of municipal landfills. Such regulations are designed in large measure to avoid pollution of ground and surface waters from leachate and overflow at landfill sites.

Regulations of the State of Hawaii[33] prohibit establishment or operation of any solid waste disposal facility without a permit from the state director of health. A permit application must be accompanied by detailed plans for the facility and by a plan of operations. Permittees are required by these regulations to compact and cover all solid waste accumulated after each day's operation with earth or other approved material so as to safeguard the environmental quality of the surrounding area; to operate monitoring equipment to detect any pollution that might result from the facility; to maintain a minimum vertical separation of five feet between deposited waste and high groundwater table; to provide for minimizing the flow of off-site drainage over the landfill; and to deposit solid wastes in such a manner as "to prevent waste materials, leachate, or eroded soil particles from entering the waters of the State without receiving the best practicable treatment or control."

Landfill regulations might also prohibit deposit of infectious or other hazardous wastes; prohibit lagooning of sewage, sludge, or septage; establish limits on the width of the working face; and require operators to meet periodic self-monitoring, recording, and reporting requirements.[34] Numerous further points of control could be cited from regulations of one or another state. Their coverage and detail can be as extensive or as selective as a state may deem practicable for its own purposes.

Direct regulation of solid waste disposal is a traditional form of government control that is fairly easy to comprehend. The difficulties it has encountered are rather of a practical nature. In some states, "grandfather clauses" exempt preexisting dumps and landfills from new state regulatory requirements. This loophole can only be filled by regulation at the local level, which is often inadequate. Moreover, regardless of the division of responsibility between states and localities, substandard operation of landfills is commonplace in many parts of the country, and compliance with strict regulatory standards has been difficult to secure. Many landfills have been located next to water bodies, or wetlands, or over aquifers, which inevitably become polluted as ever-increasing volumes of solid waste are brought to those sites for disposal. Closing down a landfill operation is a feasible remedy only if alternative disposal sites or methods are available, and often they are not because of land scarcity, obstacles to regionalization, or the impracticability of recycling. Regulation, then, needs to be accompanied by more forceful regional planning and incentives for employing different approaches to the problem of solid waste pollution. Until these steps are taken, however, state and local governments could be doing a better job of monitoring compliance with and enforcing feasible operating standards for municipal landfills.

Regulation of septic tanks is another largely local responsibility that many communities have not met adequately. An effective regulatory scheme would prevent pollution of ground and surface waters from failing septic tanks with a permit system that controls their loction, density, construction, and maintenance. State health codes routinely address these subjects but may be deficient in a number of respects. For example, rapid percolation may be required in order to avoid nuisance conditions or health hazards from surface contaminants, but if percolation of wastes is too rapid, they may pollute groundwaters. Scavengers (those whose business it is to clean out septic tanks) ought to be licensed and required to report their sludge disposal sites and methods to the licensing body, but effective regulation of scavenging practices is not practiced by many states. Local boards of health are supposed to regulate septic tanks through local health ordinances that implement, at a minimum, the standards set forth in the state code, but pressures for development and reluctance to pay for new or expanded sewer systems often result in permitting septic tanks on unsuitable soils or in excessive densities. Enforcement of standards for septic tank maintenance is also practically nonexistent in many areas. The problem lies not in learning how regulations can prevent pollution from septic systems, but in mustering the political will and administrative resources necessary to bring that pollution under control.

State and local controls for shorelands do not differ substantially from the nature of controls which can be applied to other sensitive areas. Communities may zone such areas, require special permits for activities conducted therein, or prescribe certain performance standards for development on shorelands. Also, to the extent that much of the most critical shorelands are tidal or coastal wetlands, shorelands may be protected by specifically enacted statutes.

Shorelands, like other hazardous areas, have been considered of critical concern and are protected within the context of a specific management program. The Coastal Zone Management Act of 1972, for example, provides federal funds to states to develop coastal-zone management programs which meet prescribed standards and guidelines. First, the management program must establish permissible activities within a defined zone; second, it must designate critical environmental areas; and third, it must set priorities for uses in the zone. The act thus offers states a vehicle by which to establish programs to prepare and implement plans for shorelands.

Maine's Shoreline Zoning and Subdivision Control Law[35] is an example of state controls for land within 250 feet of a water body. Under this law, the state's Department of Environmental Protection and the State Planning Office are to adopt minimum guidelines for the preservation of shoreline areas. Municipalities are then required to enact local controls consistent with these guidelines. If a municipality fails to adopt and administer satisfactory ordinances, the state will adopt and enforce rules for such communities.

Steep Slopes

Development on steep slopes or hillsides poses a threat to soil erosion and may trigger slippage of soil and rock. Because of increased development costs in such areas, there is a tendency for some developers to flatten small hills or fill valleys, changing natural drainage patterns and contours. Development regulations in these areas are designed to protect the public health and safety from potential effects of development on other land downhill and to shield the residents of such areas from their own folly.

There are three principal approaches to the regulation, by traditional land-use controls, of hillside development. One method is slope-density provisions, which state the degree of density that may be built on a particular slope by defining the percentage of a particular parcel of land, lot size, or number of units which may be developed on the basis of that parcel's average slope. A second approach to the regulation of hillside development is through the use of soil overlay maps showing which areas are suitable for particular types of development based on soil content. Finally, a regulatory approach, perhaps involving a case-by-case evaluation on the basis of specific criteria and policies, requires protective measures be instituted during construction. Such measures include grading and erosion controls, vegetative requirements, or relating the design of hillside development to topographic conditions.

Hillside restrictions are fairly common in California, where there is a tradition of building on steep slopes. The Town of Corte Madera, in Marion County, established a "slope conservation district" as an overlay to be mapped along with the most restrictive residential districts. The required lot area for residential development in the latter districts was increased up to a maximum of one acre with a special formula based on the degree of slope. Moreover, the ordinance also established certain restrictions on removing vegetation, such as allowing removal of trees of only certain sizes and only for the purpose of improving growth conditions; removing diseased material; and eliminating hazards. Similarly, subdivision-control regulations in Riverside, California, require the design of hillside subdivisions related to topographic conditions and with minimum disturbance of natural topography and vegetative cover.

State and Regional Land-Use Controls

Because the American system of land-use controls relies heavily on the local level of government to administer regulations consistent with comprehensive plans, many developments that have regional consequences or have sprung up in sensitive areas have been approved by localities without concern for the larger public interest. Within the last decade, a "quiet revolution" has been shifting responsibility for planning and land-use controls to the state and/or regional levels of government.[36] Responsibility for the implementation of plans, at least in part, has also shifted from local to regional and state governments.

A common aspect of these controls has been their attempt to define and distinguish between the nature of interests appropriate to the state, the region, and the locality. The aim is to make the controls more manageable and less expensive, to provide deference to local familiarity with local affairs, and to improve the nature of decisions made with regard to certain kinds of development in certain areas.

Many of the new pieces of legislation are based on the American Law Institute's Model Land Development Code. Although much of the Model Code is devoted to strengthening the regulatory and planning capability of local government, Articles 7 and 8 are premised on the idea that certain land-use decisions are not appropriate for determination by local systems of regulation.

The code attempts to delineate the limited categories of land-use decisons in which more than local interests are present and to establish another system of regulation. The first regulatory category in the code's nonlocal system includes those areas where development might affect citizens beyond the locality in question. "Areas of Critical State Concern," as these areas are termed, are identified (a) when historical, natural, or environmental resources of regional or statewide importance are present; or (b) when an area is significantly affected by or has a significant effect upon a major existing or proposed public facility or on other areas of major public investment. The second category includes those types of development which, wherever they occur, are likely to have an effect upon the citizens of more than one locality. These are called "Development(s) of Regional Impact." and they are of considerable size, create substantial environmental problems, attract large numbers of persons or vehicles, and generate associated development. Having defined these categories of land-use decisions which call for something more than relatively exclusive local control, the code assigns responsibilities within such a system to the state and local levels, omitting a regional role because of the inherently weak powers of existing regional bodies.

Almost all of the examples of recent land-use legislation which embody the concepts of ALI Code tend to fall into four categories:

(1) Direct state assumption of responsibility for regular zoning and/or subdivision control, sometimes in areas otherwise unzoned;

(2) Statutory provisions ensuring that most new development not cause any serious environmental damage, by means of (a) state-level administrative review under general standards and/or (b) the issuance of permits subject to conditions;

(3) General requirements for regional-level review and permits, applying generally to specified geographic areas; and

(4) Special requirements for protection of particular types of landscapes.

Two states, Maine and Hawaii, have taken over direct responsibility for land-use controls. In Maine,[37] a special land-use commission was authorized to enact zoning and subdivision regulations in unorganized territories. Under the Hawaii law, the oldest in the country, the state was divided into four categories: urban, rural, agricultural, and conservation. The state administered development controls in these categories through the counties and the localities.

Two examples of the kind of regional arrangements envisioned in category three operate in New Jersey and Massachusetts. In the Hackensack Meadowlands in Northeastern New Jersey, a special regional commission was established to supervise development in an area which included fourteen municipalities. An essential feature of this arrangement was the pooling of receipts from new tax "ratables" by the municipalities. Under the Martha's Vineyard Land Use Law, a twenty-one-member regional commission was established to pass on all applications to construct developments of regional influence, to designate districts of critical planning concern, and to oversee local regulation of these districts.

Developments of Regional Impact

The regulation of certain kinds of development on a state and regional basis makes it possible to see their entire range of effects and to render decisions about them accordingly. In fact, two clear cases of the inability of local land-use controls to assess regional consequences are the air and water pollution resulting from large-scale developments. Situations also arise in which development needed by an entire region brings disadvantages to the community where it is to be located. Two examples of this dilemma are low- and moderate-cost housing and the location of public utility services.

The principles of the ALI Code and the mechanics of regulation developments of regional impact are demonstrated in Florida's Environmental Land and Water Management Act of 1972. In addition to a category for "Areas of Critical State Concern," the law establishes a category for development that — because of its character, magnitude, or location — would have a substantial effect on the health, safety, or welfare of citizens of more than one county. The governor and cabinet are charged with establishing guidelines and standards to define the nature of these developments after they receive recommendations from the state planning agency.

The DRI process operates only where local zoning or subdivision laws are in effect. If a DRI is planned in a jurisdiction with such controls, specific requirements for notice and hearings are to be in effect. If there are no controls, the local government is given ninety days to enact them. If it does not, the developer can go ahead, subject to any other state permits he must obtain. Where such controls exist, the regional planning agencies have thirty days to prepare an impact review and recommendation, which the local government must consider before deciding how to approve the DRI. This impact review is triggered by the developer, who supplies the locality, state, and region with detailed information on how the DRI will affect the region's environment and natural resources, public facilities, and economy. Once the local government makes a decision, the state, the developer, or the region can appeal to the governor and cabinet.

Areas of Critical Concern

Some geographical areas are ecologically more fragile, or more important for economic or cultural reasons, than others. Interest in what happens to these areas extends beyond the locality in which they happen to be located. Although they are commonly referred to as areas of critical concern, some states have limited their application to environmental areas, and some have broadened the definition to include areas of critical concern to the state. For the most part, however, these are areas which include the hazardous and sensitive areas discussed earlier; when included in state and regional land-use control programs, such areas are seen not only as areas to be regulated, but as components of a total management system.

Commonly, states have enacted general-purpose environmental-protection statues establishing nonspecific criteria for environmental damage and requiring a permit and regulated development for most new projects over a specific size in such areas.[38] Other states have enacted legislation creating bodies to administer general-purpose land-use controls over a specified geographic area. An example of such statutes is California's San Francisco Bay Conservation and Development Commission which, after preparing a plan for the shoreline of the bay, was granted authority to restrict new development along its shores by passing on permits to fill in the area. The Adirondack Park Agency in New York and the Lake Tahoe Regional Planning Agency around Lake Tahoe on the California-Nevada border are examples of regional commissions with general powers over land use in particular areas.

In Florida, however, controls over areas of critical state concern were integrated with controls for developments with regional effects. An area of critical state concern must meet one of three statutory criteria: (1) it contains environmental, natural, or archeological resources of regional or statewide importance; (2) it is affected by or has a significant effect on a major public investment; or (3) it is an area of major development potential, including new towns. Such areas are to be designated and principles for guiding the development of such areas established by the governor and the cabinet after a review of recommendations from the state planning agency. The local government with jurisdiction over the area has six months to draft regulations implementing the principles. If it does not act or if its regulations are inconsistent with the state's principles, the state planning agency will prepare and enact appropriate regulations with the approval of the governor and cabinet. Actual administration of these regulations is local, although it is subject to some state supervision.

Regional Fair-Share Allocations

Another emerging issue in the field of land-use controls which results from their local administration is the attempt by municipalities to prevent undesired change in neighborhoods and, specifically, to prevent unwanted segments of the population from moving in. Indeed, the original cases upholding the constitutionality of zoning, the primary tool by which municipalities sought to achieve these ends, assumed the legitimacy of economic segregation, particularly between multifamily and single-family housing. Although courts have continued to recognize the primacy of local legislative judgments, they have invalidated local land-use regulations that clearly attempt to deny housing opportunities to racial minorities as denials of the equal-protection-under-the-law clause of the Fourteenth Amendment.

Overcoming economic discrimination in housing opportunity has been more difficult, and only recently have some state courts mandated community responsibility for meeting the housing needs of a regional population, including low- and moderate-income families.

In a number of metropolitan areas — notably Dayton, Ohio, which was the first to do so — central cities and suburbs have voltarily agreed to adopt plans for the allocation of lower-income housing units on a fair-share basis. In Montgomery County, Maryland, a suburb of Washington, D.C., ordinances require subdivision builders to allocate specific percentages of units for low- and moderate-income housing as a condition of receiving building permits.

At the state level, efforts have been made to provide low- and moderate-income housing in nontraditional areas. The New York

State Urban Development Corporation was granted authority in its enabling legislation to acquire land by eminent domain for the purpose of constructing such housing and overriding local zoning. This power was never used, however, and was eventually repealed. In Massachusetts, the Anti-Snob Zoning Law gives the state limited authority to review and override local zoning decisions that prevent construction of low-income housing. This law, too, has had little effect on exclusionary practices.

Probably the most explicit statements of the community's obligation to assume its part in providing regional housing needs were made in two recent cases in New Jersey. In *Southern Burlington County NAACP* vs. *Township of Mount Laurel*,[39] the New Jersey Supreme Court unanimously held that the township's general zoning was invalid to the extent that it failed to provide a realistic opportunity for the development of a variety and choice of housing for its regional fair-share of all classes of people. The court found that the zoning ordinance, in effect, prohibited multifamily housing. In *Oakwood at Madison* vs. *Madison*,[40] the New Jersey Superior Court struck down an ordinance — adopted by the township to curb its population growth and stabilize tax rates — which sought to enforce restrictive minimum-lot and floor requirements. The court cited the law's failure to promote a reasonably balanced community in accordance with the general welfare.

These cases are significant because, for the first time, courts interpreted the general welfare concept found in zoning-enabling statutes as an affirmative requirement to which all zoning must conform and recognized that a housing shortage in a metropolitan area is an important element in the general welfare. In *Mt. Laurel*, the court's remedy went beyond invalidating the ordinance; it required the municipality to determine existing housing needs of low- and moderate-income residents in the region, to estimate the number of units required, and to submit an affirmative program to meet its share of those needs.

Recent federal legislation has also attempted to achieve fair-share allocations. Under the Housing and Community Development Act of 1974 (PL 93-383), a community's block grant assistance is conditioned upon local adoption of a Housing Assistance Plan (HAP). The HAP must assess the needs of lower-income persons "residing or expected to reside in the community," requiring communities to look beyond the immediate needs of their residents. The HAP must also adopt dispersal policies for lower-income housing. The failure of the community to adopt or implement a HAP exposes it to the risk of losing its federal funds. With a HAP, the community is given enhanced power to control the location of federally subsidized housing.

One lawsuit[41] seeking to enforce these provisions has been brought by the City of Hartford, Connecticut. The test case challenged HUD's approval of community development block grants to seven surrounding suburbs because they did not accurately reflect regional housing needs, especially those of the inner city and of lower-income residents. The challenge was based on language in the preamble of the act, which states as its purpose the reduction of the isolation of income groups through the spatial deconcentration of housing opportunities and through the requirement that HAP's assess the housing needs of lower-income persons "residing or expected to reside in the community." Although a Federal District Court in Hartford temporarily enjoined the suburban towns from spending any of the money, the Court of Appeals dismissed the suit in a subsequent opinion on the grounds that Hartford lacked "standing" to challenge the approval of the grants, and thus failed to address the substantive issues of the case.

Air Quality

The Clean Air Act amendments of 1970 and 1977 set the groundwork for administratively set, rationally uniform, ambient air-quality standards. Although primary responsibility to control air pollution at its source was placed on states and local governments, it was recognized that there was a need to establish uniform federal standards to be promulgated by EPA. The regulatory connection between these federally imposed standards and the desire for local control is the state implementation plans (SIP's). These plans, required of each state and subject to EPA review and modification, were to describe the local "control strategies" to assure attainment and maintenance of federal ambient air-quality standards.

The act preempted emission regulation of vehicles, or mobile sources, from all states except California and set a timetable that would result in a 90% reduction in certain auto emissions. State implementation plans are designed to curtail emissions from most stationary sources and are to include emission limitations, schedules for compliance, and other measures to secure attainment including transportation controls and "preconstruction review of direct sources of air pollution." Under EPA guidelines, this requirement had been interpreted to mean that the agency carrying out the plan was to have the power to review new sources of pollution and modifications thereof and to disapprove any sources which would interfere with the state's control strategy.

As a result of *NRDC* vs. *EPA*,[42] EPA was ordered to review SIP's and to disapprove plans that do not ensure maintenance of the primary standard, once attained. This decision led to the promulgation of regulations requiring local authorities to control "indirect sources," or those sources which generate increased mobile and fixed sources of pollution, such as highways, airports, and parking facilities. This requirement clearly makes the spatial distribution of public and private facilities the responsibility of local air-pollution control authorities.

Just as methods of implementation of other environmental plans involve land-use controls, air-pollution plans also depend for their implementation on coordinated use of traditional land-use control strategies. In the absence of regionally centralized land-use control authority, planning of open space or buffer zones, creative use of public facility and service policies, and decentralization of low- and moderate-income housing, all become more important devices to implement control strategies over metropolitan areas.

Despite certain drawbacks, local zoning regulations can be used to promote the reduction of air pollution by dispersing pollution sources. Performance standards are another method for encouraging dispersion. Such standards are established by districts according to scientific measurement of various criteria. Development permission is granted only if it is shown that the use will not violate any performance standards, insofar as they relate concentration of development to emission of air pollution and seek to regulate emissions through limitations on density of emissions. Finally, using the zoning power, a community can establish air-quality zones restricting all pollution-producing uses. Identification of such zones is based on an evaluation of current ambient air-quality, topography, land-use, population-density, and atmospheric-dispersion characteristics. In Britain, "smokeless zones" have been legislated to eliminate aerial wastes within designated areas.

Air-pollution considerations must not only affect the day-to-day granting of construction permits. They must be taken into account when evaluating long-range growth strategies. Implementation of these strategies is likely to take the form of state legislation permitting the state to determine the type and amount of developmental growth authorized to "use" the allowable air-quality increment. This, of course, must be based on comprehensive long-range planning (HUD Section 701) to determine the type of growth desired, other constraints on growth, and other means for air-quality improvements.

Noise Controls

Implementation of local plans regarding noise abatement involve enforcement of noise-source ordinances established under a municipality's police power. Traditional noise-source ordinances have banned such subjectively defined problems as loud and unnecessary noises at various times of the day. They have been poorly enforced. More recent local statutes define noise violations in measurable units such as decibels and use technical measurement instruments in enforcement.

An example of an innovative approach to noise control is the City of Chicago's ordinance.[43] One section contains curfews and prohibitions against certain types of noise-making activities. A second section prohibits within the city the sale of motor vehicles and construction equipment exceeding a certain decibel limit fifty feet from the street center-line under clearly described testing procedures. Essentially, this section regulates the manufacture of noise producers. A third section prohibits vehicles and equipment from operation beyond certain decibel limits even after they are sold. The standards for sale and operation comprise a systematic attempt to control transportation noise. A final section includes performance standards relating to noise within a zoning framework. The ordinance requires that a land use within a manufacturing zone not cause noise above a certain level at the boundaries of a residential or commercial zone. Testing procedures are based on decibel standards developed by the Society of Automotive Engineers which are measurable on a single sound meter. Easily measured, these standards make for more certain enforcement. Mobile teams cruise the city with portable sound meters to enforce violations.

Promulgation of standards. The Noise Control Act of 1972[44] was the first major federal attempt to eliminate potential excess noise in the design of a wide variety of consumer products. It authorized the EPA Administrator to develop and publish information about permissible levels of noise, and then to set noise standards for products identified as major sources of noise. Although aircraft noise control remains under the administration of FAA, the law gives EPA an advisory role in formulating criteria and standards for controlling this source of noise. Also, HUD established uniform policies on noise exposure applicable to its own programs.[45] The keystone of the noise circular is a prohibition of HUD support for new construction on sites having unacceptable noise exposures. The circular establishes three categories of noise exposure defined by numerical standards and expressed in decibels. The Federal Highway Administration has established design noise levels for highways, and the Air Force issues guidelines for compatible land-use designations for areas around military airports.

Design solutions. Probably the most effective way to reduce noise is through the use of design standards. Construction standards for sound insulation could provide occupants protection against noise. Such acoustical-insulation standards and their enforcement would be the responsibility of the municipal department with jurisdiction over the building code. Exterior screening or buffering is also effective in certain situations; such buffers would include trees, shrubs, fences, and walls. Similarly, location of the structure on a particular site also can reduce noise by increasing the distance from noise sources. Still another way of controlling noise is by regulating land use. Locating noisy land uses such as industry away from areas that seek relative quiet is a legitimate purpose of zoning and should result from proper planning.

However, federal, state, and local noise regulations have been influenced by the constitutional limitation on taking private property. Governmental action may amount to a taking if it so seriously interferes with the use of the property that it has little or no value to its owner. In *U.S. vs. Causby*,[46] the Supreme Court held that severe noise from airplane flights could constitute a taking if government is involved in the location of the offending airport. Later, in *Griggs vs. Allegheny*,[47] the Supreme Court decided that a municipality had taken property when damage resulted from the take-offs and landings of private commercial aircraft at a municipally owned airport subject, as is all civil aviation, to regulation by the federal government. Any regulatory program for noise control should balance public interest and private property rights within this context.

INDIRECT INCENTIVES AND DISINCENTIVES

The third major category of government activity to implement plans includes public-policy actions that influence private development indirectly. Because of the constitutional shortcomings of government's regulatory authority and because of the financial constraints in which governments often find themselves, indirect public incentives and disincentives often are more effective in implementing plans and shaping private behavior than regulatory and/or direct governmental actions. Three kinds of incentives are examined below: public investment policy, public fiscal and tax policy, and development incentives.

Public Investment Policy

As indicated in earlier sections of this chapter, public investment in public facilities and development often has spillover effects which induce associated development in nearby areas. The classic example of this phenomenon is the development that follows the construction of highway interchanges. Thus do such government decisions as those on the location of federal installations have direct effect on the location of growth.

The consequences of a lack of an explicit policy at the federal and state levels have long been recognized.[48] The congeries of policies and programs, many of them redundant or contradictory, add up to a policy which, perhaps unintentionally, (1) reacts to, rather than shapes, the economic and social consequences flowing from patterns of private investment; (2) favors the construction of new housing and infrastructure or underdeveloped outlying suburban tracts (urban sprawl) over the conservation and rehabilitation of existing housing and infrastructure; (3) provides the benefits of appreciated land prices resulting from public improvements to private landowners rather than to the general community; and (4) encourages the concentration of low-income minorities in inner cities while subsidizing the location of employment and housing of middle- and upper-income groups in outlying areas.

Recent activities in Vermont are an example of what could be done to coodinate public investment policy to service public objectives. Noting that Vermont's investment in public facilities is instrumental in determining land-use patterns, resource-management opportunities, and private investment, the governor of Vermont stated, "If it is the state's policy to reduce the impact of new development on the environment and on the need for government spending, then . . . . an important place to begin is with our own actions in this regard.[49]

In Vermont, strip development and scattered residential sprawl are considered inefficient land uses which can cause the loss of agricultural lands and which are partially to blame for the decline of community centers. The state's public investment policy gives first priority to investments that serve existing settlements and growth centers, including development that contributes to the rehabilitation and reuse of existing facilities. Decisions concerning the need for public facilities must take into consideration the State Planning Office's plans and population figures as well as local plans and policies. First priority for facilities development is given to municipalities which have adopted comprehensive plans for guiding future growth and land-use control for their implementation. Thus, as a first step to bringing about development in accordance with public plans, coordinated public investment policies must be developed and carried out.

Public Fiscal and Tax Policy

Although the primary function of taxation is to raise revenue, recent concern over the environment has focused attention on the use of tax laws to encourage desirable land-use development. Land has been protected consistent with public objectives through various methods of property taxation, such as tax deferral, preferential assessment, and capital-gains taxes on the sale of land. These methods are designed to encourage landowners to refrain from developing their property by offering them tax relief or, in the case of a capital-gains tax, by imposing an added tax burden on landowners seeking to sell their property for development.

Preferential Assessment

Preferential assessment provides for the assessment of land at its value as used or restricted for open space rather than at its highest possible value. This policy encourages landowners to keep their land undeveloped by offering them a lower tax assessment. Massachusetts, for example, has used this method to encourage the preservation of forests and wildlands under the Forest Tax Law, and of agricultural and horticultural lands under Massachusetts General Laws, Chapter 61A.

One of the major problems that has to be dealt with in preferential assessment is the typical state constitutional provision requiring taxation to be uniform. Uniformity requires all property to be assessed at the same proportion to value and at the same rate. This prohibits classification of property for taxation purposes. The Massachusetts "uniformity" provision requires real-estate taxes to be "proportional and reasonable" and every taxpayer to contribute his or her "share" to support the government. These provisions and their interpretation required that the Massachusetts Constitution be amended in order to provide a preferential tax assessment for agricultural and horticultural land (Mass. Const. Amend. XCIX.).

Another way of protecting land through property taxation is to designate a partial tax exemption for special categories of land. This alternative might avoid the necessity for a constitutional amendment, but it would involve the risk that the courts would declare the exemption unconstitutional. Furthermore, unless the legislation were accompanied by a restriction on the use of the property to ensure preservation of its use (such as requiring landowners to pay back abated taxes with interest if they subsequently develop the land), the legislation would probably be ineffective, deferring taxes, not eliminating them.

Tax Deferral

Under a tax deferral scheme, taxes are not abated; rather, they are only deferred until a change in use occurs. Basically, deferral provides that the local assessor evaluate land both as to its use as undeveloped land and as to its potential development use. Landowners may choose to keep their land in open space and have the lower valuation applied to their property, but if they convert the land to another use, they are charged with the back taxes they were previously spared.

The inadequacies of tax assessment and deferral programs are due primarily to two factors. First, preferential assessments operate for the benefit of land speculators, undermining the intent of the program. Developers purchase open-space land, enroll in the preferential assessment program, and wait until development is sufficiently profitable. They benefit from the lower taxes, and land is not preserved. A second inadequacy of these programs is that most preferential taxation schemes may be declined by the landowner if potential sales are in the offing. This is particularly true of property located near urban areas where the potential economic value of the land is too great a temptation to resist.

The problem of the benefit of preferential assessments to land developers can be alleviated by the use of a "roll-back" charge when a change in use occurs or by imposing a capital-gains tax on sale profits. Roll-back involves charging the landowner the difference between the tax based on the property's preferential assessment and the tax based on what the property was assessed at based on the highest and best use for the number of years preferential assessment was enjoyed. However, even this may not be effective because the developer can easily recoup the loss in his sale price. Thus, some further penalty might be provided — perhaps an interest charge on the roll-back amount or an increase in the number of years to which the roll-back applies. For example, Hawaii imposes a roll-back plus a 5%-per-year penalty surcharge. California imposes a charge based on 50% of assessed value at highest and best use. In Washington, the roll-back period runs to fourteen years.

The second major reason for the failure of open-space taxation programs is that participation is voluntary. Many towns fail to encourage landowners to participate out of fear of a negative effect on the local tax structure or loss of revenue. To remedy this situation, most states have made participation mandatory. That is, if the land falls within the definition of protected land, the tax effect becomes automatic. Consideration should also be given to state compensation for local property-tax revenue lost through open-space tax abatement.

Capital-Gains Tax

An easier method to administer, and one which would recover more than the roll-back charge, would be a state capital-gains tax on profits realized when real property is sold. The rationale behind such a tax is that the increase in land value which earns the profit is largely due to the spending of public money contributed by taxpayers; therefore, the taxpayers are entitled to a substantial portion of the landowner's profit. Connecticut has enacted an open-space conveyance tax which imposes a cost ranging from 10 to 1% of the total sales price of open-space land. The charge decreases at the rate of 1% a year for each year the land is held by the owners. If sold in the first year, the full 10% tax is charged. In the second year, the tax is 9%, and so on. Recent Vermont legislation imposes a capital-gains tax on almost all land held by the landowner less than six years. A tax of anywhere from 5 to 60% of the sale profit is imposed, depending on the number of years the land is held and the amount of profit realized. It is too early to tell what effect the Vermont and Connecticut measures will have on slowing development and land speculation. Undoubtedly they will have some beneficial effect, but the taxes they impose seem too small to have any great power to slow development. The provision for a decreasing tax according to the number of years land is held may not deter speculators seeking long-term returns on investment.

Transfer of Development Rights

Development rights in land can be effectively used for public benefit through a new technique termed the "transfer of development rights." (TDR). TDR involves private parties buying and selling development rights in order to be permitted to build to a higher density than would otherwise be allowable. To establish a TDR scheme, a municipality designates those areas to be preserved and those to be developed, and it sets development limits on the latter. The development potential in one restricted area can be transferred to another district where development is feasible. Landowners in the preservation area who continue to own their land may sell their rights for further development to other landowners who wish to develop areas designated as feasible for development. This arrangement preserves environmentally important areas while equitably compensating landowners. The landowners also receive a reduction in their real-estate tax because their land is valued at a lower amount. There is no cost to the taxpayer since the government acquires no land; yet housing demand can be met.

TDR is designed to solve the dilemma of a municipality wanting to take advantage of increased taxes through development but also wanting to ensure that the community continues to be a desirable place to live by preserving open space and critical natural areas. Without violating the constitutional guarantee of due process, TDR provides equitable compensation, in the form of development rights, to the owners of restricted open-space land. TDR schemes are presently in use in Chicago; New York; Suffolk County, Long Island; Puerto Rico; St. George, Vermont; and Maryland. They appear to be working successfully, although still-unresolved legal and planning problems persist.

Compensable Regulations

The compensable regulation is a hybrid technique, a cross between regulation and acquisition of property easements. Traditionally, if a landowner challenges a regulation as a taking of property without just compensation and succeeds, the court permits him to undertake development. If he loses, the regulation is upheld. Under a system of compensable regulations, the court could determine a financial award for the landowner's compensation, and the regulation would continue in effect. Specifically, an administrative procedure could be provided whereby claims alleging unconstitutional taking could be filed. If the taking were proved, the government would have to raise funds to pay the landowner or allow the proposed development to take place.

The American Law Institute's Model Land Development Code proposes a system in which the government could choose to pay compensation for any land-use regulation held to be a taking. If a taking is found, the court would withhold relief until the government had an opportunity to provide compensation through the purchase or condemnation of a development right, paying the landowner the value of the interest acquired. Thus, compensable regulations postpone payment until after the need for payment has been determined and so avoid the requirement of large quantities of "front money." Massachusetts presently employs a similar system in its wetlands legislation, as does Rhode Island under its Fresh Water Wetlands Act. In both states, the state is authorized to take the fee or any lesser interest in the land, such as an easement by eminent domain, if a taking of property is found. However, property owners in both states have not taken advantage of statutory review, so the states have not made much use of the compensable-regulation provisions.

Development Incentives

Direct incentives of granting favorable development conditions can encourage private actions to conform to public objectives. Two such techniques — incentive zoning and impact zoning — are discussed below.

Impact Zoning

Impact zoning is a regulatory system in which development is evaluated in terms of its effects on a particular site and a particular community rather than on the category of use. Each proposed development, regardless of its categorization, is required to meet certain performance criteria in terms of maximum allowable effects on the site, but the particular manner of meeting these criteria is not prescribed. For example, a developer could choose to fulfill requirements by lowering the density of development or by providing engineering safeguards against environmental damage. Such performance requirements are usually imposed under existing law through the special permit procedure. As adopted in Duxbury, Massachusetts, uses are permitted through the zoning bylaw depending upon their effect on site topography, soil, and required municipal services.

Incentive Zoning

Under the special permit process, a municipality may approve particular uses contingent upon the developer's agreement to incorporate certain design considerations in the development. Usually, for example, a municipality encourages the provision of more open space by granting the developer permission for a great floor-area ratio, or additional floorspace, depending upon the height of the building. Another possible incentive is to grant developers permission to build at greater densities in exchange for their construction of more units of low- and moderate-income housing. This approach has been employed in Fairfax, Virginia, and Montgomery County, Maryland. As a practical matter, incentive zoning offers a way to combine police power regulations with some form of compensation.

COORDINATION OF IMPLEMENTATION

Two important intergovernmental mechanisms for coordinating federal, state, and local implementation activities are the environmental impact statement process, discussed in an earlier chapter, and the review procedures required by Circular A-95 and administered by the Federal Regional Councils.

The Office of Management and Budget issued Circular A-95 to implement the requirement of the Intergovernmental Cooperation Act of 1968 that:

> the President shall . . . establish rules and regulations governing the formulation, evaluation, and review of Federal programs and projects having a significant impact on area and community development, including programs providing Federal assistance to the states and localities.[50]

Circular A-95 establishes procedures for the review and coordination of many federal activities which concern state and local government. This review process brings together the requirements of parts of four federal acts: Section 204 of the Demonstration Cities and Metropolitan Development Act of 1966, Title IV of the Intergovernmental Cooperation Act of 1968, Section (2)(c) of the National Environmental Policy Act of 1969, and Title VI of the Civil Rights Act of 1964.

Four different reviews and evaluation processes are required by the circular:

(1) *Project notification and review system.* Applications for federal grants, loans, guarantees, and other assistance are subject to review by state and areawide "planning and development clearinghouses." This review evaluates the proposed application in terms of other plans, projects, or activities, and it obtains and forwards the comments of other interested parties.

(2) *Direct federal development.* Federal agencies are required to consult with governors and state and local officials before undertaking projects that involve construction of buildings and facilities or the acquisition, use, and disposal of federal land. The purpose is to ensure that their plans or projects are compatible with various other plans.

(3) *State plans and multisource programs.* Plans prepared by state agencies as a condition of federal assistance must be submitted to the governors for review and comment. Multisource programs are applications for assistance from more than one federal source and are prepared and submitted on a consolidated basis. The Integrated Grant Administration Program is one example of such programs.

(4) *Coordination of planning in multijurisdictional areas.* Where states establish planning regions or development districts, federal agencies administer their programs in conformance to these areas unless there is some clear justification for not doing so. Where planning agencies serving these areas have been designated as areawide clearinghouses for the Project Notification and Review System, federal agencies are encouraged to use these agencies in their planning programs or requirements. The objective is to establish a consistent geographic base for the coordination of federal, state, and local programs.

Although these requirements are advisory, they do establish an intergovernmental coordination system for many activities which affect growth and development. In practice, most federal agencies do carefully consider, and attempt to follow, the recommendations formulated through the review process. However, because federal financial support has not been specifically provided to the reviewing agencies, the attention devoted to this process has been limited.

REFERENCES

1. M.G.L. Ann. Ch. 184 § 31-33 (Supp. 1974). The description of the Massachusetts law in the text is taken from Russell R. Sicard, "Persuing Open Space Preservation: The Massachusetts Conservation Restriction." *Environmental Affairs* IV:481-514 (Summer 1975). Mr. Sicard's article discusses various legal ramifications of the device in some detail.

2. One important effect of this statute is to supersede ancient common-law limitations on the extent to which the alienability and use of land can be restricted over time.

3. Sicard, Ibid.

4. N.J. Stat. Ann. 15: 8A-20(d) (Supp. 1973).

5. Bucks County Planning Commission, "Plan for Implementation of Provisions of Act 515 of 1965" (Doylestown, Pennsylvannia: Bucks County Planning Commission, 1971).

6. See Office of Management and Budget, *Federal Catalogue of Domestic Assistance* (Washington, D.C.: Government Printing Office, 1976).

7. 30 NY2d.359, 385 NE2d.291, appeal dismissed, 409 US 1003 (1972).

8. United States Court of Appeals for the 9th Circuit, 8 ERC 1001 (1975).

9. The description in the text is taken from U.S. Department of Housing and Urban Development, Office of Small Town Services and Intergovernmental Relations, "Capital Improvements Programming in Local Government" (Washington, D.C.: Government Printing Office, 1970).

10. E.G., *Turnpike Realty Co.* vs. *Town of Dedham*, 284 NE2d. 891 (Mass., 1972). See also Fred Bosselman, David Callies, and John Banta, *The Taking Issue* (Washington, D.C.: Council on Environmental Quality, 1973).

11. See discussion of *Ramapo* and *Petaluma* cases above, pp. 160-161, and *Mt. Laurel* and *Oakwood* cases below, pp. 193-194.

12. Ronald M. Hershkowitz, "Local Environmental Protecton: Problems and Limitations," *Environmental Affairs* 2:4 (Spring 1975), pp. 783, 793.

13. 262 U.S. 365 (1926).

14. Supra, note 10.

15. 260 U.S. 393 (1922).

16. Ibid.

17. *Morris County Land Improvement Company* vs. *Parsippany-Troy Hills Township.* 40 N.J.539, 193 A2d.232 (1963).

18. Erica L. Dolgin and Thomas G. P. Guilbert (eds.), *Federal Environmental Law* (St. Paul, Minn.: West Publishing Company, 1974), p. 67.

19. 89 Cal. Rptr. 897 (Cal. App. Ct., 1970).

20. 201 N.W.2d.761 (Wisconsin, 1972).

21. 201 N.W.2d.761

22. 469 F.2d.956 (1st Cir. 1972).

23. 469 F.2d.956.

24. U.S. Environmental Protection Agency, *Performance Standards for Sensitive Lands: A Practical Guide for Local Administration*, EPA-60015-75-005.

25. Title 25, §102.23 of the Rules and Regulations of the Pennsylvania Department of Environmental Resources.

26. See, for example, the ordinances of Camden, N.J., described in EPA *Performance Standards*, Reference # 24, pp. 62-63.

27. For a selective list of publications on erosion and sediment control standards, see Reference #24 above.

28. EPA *Performance Standards*, Reference # 24, pp. 60-61.

29. EPA *Performance Standards*, Reference # 24, p. 63.

30. EPA *Performance Standards*, Reference # 24, p. 65.

31. For other examples of erosion and sedimentation control ordinances, see the Model Municipal Land Disturbance Ordinance prepared by the New Jersey State Soil Conservaton Committee and reprinted in EPA *Performance Standards*, Reference # 24, pp. 87-91; the Soil Erosion and Sediment Control Manual of the Pennsylvania Department of Environmental Resources (1/1/74); and the assembly of reference items entitled, "The Maryland Sediment Control Program" (College Park, Maryland: U.S. Department of Agriculture, Soil Conservation Service, 1971), and a publication of Leon County, Florida, entitled "Environmental Criteria for Erosion and Sedimentation Control" (January 1975).

32. See the model ordinance prepared by the South Branch Watershed Association of Arrington, N.J.

33. Hawaii Environmental Laws and Regulations, Vol. II, Chapter 46.

34. See New Jersey's highly detailed Solid Waste Management Regulations, adopted as Rules of the Bureau of Solid Waste Management, N.T., Code Amn. 7:26-1 et. seq.

35. P.L. 1971, Chap. 535. See also Wisconsin's Water Resources Act.

36. See, for example, Fred Bosselman and David Callies, "Quiet Revolution in Land Use Controls" (Washington, D.C.: Council on Environmental Quality, Government Printing Office, 1971).

37. Maine Land Use Regulation Commission (MLURC).

38. See, for example, Vermont's Act 250.

39. *Southern Burlington County NAACP* vs. *Township of Mt. Laurel*, 119 N.J. Super 164, 290 A2d. 465.

40. *Oakwood at Madison* vs. *Madison*, 128 N.J. Super 438, 320 A2d 223, (Law Div., 1974).

41. *City of Hartford* vs. *Hills*, 408 F. Supp. 889 (1976), rev'd___ F2d___ (C.A. 1977).

42. 475 F.2d.968 (D.C. Cir., 1973).

43. Municipal Code of Chicago, Sect. 17-1.6, Chapter 17 (July 1, 1971).

44. 42 USCA § 4901.

45. HUD Circular No. 1390.2.

46. 328 U.S. 256, (1946).

47. 369 U.S. 84 (1962).

48. See, for example, the *Douglas Commission Report: Building the American City;* and "A National Public Works Investment Policy," Background Papers for the U.S. House of Representatives Committee on Public Works (1974).

49. Vermont's Policies and Procedures for Public Capital Investment, Office of the Governor (September 1975).

50. P.L. 90-577, Sec. 401(a), 403 (1963). ·

Chapter 5
Plan Monitoring
and Management

This manual has emphasized a process-oriented approach to comprehensive planning. In the preceding chapter we focused on the importance of implementing plans and policies. We turn now to the continuing responsibilities of comprehensive planners once implementation is underway, for the process does not end once plans and policies are put into operation any more than it does with the selection of alternatives. Continuous, systematic monitoring of the results, both intended and unintended, or planned and programmed actions is crucial if planners are to profit from past experience and better guide community development in the future. Monitoring for this purpose, then, is not a crash effort mounted spasmodically every few years, but rather an integral part of an iterative planning process in which "review becomes simply a longer beat in the rhythm of the whole process of implementation."[1]

An analogy is often drawn in the urban planning literature between the servo-mechanism used to keep a guided missile on course and the concept of monitoring changes in a dynamic urban system at regular intervals in order to provide feedback to planners and policy-makers. The actual state of the system is compared with the intended state, and adjustments are then made on the basis of detected disparities. Or, the very course of the system may be redirected in response to changes in people's goals and objectives for their environment. Melville Branch has described the role that monitoring should play in the comprehensive planning process as follows:

> Planning must incorporate analytically current information, conditions, and decisions to a much greater extent than is now the case . . . . The city plan must incorporate information and projections for each principal urban element separately, and portray their synthesis into a combined pattern of actions and objectives over time for

the best benefit of the city as a whole. It must be maintained and displayed in such a form that it can be revised regularly and completely and quickly changed when need be. Above all, it must always be sufficiently up-to-date to serve as the basic analytical simulation of the municipality and the official reference for discussing and deciding many different matters. It is ahead of the game rather than running to catch up.[2]

The greater the comprehensive-planning agency's ability to describe the current situation with undisputed facts, the better will be its chances of (1) obtaining support for its plans/policies from public officials and citizens, (2) having a legally defensible basis for land-use and other control ordinances, and (3) helping private sector developers, through information sharing, make better development decisions.

Elsewhere in this manual, three important techniques for integrating environmental-planning concerns have been noted: (1) the conduct of planning studies that furnish a basis for decision making about community development, (2) decisions regarding public investments, and (3) policy guidance provided to private-sector development. A fourth, closely related technique is the maintenance in a central location of up-to-date information on the planning area that is accessible to agencies, public officials, and private citizens.

Monitoring the state of the planning-area environment, in turn, consists of four basic elements:

Strategies for continuous monitoring of both environmental conditions and trends, and the consequences of specific comprehensive-planning policies and programs

A system for updating the planning information base

Procedures for periodically sounding public opinion regarding both the results of policies and programs and basic goals and objectives for the area

Revision of planning goals and objectives in light of the monitoring information

These four elements of plan monitoring and management are discussed below. Specific examples of environmental monitoring systems currently in use in urban areas are also provided.

MONITORING THE PLANNING AREA ENVIRONMENT

The major considerations in formulating any program for continual monitoring and updating of essential planning information revolve around the following:

Information needs

Data availability and sources

Data quality and format

Updating and report generation procedures

Citizen input

These considerations are discussed briefly in terms of monitoring and updating environmental data within the framework of comprehensive planning.

Determination of Information Needs

To a large extent the data base created by the planning studies conducted in the first phase of comprehensive planning and management provides the framework for collection of environmental monitoring data. However, some of the elements of that data base require more frequent updating than others, depending on the use to which they are put in ongoing planning and decision making. There may also have been gaps or inaccuracies in the data, which subsequent monitoring can correct. Presumably, monitoring and updating provide a progressive refinement of the data base, so that planning information continually improves.

In order to maximize the utility of monitoring data and avoid the costs of collecting irrelevant or inconsistent information, it is wise to interview potential users to find out in advance what their information needs are. "Users" would be, in addition to the comprehensive-planning agency, functional planning agencies responsible for air- and water-quality management, specific problems, or media; elected and appointed local public officials; and private citizens, including developers.

The comprehensive-planning agency itself must consider carefully the kind of data it needs in order to monitor the performance of specific programs and policies and to keep track of conditions and trends in the planning area's environment as a whole. Different measures apply to these two types of evaluation; Robinson terms the distinction as that between "program performance" and "systems performance."[3] In the former process, the objective is to determine how successfully a program is meeting its specific objectives. In the latter, program accomplishments are evaluated in terms of their contribution to broader community goals. Work is being done on developing "urban, social, and environmental indicators" to measure the performance of the total community system, but still lacking is a ready set of standards by which to assess the overall status of broad social/environmental concerns.[4] For now, planners must content themselves with measuring as accurately as possible those dimensions of community goals directly within their area of responsibility — for example, legislated thresholds for known pollutants; housing quality, diversity, and availability; the quality and distribution of public services and facilities; and the protection of historic and cultural resources.

Data Availability and Sources

Once information needs are ascertained, the source of that information must be identified and arrangements made to collect it regularly. In many cases needed data are already compiled routinely by various agencies and must simply be transmitted periodically to the comprehensive-planning agency or to the office for centralized storage and analysis. Where data are not already collected as a matter of course, and where they are not collected as often as necessary, manpower and procedures must be provided to do this work.

One of the clear benefits of a monitoring program that involves regular data input from different functional agencies to one central system is that public agencies and officials, citizen groups, and the business community may all use the same information base for their planning and decision making. Also, closer coordination and better communication are stimulated between the comprehensive-planning agency and the functional agencies since they both are suppliers and users of the data base.

One promising tool for monitoring programs which is frequently mentioned in the literature is aerial and satellite photography. NASA is experimenting with remote-sensing techniques for land-use monitoring at the Manned Spacecraft Center in Houston and the Goddard Space Flight Center. Aerial photography yields up-to-date information on land use that might not be available from other sources. An aerial survey recently made of a Massachusetts community revealed, among other things, the existence of scores of residential swimming pools for which the building permit department had no records.

Data Quality and Format

One of the most important considerations in system development, particularly if the system is to be computerized, is the quality and form of the data collected and updated. It is critical to establish consistency between the monitoring data collected and the information base to be updated; no useful feedback results unless the incoming data — in form, condition, and accuracy — permit combining data for desired analyses.

Examples of desired types of analysis include:

Comparing the existing situation with past and predicted states

Assessing the performance of current policies and programs against immediate objectives and broader social goals

Predicting the effects of proposed actions on the public and private sectors

Establishing justification for making changes in current plans, policies, programs, and regulations

Anticipating needs for capital investments and controls

It is helpful if data are in a form that allows direct combination with state and regional systems.

Updating, Analysis, and Reporting

A system for receiving the monitoring data, updating the information base, and conducting the analyses to yield desired feedback must be established, and clerical and analysis staff are necessary to run the system. Regular reports would be generated for comprehensive-planning staff as well as for other agencies and departments. A capability for handling special requests — from private developers, for instance — should be built into the system in order to make fullest use of the information.

Citizen Input

Regular collection of data on the state of the planning area's environment and the effects of comprehensive plans and programs is necessary to monitor the extent to which stated goals and objectives are being achieved. But community development goals and objectives also change as people's attitudes and aspirations evolve and as federal and state environmental legislation establishes new goals and standards to be met. Periodic citizen review and feedback regarding policies, programs, and goals for the community should be provided for in the monitoring program, thus continuing the dialogue between planners and citizens. Public meetings and workshops similar to those held in the initial planning stage can generate citizen input. However, the comprehensive-planning agency should also aim to continually expand its outreach to less vocal, less visible groups who have been underrepresented in the past. A technique for reaching citizens who might not attend workshops or public meetings is to survey a sample of the population with questionnaires. In recent years, solicitation of public input through extensive citizen surveys has been undertaken in San Diego County, California;[5] Oregon's Willamette Valley;[6] Boulder, Colorado;[7] Dallas, Texas;[8] and the New York City area.[9]

Although extensive public participation in initial goal setting for planning purposes has become fairly common practice, ongoing provision for citizens to review progress being made toward attaining goals and to revise the goals themselves is much less common. One program that does provide for systematic citizen input to the monitoring of planning achievements is Goals for Dallas, a citizen-based program first organized in 1965. The third stage of this program set up a system "to evaluate progress being made toward the goals and to revise goals periodically as changed circumstances warrant." The system established to monitor goal progress and report to the public consists of twelve "achievement committees" corresponding to the twelve sets of goals established in the program's first stage. Each committee, composed of citizen volunteers knowledgeable about technical aspects of their goal subject area, makes quarterly reviews and an intensive annual study of progress. The committees consult with relevant action agencies and decide whether progress is satisfactory. If they find it is not, they may recommend steps to accelerate progress. To inform the citizenry about their findings and elicit feedback, the achievement committees prepare detailed annual reports and publicize them in the news media. Heads of agencies are also given the opportunity to report on their progress on radio, on television, and in newspapers. The program allows citizens to ask questions and make comments and suggestions on the goals and their achievement.

The environmental concerns of Goals for Dallas are expressed in the broad goal sets listed under the heading "Design of the City." These include open space, effective flood control, preservation of historic landmarks, air and water quality, land use, urban design, protection and improvement of neighborhoods, renewal of blighted areas, and improved public housing.

Unsolicited citizen complaints about environmental concerns can also be useful to a monitoring program. The frequency of complaints about a given situation is an often-used supplemental measure in environmental impact assessments. Although such data are obviously biased and should be interpreted and weighed cautiously, complaint files can nevertheless be useful as sources of planning information.

A range of responses by both comprehensive- and interested functional-planning agencies is possible, based on the findings of a monitoring program. These responses should include:

Identification of problem areas to be made the subject of an in-depth study to obtain more data

Minor adjustments to programs and policies found to be falling short of their intended purpose and/or having unanticipated secondary effects

Major revamping or elimination of programs that prove to have been ill-conceived or that have seriously "misfired" in actual operation

Revision of planning goals, objectives, and assumptions where warranted by the results of citizen review and feedback

ENVIRONMENTAL MONITORING PROGRAMS

One of the main thrusts of planning in recent years has been the development of computerized data-storage and retrieval systems to provide planning information that is ever more accurate, accessible, and up-to-date. One ambitious system recently developed and put to use is the Urban Development Information System (UDIS) created for Fairfax County, Virginia. The UDIS project, which was supported in part by HUD, has been described fully in a handbook for other planning jurisdictions.[10]

UDIS is a process for monitoring the physical growth and condition of specific geographic areas in the county and for projecting new development and associated needs for county services. The system is land-use oriented; all of its data inputs are designed around the county's unique land parcel identification numbers. A separate record is maintained for each of the county's approximately 157,000 parcels. Detailed running inventories are kept of population, housing, construction activity, and land use.

There are six primary data files, updated regularly by a small clerical staff (see Figure 11).

The parcel file contains a current inventory of all land parcels, listing geographic identifiers, zoning, land use, physical and structural characteristics, water consumption, financial data, and the planned land uses designated in the county's comprehensive plan. The file is updated biweekly.

The sanitary sewer network file contains an inventory of all components of the county's entire sanitary sewer network system, such as treatment plants, sewersheds, pumping stations, and pipe segments. These components are linked to individual parcels in the parcel file. This file furnishes data for detailed location-specific flow, infiltration analyses, and facility planning. The file is updated weekly.

The rezoning case file is a separate record of each rezoning petition. File data include acreage, existing and proposed zoning and allowable densities, likely density yields, expected date of rezoning, and estimated construction schedule.

The building permit file contains a record of each residential building permit, which includes descriptive data from the permit application, data of permit issue, construction starts and completion, and geographic identifiers.

The residential builder plans file holds the status of each active subdivision in the county, in terms of number and type of housing units, vacant lots, state of approval in the construction process, and estimated completion date. The file also contains a summary of all county documents originating in the various agencies that relate to the development process.

FIGURE 11

Urban Development Information System, Fairfax County, Virginia

The basic system is designed to monitor, inventory, and project changes in the development of the county, using six primary data files to produce reports, analyses and graphics.

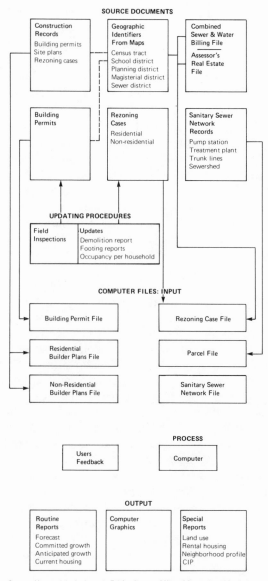

Source: Hysom, John L. Jr. et.al. Fairfax County, Office of Research and Statistics, **A Handbook for Creating an Urban Development Information System**, 1974.

The nonresidential builder plans file contains an inventory of every commercial and industrial project, including name, owner, size, cost, location, and applicable data on zoning, site plans, subdivision plans, building permits, and construction inspections.

Published output from the system consists of standard reports, special reports, and computer graphics. Standard reports, which cover information on housing, construction, population, and land use, are routinely distributed to elected officials, county agencies, libraries, and newspapers, and are available for other members of the public. UDIS staff produce numerous special reports addressing particular planning problems.

Notably missing from the system at present is a capability for monitoring natural environmental factors. Expansion plans for UDIS call for a physical analytical subsystem which will include five models: land-use allocation (which will provide the primary data base and input to the other four models), stormwater runoff, water quality, air quality, and the transportation network. Also planned is a fiscal analytical subsystem which will calculate the cost and revenue consequences of simulated changes in the physical models. An economic impact model and demographic factor library are also to be added.

The Houston-Galveston Area Council's Environmental Decision Assistance System (EDAS) uses economic and ecological modeling to project and monitor growth and associated environmental conditions.[11] The system combines an input-output model for the region; a regional land-use simulation model; and several interrelated technical submodels, including ones for water supply, Galveston Bay water quality, drainage and flood control, and solid waste. The input-output model is one of eight estimated for regions of the State of Texas; together they form the statewide input-output model. The system's dynamic data base, which is systematically updated for monitoring purposes, includes environmental deficiencies, population and housing characteristics, employment and wage data, subdivision and other new construction activity, subsurface hydrology, water supply and consumption, surface hydrology and drainage, water-quality sampling data, sewage-treatment permit data, and quality and volume reports on wastewater. The system is a new one, still undergoing development and refinement, and hence the status of the system's updating procedures and technical models varies.

In line with the trend toward using large computerized information systems to aid ongoing planning, San Diego County several years ago set out to develop a regional environmental-quality information system featuring computer access and computer graphics. The County Office of Comprehensive Planning subsequently backed off from the computer approach after finding that a manual-access data system was more workable.

Examples of environmental media monitoring systems are the national air- and water-quality sampling and analysis programs run by the Environmental Protection Agency. Actually, most of the air-quality data in the National Aerometric Data Bank derive from state and local monitoring networks. To correct past problems associated with data collected by unacceptable methods, EPA has now developed and issued measurement techniques and analysis guidelines for monitoring. The agency also provides training and technical assistance to state and local agencies, and it plans soon to publish guidelines for performing quality-assurance tests.

The National Water Quality Surveillance System (NWQSS), established under Section 104(a)(s) of PL 92-500, is a national monitoring program designed to evaluate the relation between land-use conditions and stream quality. The program's findings and analysis methods can be valuable to agencies in their own planning and monitoring activities. The approximately seventy pairs of monitoring stations now operating were selected to reflect different types of land-use conditions (characterized according to industrial and agricultural activity and population density) and stream sizes (large, medium, and small). At each site, a pair of monitoring stations brackets a drainage area. Each station reports on at least thirty water-quality variables every two weeks, and the effects of adjacent land use on water quality are estimated by comparing upstream and downstream differences in the variables. EPA also operates the National Stream Quality Accounting Network (NASQUAN), which assesses inland stream quality at 345 monitoring stations across the nation.

REFERENCES

1. J. Brian McLaughlin, "System Guidance, Control, and Review" in Ira M. Robinson (ed.), *Decision-Making in Urban Planning: An Introduction to New Methodologies* (Beverly Hills: Sage Publications, 1972), p. 406.

2. Melville C. Branch, "Continuous Master City Planning," in Robinson, Ibid., p. 410.

3. Ira M. Robinson, Ibid., "Plan Review and Feedback," pp. 391-394.

4. See, for instance:

   Raymond A. Bauer (ed.), *Social Indicators* (Cambridge, Mass.: The MIT Press, 1966).

   Norman C. Dalkey et al., "Measurement and Analysis of the Quality of Life" (Santa Monica: The RAND Corporation, 1970). Prepared for the U.S. Department of Transportation.

   Bertram M. Gross, "The City of Man: A Social System Accounting," in William R. Ewald, Jr. (ed.), *Environment for Man* (Bloomington: Indiana University Press, 1967).

   U.S. Environmental Protection Agency, *The Quality of Life Concept: A Potential New Tool for Decision Makers* (March 1973).

   "Environmental Indices and Interpretive Techniques" in *Environmental Quality, The Fifth Annual Report of the Council on Environmental Quality* (December 1974), pp. 331-334.

5. San Diego Regional Goals Committee, *Goals and Objectives for the San Diego Region* (1973).

6. State of Oregon, Office of the Governor, Willamette Valley Attitude Survey (1970). Undertaken preparatory to development of an environmental protection plan for the Willamette Valley.

7. Boulder Area Growth Study Commission Citizen Survey (Boulder, Colorado: 1972). The questionnaire was printed in three local newspapers and also made available in business and public places.

8. Graduate Research Center of the Southwest, *Goals for Dallas*, four volumes (Dallas, Texas: 1966).

9. Regional Plan Association project entitled "Choices for '76," conducted in 1973. Results of the survey were reprinted in *Metropolis Speaks* (New York: Regional Plan Association, August 1974, 34 pp). A second report, *Listening to the Metropolis* (December 1974, 96 pp.), is an evaluation of the project.

10. John L. Hysom, Jr., et al., Fairfax County Office of Research and Statistics, *A Handbook for Creating an Urban Development Information System*. (Springfield, Virginia: National Technical Information Service, November 1974). Prepared for the Department of Housing and Urban Development. NTIS No. PB-238 815.

11. Applied Decision Systems, Inc., *Small Area Model of the Houston-Galveston Area, Volume I, Summary of the Project*. Prepared for the Houston-Galveston Area Council, sponsored in part through a Comprehensive Planning Grant from the Department of Housing and Urban Development (May 1973).

CONCLUSION

The preceding sections of this manual have illustrated how the practicing planner can draw on various environmental-planning techniques during the different phases of comprehensive planning. Although environmental considerations are just one of a number of functional areas that must be considered in such planning, an environmentally sensitive comprehensive plan can identify and evaluate potentially adverse effects and trade-offs among natural, economic, and social concerns in advance of specific project planning. It also allows project-level planning to concentrate on local natural factors. Projects conceived as part of an environmentally sound comprehensive plan may be less likely to encounter problems and delays in the permit-issuance and impact-assessment stages of the development process.

No amount of guidance will make a plan work. What is required on the part of planners is hard work, sensitivity to community attitudes, a spirit of accommodation to the local political process, and the creativity to adopt proven techniques in particular situations. Planners manage the skills of several disciplines in order to improve the community's well-being. We hope that this manual will enable planners to do their work more easily and creatively, and that it will stimulate new methods of applying environmental considerations to improve comprehensive planning.

Appendix
Legislative Mandates

A substantial body of federal legislation mandates certain general as well as very specific environmental planning considerations be incorporated into comprehensive planning and management. These statutes provide the basic legal framework within which regional and local planners must operate.

This appendix briefly summarizes the federal statutes that affect local planners. Examined first is the National Environmental Policy Act, which places significant comprehensive conditions on all major federal actions for impact assessment. Next, statutes which are directly related to comprehensive planning are summarized. Finally, legislation which affects comprehensive planning and management in these seven specific areas of environmental concern is examined:

Land use

Water quality and resources

Air quality

Noise abatement and control

Flood and other hazards management

Historic preservation

Social equity

Each discussion of federal legislation relates this legal framework to three important comprehensive planning and management functions:

Collection and analysis of data

Planning and implementation of public facility and other infrastructure investment

Policy guidance to private development activities

LEGISLATION FOR COMPREHENSIVE PLANNING AND ENVIRONMENTAL CONCERNS

The National Environmental Policy Act
(42 USC 4341, as amended by PL 94-52 and PL 94-83)

Public concern over the deteriorating state of the environment heightened considerably in the 1960's and culminated in passage of the National Environmental Policy Act, which became law on January 1, 1970. This far-reaching legislation made systematic consideration of all aspects of environmental quality — natural, built, and social — a matter of national policy. The purposes of the act, as enunciated in Section 2, were to:

> declare a national policy which will encourage productive and enjoyable harmony between man and his environment; to promote efforts which will prevent or eliminate damage to the environment and biosphere and stimulate the health and welfare of man; to enrich the ecological systems and a natural resources important to the Nation; and to establish a Council on Environmental Quality.

Data Collection and Analysis

In order to carry out the policies of the act, all agencies of the federal government are directed to use a "systematic, inter-disciplinary approach which will insure the integrated use of the natural and social sciences and the environmental design arts in planning and in decision-making which may have an impact on man's environment" [102(2)(A)] and to identify and develop methods and procedures to "insure that presently unquantified environmental amenities and values may be given appropriate consideration" with economic and technical considerations in decision making [102(2) (B)]. Every recommendation or report on proposals and every "major federal action" is required to have a detailed statement describing the environmental impact of the proposed action, alternatives thereto, and any irreversible commitments of resources involved [102(2)(C)]. Paragraph 4 of Section 102 requires federal agencies to "initiate and utilize ecological information in the planning and development of resource-oriented projects."

Planning for Public Facilities and Infrastructure

As stated above, federal agencies are required to prepare environmental impact statements for "major Federal actions significantly affecting the quality of the human environment." Section 102(2)(D) stipulates that environmental impact statements prepared after January 1, 1970 "for any major Federal action funded under a program of grants to States" are not legally insufficient solely because they are prepared by a state agency or official as long as that agency or official has statewide jurisdiction and the responsibility for such action, and as long as the responsible official is involved in the preparation of the statement in certain ways as provided in Section 102(2)(D).

Guidance for Private Development

The act focuses on public actions and development, primarily at the federal level. However, general policies are expressed in the purpose and declaration of the policy sections of the act. The act declares that one of its purposes is "to promote the efforts which will prevent or eliminate damage to the environment and biosphere and stimulate the health and welfare of man." Further, Congress recognized the "profound influences" of high-density urbanization, industrial expansion, and resource exploitation "on environmental quality and the welfare of man," and declared it to be the national policy "to create and maintain conditions under which man and nature can exist in productive harmony." To carry out this policy, Congress placed on the federal government the responsibility to use all practical means to ensure safe, beautiful, productive, and aesthetically and culturally pleasing surroundings, to attain the widest range of beneficial uses of the environment without degradation, and to preserve important historic, cultural, and natural aspects of our national heritage [101(b)(2)(3)(4)].

One of the significant effects of NEPA has been its impetus to state laws and regulations which require similar kinds of environmental impact statements. As of April 1976, twenty-six jurisdictions had distinct impact statement requirements of their own. Known as "little NEPA's," the scope of these statements varies considerably. Fourteen states and Puerto Rico have enacted impact statement requirements of general application;[1] five states have environmental analysis requirements of limited application;[2] and six have procedures adopted by administrative regulations, roughly equivalent to NEPA.[3] Among the twenty-six jurisdictions, some require environmental analysis only for certain limited activities, such as power plant siting (Nevada). Others, like Massachusetts, cover only state-initiated actions, omitting those that require a state permit or license. Michigan, as another example, requires an impact statement for any state activity which "raises public concern or controversy," while North Carolina authorizes local governments to require statements from special-purpose districts and private developers of major projects.

Most of the state acts follow NEPA in its specification of the items that must be discussed in the impact statement. Elements added to the requirements by state laws include discussion of the measures proposed to minimize the effects of projects (California), analysis of the growth-inducing consequences of the proposed action (Montana, California), energy conservation measures (New York, California), and economic impacts (Michigan, Minnesota).

To date, implementation of state programs has moved slowly because of limited funds and staff to administer the requirements of the programs. States with the most experience in using the impact statements, such as California, have claimed their usefulness as a framework for environmental analysis and decision making and public participation in government.

Housing and Community Development Act of 1974
(PL 93-383, as amended by the Housing and Community Development Act of 1977, PL 95-128)

Among the objectives of the 1974 act was an important set of revisions to the existing Section 701 Comprehensive Planning Assistance Program. The 1977 act revised the formula by which Community Development Block Grants are allocated to consider on a weighted scale growth, lag, poverty, and age of housing; and authorized Urban Development Action grants for severely distressed cities and urban counties.

Data Collection and Analysis

In order to apply for a grant under Title I of the 1974 act, communities must have already completed a substantial data collection and analysis effort. Applications are required to contain the following features:

A summary of a three-year plan that identifies community development needs and objectives (developed in accordance with areawide development planning and national urban growth policies) and that demonstrates a comprehensive strategy for meeting those needs [Section 104 (a)(1)]

A program that includes activities to meet the community development needs and objectives (and which identifies other resources available to meet the needs), and "takes into account appropriate environmental factors" [Section 104 (a)(2)]

A housing assistance plan which surveys the condition of the community's housing stock and assesses the assistance needs of lower-income persons in the community, sets realistic annual goals for units or persons to be assisted, and indicates the general locations of proposed housing for lower-income persons [Section 104(a)(4)]

Title IV of the 1974 act, which revised Section 701 of the Housing Act of 1954, contains the provisions pertinent to comprehensive planning conducted with community development grant assistance. Comprehensive plans must include a housing element that takes into account all available data regarding the area's housing needs as they relate to population growth [401(c)(1)] and a land-use element which includes "(A) studies, criteria, standards, and implementing procedures necessary for effectively guiding and controlling major decisions as to where growth should take place within the recipients' boundaries, and (B) as a guide for governmental policies . . . and laws with respect to the pattern and intensity of land use for residential, commercial, industrial, and other activities" [401(c)(2)]." The term "comprehensive planning" is defined to include:

Preparation of general plans with respect to the pattern and intensity of land use, the provision of public facilities (including transportation facilities) and other government services, and the effective development and use of human and natural resources

Identification and evaluation of area needs (including housing, employment, education, and health) and formulation of specific programs for meeting them

Surveys of structures and sites which are determined by the appropriate authorities to be of historic or architectural value

Long-range physical and fiscal plans for such action

Programming of capital improvements and other major
expenditures based on a determination of relative urgency,
together with definite financing plans for such expenditures in the earlier years of the program

Coordination of all related plans and activities of the
state and local governments and agencies concerned

Preparation of regulatory and administrative measures in
support of the foregoing 401(M)(4)

Planning for Public Facilities and Infrastructure

Section 104 (a)(3) requires the applicant for grants under
Title I to "describe a program designed to (A) eliminate or prevent
slums . . . " and "(B) provide improved community facilities and
public improvements, including the provision of supporting health,
social, and similar services where necessary and appropriate." Activities eligible for assistance under the Community Development
program include, but are not limited to "the acquisition, construction, reconstruction, or installation of public works, facilities, and
site or other improvements" [Section 105(a)(2)] as well as the
"provision of public services not otherwise available in areas where
other activities assisted under this title are being carried out" [Sec-
tion 105(a)(8)].

Planning grants are also authorized under Section 401(h) for
"activities relating to all the developmental aspects of the total
metropolitan area . . . including but not limited to . . . land use,
transportation, . . . economic development, . . . community facilities, and the general improvement of living environments." As defined in the act, comprehensive planning also includes planning for
the provision of public facilities and other government services
[401(M) 4] (A)(ii).

Guidance for Private Development

Among the purposes of the act is to encourage the development
of "viable urban communities, by providing decent housing and a
suitable living environment . . . principally for persons of low and
moderate income" [101(c)]. Federal assistance is provided to
support "a more rational utilization of land and other natural resources and the better arrangement of residential, commercial,

industrial, recreational, and other needed activity centers" [101 (c)(5)], and to further the development of a national urban-growth policy which "encourages community development activities consistent with comprehensive local and areawide planning" [101(d) (2)].

Also eligible for assistance by the 1977 act, when carried out by public or private nonprofit entities or by small minority investment companies, are financing public or private acquisition for and rehabilitation of privately owned properties; planning; and assistance to local development corporations "when such activities are necessary or appropriate to meeting the needs and objectives of the community development plan" [Section 105(d)].

Urban Growth and New Community Development Act of 1970
[Title VII of the Housing and Urban Development Act of 1970, PL 91-609. Pursuant to Title VI of the Housing and Community Development Act of 1977 (PL 95-128), the name of the act was changed to the National Urban Policy and New Community Development Act of 1970.]

Data Collection and Analysis

The act makes no specific data requirements; however, a variety of data-collection and analysis needs are *implied* in its definition of the components of "comprehensive planning" found in Sections 109 and 806(c). These elements are essentially the same as those defined in Title IV of the Housing and Community Development Act of 1974.

Planning for Public Facilities and Infrastructure

As an element of a policy for federal programs and projects having a significant effect on community development, Section 401(c) requires that federal aid for development purposes be consistent with state, regional, and local comprehensive planning, with consideration given to "all developmental aspects of our total national community including . . . housing, transportation, economic development, natural and human resource development, community facilities, and the general improvement of living environments." Sections 401(d) and (e) require that federal agencies and

programs be coordinated with one another and that individual
planning for one program — for example, "highway construction,
urban renewal, and open space" — be coordinated with comprehensive and areawide planning.

Guidance for Private Development

Regulations promulgated under Section 401 or federal programs
that affect community development are to serve seven objectives of
development policy: (1) appropriate land uses for housing, commercial, industrial, governmental, institutional, and other purposes;
(2) wise development and conservation of natural resources; (3)
balanced transportation systems, including highway, air, water,
pedestrian, mass transit, and other modes for the movement of
people and goods; (4) adequate outdoor recreation and open space;
(5) protection of areas of unique natural beauty and of historical
and scientific interest; (6) properly planned community facilities,
including utilities for the supply of power, water, and communications and for the safe disposal of wastes; and (7) concern for high
standards of design. Local policies carried out to serve these development objectives can directly influence the quality and spatial
location of private development.

Intergovernmental Cooperation Act of 1968
(PL 90-577)

Data Collection and Analysis

Section 735 amends Section 701 of the Housing Act of 1954
to require that plans formulated under this section "include studies,
criteria, standards, and implementing procedures necessary for
effectively guiding . . . decisions as to where growth should take
place." Furthermore, these plans should take into account the need
for conserving land and other irreplaceable natural resources; population changes; housing and employment opportunities; possible
locations of new communities, large-scale development, and the
centralization of existing communities; and methods to improve
governmental structures.

Section 712 states the eligibility requirements for new community development programs. The Secretary of HUD must determine that the program "is consistent with comprehensive planning, physical and social, . . . provides an adequate basis for evaluat-

ing the new community development program in relation to other plans involving area population, housing and development trends, and transportation, water, sewerage, open space, recreation, and other relevant facilities" [712(a)(4)], and that it "will make significant use of advances in design and technology with respect to local utilization, . . . and the provision of community facilities and services." [712(a)(8)].

Finally, Section 703(a) requires a biannual report to Congress on urban growth [now the National Urban Policy Report, according to Title VI of the Housing and Community Development Act of 1977 (PL 95-128)], which is to include information, "statistics and significant trends relating to the pattern of urban development . . ."; a status assessment and evaluation of interstate, state, local, and private policies and plans regarding a national urban policy; and recommendations for programs to carry out such a policy.

Planning for Public Facilities and Infrastructure

Section 718(a) authorizes the Secretary of HUD to make supplementary grants to a state or local agency carrying out a new community-assistance project [(defined to include public facilities financed by other federal programs, as listed under Section (c)] if the project is necessary to carry out a new community development program. Also, in Section 715, the Secretary is authorized to make "public service grants" to a state or local agency responsible for providing essential public services (including educational, health, and safety services) which the Secretary determines are necessary to serve the needs of the residents of the new community prior to completion of permanent arrangements.

Implicit in the provision of both of these grants is the notion that some funds will be used to support planning for public facilities. Section 719 authorizes the Secretary to provide public or private developers of new communities with technical assistance "in connection with planning and carrying out new community development programs." Finally, Section 720 authorizes the secretary to provide grants for special planning assistance to state land-development agencies and private developers in order that they will be "responsive to social or environmental problems related to the public purposes of new community development or will adequately provide for or encourage the use of, new or advanced technology." This provision has authorized innovative methods of providing public facilities and services.

Guidance for Private Development

Section 710(f) states that the purpose of this act is "to provide private developers (and state and local public bodies) . . . with financial and other assistance necessary for encouraging the orderly development of well planned, diversified, and economically sound new communities, including major additions to existing communities, and to do so in a manner which will rely to the maximum extent on private enterprise." If this section is read together with Section 712, some general policies regarding new community development become clear. They are to provide an alternative to disorderly urban development; preserve and enhance the natural and urban environment; increase everyone's choice in residential and employment opportunities and thereby encourage full use of the potential of existing development; assist in the production of housing at reasonable cost; increase the capability of the housing industry to make use of improved technology; provide neighborhoods with easier access among living and working places and recreation areas; and encourage innovation in meeting domestic physical, social, and economic problems.

LEGISLATION FOR SPECIFIC ENVIRONMENTAL CONCERNS

Planners must also be aware of the body of federal legislation that establishes goals, policies, and standards for specific environmental-planning considerations. The following sections briefly summarize the major federal statutes that affect the environmental planning concerns addressed in this manual: land use, water quality, noise abatement and control, flood and other hazards, and historic preservation. As before, the discussion is limited to those aspects most relevant to the responsibilities of comprehensive-planning agencies for data collection and analysis, planning for public facilities and infrastructure, and guidance for private development.

Coastal Zone Management Act of 1972
(PL 92-583, as amended by PL 94-370)

The purpose of the act, administered by the Department of Commerce, is to foster more effective and beneficial management, use, and protection of the nation's coastal zone. The act authorizes provision of funds to coastal states to prepare and administer prog-grams "to achieve wise use of the land and water resources of the coastal zone, giving full consideration to ecological, cultural, historic, and aesthetic values as well as to needs for economic development" [303(b)].

Data Collection and Analysis

Section 305 authorizes grants to states for preparation of a coastal zone management program, which must include:

Identification of the boundaries of the coastal zone subject to the management program

Definition of permissible land and water uses having a direct and significant effect on the coastal waters

Inventory and designation of areas of particular concern within the coastal zone; such as natural or estuarine areas, transitional and intensely developed areas where reclamation is needed or where public access should be increased, areas especially suited for intensive use or development, etc.

Identification of the means by which the state proposes to exert control over the land and water uses referred to in paragraph (2) above, including a listing of relevant constitutional provisions, legislative enactments, regulations, and judicial decisions

Broad guidelines on priority of uses in particular areas

Description of the organizational structure proposed to implement the management program, including the responsibilities and interrelations of local, areawide, state, regional, and interstate agencies in the management process [305(b)]

A definition of the term "beach" and a planning process for the protection of, and access to, public beaches and other public coastal areas of environmental, recreational, historical, aesthetic, ecological, or cultural value

A planning process for energy facilities likely to be located in, or which may significantly affect, the coastal zone, including but not limited to a process for anticipating and managing the effects from such facilities

A planning process for assessing the effects of shoreline erosion (however caused) and for studying and evaluating ways to control or lessen the impact of such erosion and to restore areas adversely affected by such erosion

Under Section 306, grants are provided for administering the state management program. Before approving a program for funding, the secretary must find that the program, among other things:

Has been coordinated "with local, areawide, and interstate plans applicable to areas within the coastal zone"

"Provides for adequate consideration of the national interest involved in the siting of facilities necessary to meet requirements which are other than local in nature"

"Makes provision for procedures whereby specific areas may be designated for the purpose of preserving or restoring them for their conservation, recreational, ecological, or aesthetic values"

Will be managed by an authority empowered "to administer land and water use regulations, control development . . . and . . . resolve conflicts among competing uses "

Planning for Public Facilities and Infrastructure

Section 307 of the act, which relates to interagency coordination and cooperation, states that the requirements of the Federal Water Pollution Control and Clean Air Acts, as amended, are to be incorporated in any program developed pursuant to the Coastal Zone Management Act. Furthermore, the Department of Housing and Urban Development has signed an Interagency Agreement with the Office of Coastal Zone Management that requires coordination of Comprehensive Planning Assistance applications with Coastal Zone Management grant applications and provides guidelines for determining consistency between the required land-use element of the comprehensive plan and of coastal-zone management programs.

In addition to land-use regulations pertaining to private development in coastal zones, planning agencies should consider, in connection with public investment planning, such environmental strategies as land acquisition; conservation easements; utility extension policies; utility pricing policies, including effluent surcharges; and state or regional control over the location of major facilities.

Guidance for Private Development

Section 302(h) of the act states that "the key to more effective protection and use of the land and water resources of the coastal
zone is to encourage the states to exercise their full authority over
the lands and waters in the coastal zone, including unified policies,
criteria, standards, methods, and processes for dealing with land
and water use decisions of more than local significance." Also,
provisions for federal funding of coastal-zone management programs
under Section 306 include a requirement that the program provide
for "state administrative review for consistency with the management program of all development plans, projects, or land and water
use regulations, including exceptions and variances thereto, proposed
by any state or local authority or private developer [306(e)(c)]."

It is clear that comprehensive-planning agencies must integrate
their plans and policies with state coastal-zone planning objectives
and coordinate their land-use management strategies with the state
coastal-zone management plan. Environmental controls that planning
agencies should consider include the following: mandatory shoreline ordinances, including zoning; sanitary and subdivision ordinances and building permits to control minimum lot sizes, setbacks
from the water, vegetation clearing and removing, filling, draining,
dredging, and the size, location, and operation of septic tanks;
zoning and subdivision ordinances based on vulnerability criteria;
state or regional review of local plans and enforcement measures;
coastal wetland alteration laws that prohibit dredging, filling, or
altering of coastal wetlands without a permit (as in Massachusetts,
Maine, Connecticut, and North Carolina); establishment of aquatic
preserves (as in Florida) where there can be no more selling, filling,
or dredging of submerged land to create waterfront real estates;
and regional permit systems for shoreline development (as in the
San Francisco Bay Area).

Amendments to the act passed in 1976 are specifically designed to assist those states facing Outer Continental Shelf (OSC)
oil and gas development or other energy-related developments and
facilities affecting the coastal zone. Assistance is provided in the
form of grants or loans to coastal states from a new Coastal Energy
Facility Impact Fund, authorized at $250 million for three fiscal
years. Up to 20% of the fund may be used for planning grants. The
act also provides for automatic grants to be given to any state which
is actually landing OCS oil or natural gas in its coastal zone, based on

the number of barrels of oil or natural gas equivalent produced, to be used to ameliorate adverse effects of energy resource development and related facilities. A federal guarantee for state and local government bonds for such purposes is also provided in the act.

Funds may be used for planning and carrying out projects in impacted states to provide new or improved public facilities and services required as a result of OCS activity. Although such facilities and services are to be approved by the Secretary, they include highways and secondary roads, docks, navigation aids, fire and police protection, water supply, waste collection and treatment (including drainage), schools and education, and hospitals and health care [Section 308(b)(4)(B)(i) & (ii)].

Resource Conservation and Recovery Act of 1976
(PL 94-580, 42 USLA 3251 et seq.)

The act amends the Solid Waste Disposal Act of 1972 and directs the Administrator of EPA, in conjunction with other federal, state, and local agencies, to develop and publish guidelines for solid-waste management (Section 1008); to provide technical and financial assistance to state or regional agencies in the development and implementation of solid-waste plans and hazardous-wastes management programs (Section 4008); to promulgate regulations establishing standards for generators of hazardous waste as may be necessary to protect human health and the environment (Section 3002); to establish a procedure for the issuance of permits to facilities for the treatment, storage, or disposal of hazardous wastes (Section 3005); to require that each state adopt a solid-waste disposal plan in order to be eligible for grants under the act and that such plan prohibit open dumping of solid wastes within five years [Sections 4007, 4005(c)]; and to carry out a program of special study and demonstration projects on the recovery of useful energy and materials (Subtitle H).

Data Collection and Analysis

The planning provisions of the act are contained in Subtitle D. Detailed guidelines for the plans, including data collection and analysis, are found in Section 4002(c). The plans are to consider:

The varying regional, geologic, hydrologic, climatic, and other circumstances under which different solid-waste practices are required in order to ensure the reasonable protection of the quality of the ground and surface waters from leachate contamination, the reasonable protection of the quality of the surface waters from surface runoff contamination, and the reasonable protection of ambient air quality

Characteristics and conditions of collection, storage, processing, and disposal, taking into account the nature of the material to be disposed

Methods for closing or upgrading open dumps for purposes of eliminating potential health hazards

Population density, distribution, and projected growth

Geographic, geologic, climatic, and hydrologic characteristics

The type and location of transportation

The profile of industries

The constituents and generation rates of waste

The political, economic, organizational, financial, and managerial problems affecting comprehensive solid-waste management

Types of resource-recovery facilities and resource-conservation systems which are appropriate

New markets for recovered material

In addition to procedures for designating regions and state and local agency responsibilities, Section 4006(b) states that "where possible, designation of the agency for the affected area designated under Section 208 of the Federal Water Pollution Control Act shall be considered" . . . as an agency to plan and carry out solid waste functions under the act.

The plans prepared under Subtitle D are to:

Identify the responsibilities of state, local, and regional authorities in the implementation of the state plan; the distribution of federal funds to those authorities; and the means for coordinating regional planning and implementation under the state plan

Prohibit the establishment of new open dumps within the state require that all solid waste be used for resource recovery or be disposed of in sanitary landfills or in another environmentally sound manner

Provide for the closing or upgrading of all existing open dumps within the state

Provide for the establishment of state regulatory powers as may be necessary to implement the plan

Provide that no local government within the state be prohibited under state or local law from entering into long-term contracts for the supply of solid waste to resource-recovery facilities

Provide for such resource conservation or recovery and for the disposal of solid waste in sanitary landfills or for any combination of practices necessary to use or dispose of waste in a manner that is environmentally sound

Guidance for Private Development

Since the act is directed to public activities with respect to resource conservation and recovery, there are limited pronouncements of policies for private development. Relevant portions of Section 1003, however, state that the objectives of the act are to:

Prohibit future open dumping on the land and require the conversion of existing open dumps into facilities that do not pose a danger to the environment or to health [Section 1003(3)]

Regulate the treatment, storage, transportation, and disposal of hazardous wastes that have adverse effects on health and the environment [Section 1003(4)]

Establish a cooperative effort among federal, state, and local governments and private enterprise in order to recover valuable materials and energy from solid waste [Section 1003(8)]

Federal Water Pollution Control Act Amendments *(PL 92-500) and the 1977 amendments, PL 95-217)*

PL 92-500 and its amendements, administered by EPA, greatly expand the federal emphasis on water-quality management planning, particularly coordination among water-pollution control activities at the different levels of government. Specifically, the law calls for the integration of the NPDES permit program into a three-tiered structure of planning operations, which includes:

Municipal facilities planning at the local government level (Section 201)

Areawide wastewater management planning by regional planning agencies

Basin planning at the state level [Section 303(e)]

To a large extent, PL 92-500 prescribes similar planning objectives for all three levels, the principal distinctions among the objectives being geographic scope and the level of planning detail required. Coordination is to be achieved by requiring local facilities plans to be incorporated into the areawide plan, which in turn must be incorporated in, and consistent with, the state-level basin plan.

To ensure further that water-quality management planning conducted under PL 92-500 is integrated with HUD-assisted comprehensive planning, EPA and HUD have signed an interagency agreement that requires coordination and consistency between these planning activities and that provides guidelines for compliance. The A-95 review process provides another mechanism for reviewing consistency between these programs; and the required environmental assessment of comprehensive plans and policies should also consider whether these plans and policies are consistent with water-quality management plans.

Data Collection and Analysis

Section 208 authorizes the preparation and implementation of areawide waste-water management plans. Data must be collected and analyzed in order to determine:

Treatment works necessary to meet anticipated municipal and industrial waste treatment needs for a twenty-year period with provision for annual updating [208(b)(2) (A)]; construction priorities for such treatment works with time schedules for initiation and completion [208 (b)(2)(A)]

A regulatory program to control or treat all point and nonpoint pollution sources, including in-place or accumulated pollution sources; control the location, modification, and construction of any facilities within the area; and assure that industrial or commercial waste discharges into any publicly owned treatment works meet applicable pretreatment requirements [208(b)(2)(C)]

Measures necessary to execute the plan (including financing), the time required, costs, and economic and environmental effects on the residents of the area [208(b)(2)(E)]

A process to identify agriculture, silviculture, and mine and construction-related nonpoint sources of pollution, and to propose procedures and methods (including) land-use requirements) to control such sources [208(b)(2)(F)(G) & (H)]

A process to identify salt water intrusion into rivers, lakes, and estuaries, and to propose procedures and methods to control such intrusion [208(b)(2)(I)]

A process to control the disposition of all residual waste which could affect water quality [208(b)(2)(J)]

A process to control the disposal of pollutants on land or in subsurface excavations to protect ground- and surface-water quality [208(b)(2)(K)]

It is not entirely clear how regional planning under 208 will mesh with basin planning under 303(e), except that the legal requirements of each must take cognizance of and be compatible with those of the other. States are expected to consult closely with the concerned Section 208 agencies and to reflect their inputs in formulating the basin plans. The states need not, however, preempt the 208 planning process by attempting to decide the number, types, locations, and service areas of future wastewater-management facilities. When 208 is activated, such planning should be done in detail by the 208 planning agency. At the same time, the 303(e) plan can recommend basic engineering strategies for meeting water-quality standards and effluent limitations in cost-effective ways. Since Section 208 plans have to secure state approval, a state may choose to outline in its basin plan whatever engineering configurations it may be inclined to favor before 208 planning gets underway. Later on, the 303(e) plan can be amended to take account of new findings or conclusions developed in the course of 208 planning. Thus, as the overall planning process unfolds, an interactive, iterative relation can be envisaged between the respective plans of state and regional agencies.

Planning for Facilities and Infrastructure

Section 201 of the federal act is the third major planning section demanding consideration. Management agencies designated by a 208 plan would be eligible to receive Section 201 funds to prepare engineering reports, designs, and specifications for facilities which the Section 208 plans call upon those agencies to build. If for any reason 208 is not used, 201 may also serve as the vehicle for preliminary planning -- for determining the basic components of a cost-effective areawide control strategy that takes both point and nonpoint sources into account. In that event, recommendations for areawide solutions can be implemented through Sections 303(e) and 201. First, they would be incorporated into a 303(e) basin plan. Then municipalities or intermunicipal districts would apply under 201 for grants to design and build the facilities envisaged in the plan. Section 208, then, is not indispensable to implementation of areawide engineering solutions.

Guidance for Private Development

Plans prepared under Section 208 of the federal act will, in large part, be land-use plans. They will represent a cost-effective mix of structural measures (collection and treatment facilities) and nonstructural measures — especially land-use and nonpoint source controls -- for achieving water-quality objectives. They will serve, moreover, as guides for development, reflecting not merely factual projections of future growth, but policies for timing and channeling it within the 208 area. Consider the following implications of a 208 plan:

> It will prefigure the usage of land required for the wastewater-management system itself, locating its major components. The plan may well indicate which sites and which rights of way are appropriate for new transmission and treatment facilities.

> By determining locations, sizes, interconnections, and construction schedules for wastewater-management facilities, the plan will prefigure the direction and pace of

future residential and economic growth. It will encourage growth in locations that will be served by sewers and treatment plants, and discourage it elsewhere.

The plan must establish a program for regulating the locations of all "facilities" — apparently including any sort of development — that may result in point or non-point discharges within the area. What this means, by and large, is that development should be permitted only where adequate wastewater-control or disposal facilities are available. Furthermore, it may mean that develop-ment should be positively restricted in sensitive areas — such as wetlands, floodplains, steep slopes, and aquifer recharge zones — where it is most likely to have detri-mental effects on the water resource.

The plan must provide for the control of nonpoint sources of pollution in general, and of agricultural and construc-tion-related sources in particular. To control such sources, it may be necessary not only to institute performance standards for permissible uses, but to restrict or prohibit particular uses in sensitive areas and to preserve some of these areas as open spaces in their natural state.

The plan must provide for controlling land disposal of residual wastes and of other pollutants that might impair ground- or surface-water quality. Septic tanks, dumps, scavenging, and disposal of septage are the principal operations to be considered here. Performance standards will have to be implemented, but also controls over the location of disposal sites.

Those parts of a 208 plan which relate to point sources will be enforced through the requirements that all discharge permits and construction grants conform to the plan. There is no assurance, however, that other kinds of development permitted, subsidized, or undertaken by agencies or private developers will be compatible with such a plan. Most municipalities in the 208 area will have re-solved to "proceed towards its implementation," and the 208 agen-cies can help protect the plan's integrity through A-95 reviews and project certifications; but a largely voluntary effort will be required at all levels in order to harmonize the pace and pattern of future development with the measures set forth in the 208 plan for water-quality management. The plan could easily be undermined if other elements of the region's capital infrastructure — transportation facilities, housing, shopping centers, and so forth — were built and operated at times, in places, or in ways that violated the criteria or undermined the commitments set forth in that plan. In fact, implementation of Section 208 plans (or of comparable plans for non-208 areas) presupposes that they will have been prepared and will subsequently be considered in the context of all other land-use decisions affecting the region.

Safe Drinking Water Act of 1974
(PL 92-523)

The act authorizes the Environmental Protection Agency to issue national drinking-water regulations applicable to all public water supplies. The states are charged with primary enforcement responsibility, and to protect underground sources of drinking water from contamination, they are required to establish underground injection control programs that include a permit system governing all such injections. In the interim, Section 1424(e) of the act prohibits commitment of federal financial assistance to any project that might endanger an aquifer if the aquifer is an area's sole or primary drinking-water source.

Data Collection and Analysis

The most immediate data collection requirement of the act relates to information needed by the Administrator of EPA to establish maximum contaminant levels in drinking water [see Section 1412(e) 1, 2, 3, & 4]. In addition, Section 1442 authorizes the Administrator to conduct research on a variety of aspects of drinking-water safety, including "a survey and study of (A) disposal of waste (including residential waste) which may endanger underground water . . . and (B) means of control of such waste disposal." Finally, the Administrator is directed to undertake a study of the "quantity, quality, and availability of rural water supplies" (Section 3).

Planning for Public Facilities and Infrastructure

The act contains no explicit requirements for planning. However, to the extent that it gives the states the responsibility for enforcing national drinking-water standards, the act implies that the states will be involved in planning for water-supply facilities.

Guidance for Private Development

The act contains no specific policy statements vis-à-vis private development. However, state permit programs to regulate underground injections will apply to injections not only by federal agencies, but also "by any other person whether or not occurring on property owned or leased by the United States" [Section 1421(b) (D)(ii)]. This requirement suggests an implicit policy for private development, that is, avoidance of practices that may cause contamination of underground water supplies.

Clean Air Act Amendments of 1970
(PL 91-604 and the 1977 amendments, PL 95-95)

The Clean Air Act, as amended in 1970 and 1977, established national primary and secondary ambient air quality standards and required each state to adopt implementation plans (SIPS) providing means for the attainment, maintenance, and enforcement of the national standards. The act delegated to the state primary responsibility for carrying out implementation plans within the designated air-quality control regions of each state. States may, however, authorize a local agency to administer or develop certain portions of a plan. Among other things, the 1977 amendments required the designation of all areas to be within one of three quality classes and established increments for particulate matter and sulfur dioxide to prevent significant deterioration within those areas where the air is cleaner than standards require.

The act and the Environmental Protection Agency's guidelines for SIP's suggest that strategies for air-quality management should extend beyond source control of pollutant emissions to a broader approach that incorporates transportation controls as well as "preconstruction review of direct sources of air pollution." Comprehensive plans and policies will be strategic to long-term air quality and people through the influence they exert on land-use patterns, proximity between the generators and receptors of air pollutants, and — generally — the intensity and pattern of economic growth and urbanization.

Data Collection and Analysis

Conditions for EPA approval of state implementation plans include the requirement that plans provide for "establishment and

operation of appropriate devices, methods, systems, and procedures necessary to . . . monitor, compile, and analyze data on ambient air quality" [111(a)(2)(C)].

Clearly, too, comprehensive-planning agencies, as a basis for
incorporating air-quality considerations into their land-use and
transportation plans and policies, must obtain and analyze data on
local factors affecting ambient air quality and its effects — the
sources of pollutant emissions, sensitive receptors, meteorological
and topographical conditions, and so on, as well as population and
development projections.

Planning for Public Facilities and Infrastructure

Specific reference to public facilities is made, in Section 111
of the act, in connection with performance standards applicable
to new stationary sources of pollutant emissions and the required
review of such sources prior to construction or modification. New
stationary sources are defined as "any building, structure, facility,
or installation which emits or may emit any air pollutant" [111
(a)(3)].

EPA guidelines for state implementation plans suggest a number
of land-use and transportation measures relating to public investments. Among these are emission standards for incinerators, parking
lots, and other public facilities; provision of parks and open space;
and indirect guidance of private development through strategic
timing and location of infrastructure investments.

Guidance for Private Development

Although no explicit policy regarding private development is
enunciated in the act, two provisions referred to above have relevance for private-sector activities. The first is the provision for
applying transportation controls and preconstruction review of
direct sources of air pollution where necessary to ensure attainment
and maintenance of air-quality standards [110(a)(2)(B)]. The
second is the requirement that implementation plans include a procedure for new stationary source review and a program to enforce
emission limitations and regulation of the operation or construction
of stationary sources [110(a)(2)(D)].

EPA guidelines for state implementation plans place strong
emphasis on ways to guide private development so as to promote
maintenance of air quality standards. Possible land-use and transportation planning strategies include: emission-density regulation

over the amount of pollutant emissions per unit of land area; emission-density zoning of parcels according to polluting capacity as a function of the surrounding land use; special use permits; air zoning with complete restriction of polluting activities in certain areas; nonconforming use; protective or exclusive-use zoning; emission standards for parking lots and other facilities, mechanical equipment, and appliances; parking controls; and measures to increase use of mass transit.

Also, flexible land-use regulations allowing for planned unit development, cluster subdivisions, and density zoning can contribute to air quality because the resulting development patterns tend to preserve open space and minimize trip lengths and, therefore, automobile emissions. Private development can also be guided through use of "inducements" in the form of tax policies, public land assembly, and public investment programs, as noted above.

Environmental assessments of comprehensive plans and policies are useful for determining whether the plans are consistent with state implementation plans.

HUD Circular 1390.2

In HUD Circular 1390.2, issued in 1971, the Department of Housing and Urban Development set forth an innovative policy on noise abatement and control, requiring that "noise exposures and sources of noise be given adequate consideration as an integral part of urban environments in connection with all HUD programs which provide financial support to planning" (Section 2, No. 1, Planning Assistance). The purposes of the policy enunciated in HUD Circular 1390.2 are to avoid adverse physiological and psychological effects, as well as economic losses, that may be caused by objectionable sound; to encourage control of noise at its source in cooperation with other federal departments and agencies; to encourage land-use patterns that separate uncontrollable noise sources from residential and other noise-sensitive accommodations; and to prohibit HUD support of noise-sensitive uses, particularly housing, on sites that have or are projected to have unacceptable noise exposures.

Data Collection and Analysis

Given HUD's policy to discourage construction of noise-sensitive uses wherever noise levels are unacceptable, it is advisable for all agencies responsible for housing and land-use planning to conduct background studies on which to base land-use strategies that account for noise as well as other environmental concerns. HUD Circular 1390.2 provides that "reconnaissance studies, and . . . studies in depth for noise control and abatement" are allowable costs.

Planning for Public Facilities and Infrastructure

To ensure that the interim noise standards are satisfied, HUD encourages "compatible land use planning in relation to airports, other general modes of transportation, and other sources of high noise" [Section 2(a)(1), Planning Assistance]. Construction on sites that have "unacceptable noise exposures" is to be discouraged "by withholding all forms of HUD's assistance for such units [Section 2(a)(2), New Construction].

Guidance for Private Development

The general policy of HUD Circular 1390.2 is "to foster: the creation of controls and standards for community noise abatement and control by general-purpose agencies of state and local governments." Accordingly, all forms of HUD assistance will be withheld for both new construction and major rehabilitation that (with certain exceptions) do not conform to promulgated noise-abatement standards. As a general policy, HUD promotes private development that is designed and constructed to mitigate noise [Section 2(a) (6 and 7)].

Noise Control Act of 1972
(PL 92-574)

The act delegated to the U.S. Environmental Protection Agency responsibility for coordinating federal research on noise and for establishing noise standards for products distributed in commerce (source control). Standards are authorized for construction and transportation equipment, motors, engines, and electrical devices. Noise-emission standards required for aircraft, railroads, and motor carriers are applicable only to carriers engaged in interstate commerce; the act sets forth no explicit policy with respect to local public transit systems. The only reference made to state and local governmental policies regarding noise control is the authorization, in Section 14(2), of the Secretary of EPA to provide technical assistance to state and local governments "to facilitate their development and enforcement of ambient noise standards, including . . . preparation of model state or local legislation for noise control."

Flood Disaster Protection Act of 1973
(PL 92-234, as amended by Title VII of the Housing and Community Development Act of 1977, PL 95-128)

The act substantially expands the National Flood Insurance Program in order to provide better protection to the public and to reduce annual disaster assistance outlays through the increased availability of flood insurance. Specific purposes of the act are to substantially increase the limits of the subsidized and unsubsidized flood insurance coverage; provide for expeditious identification of flood-prone areas; require states or local communities, as a condition of future federal financial assistance, to participate in the flood-insurance program; and require lending institutions to notify loan recipients that they would not be eligible for federal disaster relief unless they undertook flood-proofing measures, as a condition of making, increasing, extending, or renewing any loan for the acquisition or improvement of land or facilities located in areas having special flood hazards.

HUD must publish information on known flood-prone communities and notify them within six months of their tentative identification as such. Upon notification, the community must either promptly apply for participation in a flood-insurance program or satisfy the Secretary of HUD within six months that it is no longer flood-prone. A hearing may be granted to resolve disputed cases, but the Secretary's decision is final if supported by the record.

Data Collection and Analysis

Comprehensive plans and policies developed by HUD-assisted agencies are to be assessed for their adherence to Flood Insurance Program requirements and for their encouragement of state, areawide, and local development goals that respond to effective land management for flood- and mudslide-prone areas.

Background studies needed to furnish a basis for selecting appropriate planning and policy measures for such areas include identification and assessments of the adequacy of present management in terms of land use, flood and erosion control, zoning and damage prevention; flood-proofing and vehicular access needs of structures already located in these areas; and runoff and drainage conditions throughout the planning area.

Planning for Public Facilities and Infrastructure

HUD-assisted planning agencies are to consider, in connection with public investment decisions, the following kinds of controls for flood- and mudslide-prone areas: (1) reservation of flood-prone areas for open space or nondevelopment; (2) provision of alternative vehicular access and escape routes to be used when normal routes are flooded; (3) minimum flood-proofing and access requirements for public and quasipublic institutions already located in the flood-prone areas; (4) programming acquisition of land or land development rights for public purposes consistent with effective flood-plan management; (5) in coastal areas, programs consistent with the coastal-zone management program for building damage-abatement structures and for preserving such natural barriers to flooding as sand dunes and vegetation; (6) in mudslide hazard areas, programs to control potentially adverse effects of inappropriate hillside development; and (7) routing of public infrastructure and services in such a manner as to guide future development away from hazard-prone areas.

Guidance for Private Development

The federal Flood Insurance Program requires that participating jurisdictions adopt measures to restrict development in areas exposed to flood or mudslide hazards and to guide proposed development away from such areas. In addition to public investment strategies that promote appropriate use of hazardous areas, other types of measures for guiding private development include use of floodplain zoning, building codes, building permits, and subdivision or other land-use regulations; planning the diversion of future development to areas not exposed to flooding and mudslide hazards; use of ordinances incorporating standards and requirements regarding site exploration, design, grading, construction practices, and so on in mudslide areas; and (4) coordination of local plans and policies with relevant areawide floodplain- and mudslide-management programs.

Disaster Relief Act of 1974
(PL 93-288)

The act authorizes federal disaster-relief assistance to state and local governments to help alleviate the suffering and damage caused by floods, tsunamis, earthquakes, mudslides, and other emergencies and disasters. The Disaster Relief Act of 1974 makes three important changes in federal disaster assistance. First, financial and technical assistance are offered to states to develop plans, programs, and regulations for hazard reduction, disaster preparedness, and disaster relief. Second, property to be replaced, repaired, or restored with the assistance of federal relief funds is to be insured, if insurance is available, against future losses. Third, the receipt by a state or local government of any disaster loan or grant is made contingent on its evaluating natural hazards in the disaster area and taking actions to mitigate them.

The regulations pertaining to the administration of Federal Disaster Assistance prohibit extending postdisaster financial assistance for permanent repairs or restoration of structures within an identified flood-hazard area unless the regulations of the National Flood Insurance Program have been adhered to. The major effect of the program on flood-damage reduction efforts is to reinforce the provisions of the National Flood Insurance Program that discourage floodplain development.

National Historic Preservation Act of 1966
(PL 89-665)

The goal of the National Historic Preservation Act of 1966 is the preservation and enhancement of the nation's cultural resources: historic and cultural districts, sites, building, structures, and objects that are significant in American history, architecture, archeology, and culture. Once these resources have been identified by the Secretary of the Interior, they are listed in the National Register of Historic Places which is maintained by the Secretary and his liaison in each state, the state historic preservation officer.

Comprehensive Planning Assistance activities must be carried out in accordance with Section 106 of the act, as well as with Executive Order 11593 and Section 101(b)(4) of the National Environmental Policy Act of 1969, both of which address a similar goal. It is further required by the Historical and Archeological Data Act of 1974 that for all federally assisted activities including Comprehensive Planning Assistance, every effort be made by the Secretary of the Interior to prevent scientific, prehistorical, or archeological data from being irrevocably lost or destroyed.

Data Collection and Analysis

In order to comply with legislative requirements that federally assisted activities take into account their effects on historic and cultural resources, it is important that planning agencies identify as early as possible properties that are included in the National Register or are eligible for inclusion, and areas in which scientific, prehistorical, historical, or archeological data exist or are likely to exist.

Although Comprehensive Planning Assistance Program regulations do not specifically require participants to assess consequences on locally esteemed historic/cultural sites that have not been found eligible for a place in the National Register, agencies may nonetheless wish to investigate the existence of such sites or districts in the community under NEPA's broader mandate to "preserve important historic, cultural, and natural aspects of our national heritage."

Planning for Public Facilities and Infrastructure

Planning for any public facility or infrastructure investments must take into account effects on sites listed in the National Register, in accordance with Section 106 of the 1966 act and Comprehensive Planning Assistance regulations.

It is a goal of the act and of HUD policy not only to preserve but also to enhance resources of historic and cultural significance. Federal assistance for local enhancement efforts is made available under community development block grants and under Title I of the National Housing Act as amended. Block grants authorized by the Housing and Community Development act of 1974 may be used for a broad range of activities, including the survey, acquisition, rehabilitation, preservation, and disposition of historic properties. And they may also be used in grant and loan programs for preservation at the local level. A 1974 amendment to Title I of the National Housing Act authorizes HUD to insure loans for preserving residential properties listed in the National Register of Historic Places and for those conforming to National Register criteria.

If properties of significant historic, archeological, architectural, or cultural interest are present in the area affected by comprehensive plans or policies, Comprehensive Planning Assistance Program regulations require the preparation of a specially designed historic preservation assessment. The assessment must include: (a) a summary or abstract of the proposed plans or policies; (b) the beneficial and adverse effects of the proposed plans or policies; (c) any adverse impacts which cannot be avoided should the proposed plans or policies be carried out; (d) alternatives to the proposed plans or policies; (e) the consequences of proposed plans and policies on the long-term maintenance and enhancement of National Register properties; and (f) a statement setting forth applicable federal, state, and local controls or programs for conserving and enhancing historic properties. The determination of adverse effects should be made based on the criteria outlined in the Advisory Council on Historic Preservation's "Procedures for the Protection of Historic and Cultural Properties." Adverse impact is defined as occurring under conditions which include but are not limited to destruction or alteration of all or part of a property; isolation from or alteration of its surrounding environment; introduction of visual, audible, or atmospheric elements that are out of character with the property or that alter its setting; and neglect resulting in deterioration or destruction.

Guidance for Private Development

The Advisory Council on Historic Preservation, established under Section 201 of the act, is to encourage historic preservation by — among other things — disseminating information, recommending studies, and proposing guidelines for state and local legislation.

Furthermore, since comprehensive-planning agencies are to consider the consequences of their plans and policies on historically and culturally significant sites, any actions taken to guide private development should be assessed for their compatibility with historic/cultural preservation objectives.

SOCIAL EQUITY

The basic federal legislation concerned with social justice consists of the following:

Civil Rights Act of 1964, Title V
(PL 88-352)

This act prohibits discrimination on the basis of race, color, sex, or national origin in connection with any programs or activities receiving federal financial assistance.

Fair Housing Act of 1968 (Title VIII of the Civil Rights Act of 1968)
(PL 90-284)

This act makes discrimination because of race, color, sex, or national origin in the sale, rental, or financing of housing unlawful. Affirmative action to further the policies of this title is required on the part of all executive departments, federal agencies, and block grant recipients.

Executive Order 11063

This regulation directs federal departments and agencies to take all action necessary and appropriate to prevent discrimination, because of race, color, creed, or national origin, in the sale and rental of housing and related facilities assisted by federal funds or insurance.

Executive Order 11246 (as amended by Executive Order 11375)

The order provides for nondiscrimination in government employment, by government contractors and subcontractors, and under federally assisted construction contracts.

Executive Order 11478

The order provides for equal employment opportunity in the federal government.

Housing and Urban Development Act of 1968, Section 3
(PL 90-448)

This law provides that to the greatest extent feasible, opportunities for training and employment will be given to lower-income residents of federally assisted project areas, and that contracts for work in connection with such projects be awarded to business concerns located in, or owned in large part by, residents of the project area.

Housing and Community Development Act of 1974
(PL 93-383)

Section 109 of the act prohibits discrimination on the basis of race, color, national origin, religion, or sex in carrying out community development programs and activities.

Furthermore, the overall purpose of the Community Development program, as stated in Section 101, is "the development of viable urban communities, by providing decent housing and a suitable living environment and expanding economic opportunities, principally for persons of low and moderate income."

Applicants for community development block grants are required to analyze the special needs of minorities and women apart from needs of the low-income population in general, making use of census and other existing data in the analysis. The application must spell out what is being done to address these special needs, including how proposed programs will alleviate problems caused by past discrimination against minorities.

REFERENCES

1.   California (Pub. Res. Code § 21000 et seq.); Connecticut (Pub. Act No. 73-562, approved June 22, 1973); Hawaii [Haw. Rev. Stat. Ch. 334 (1974)]; Indiana (§ 35-5301 et seq.); Maryland (Ch. 702, Md. Laws of 1973); Massachusetts (C. 30, § 61 et seq.); Minnesota (Chap. 412, Laws of 1973); Montana (§ 69-6501 et seq.); New York [Art. 8, Environmental Conservation Law (1975)]; North Carolina (Sess. Laws-1971, Chap. 1203); Puerto Rico (T. 12 § 1121 et seq.); South Dakota [S.D. Comp. Laws 1967 Ch. 11-1A (Supp. 1974)]; Virginia (Chap. 384, approved March 15, 1973); Washington (§ 43.21C010 et seq.); and Wisconsin (Chap. 273, Laws of 1971).

2.   Delaware (7 § 7001 et seq.); Mississippi [§ 49-27-11(i), Coastal Wetlands Protection Law]; Georgia [GA Code Ann. Ch. 95-A-1, § 241(e)(1)]; Nevada (§ 704.820 et seq). Also see Nevada Air Quality Regulations (Article 13), and North Dakota (§ 54-01-05, 4 N.D. Century Code).

3.   Arizona (Game and Fish Commission policy of July 2, 1971; *Policy Memo, Requirements for Environmental Impact Statements* of June 9, 1971); Michigan (Executive Directive 1971-10, issued by governor); Nebraska [Neb. Dept. of Roads, Department of Roads Action Plan (1973)]; New Jersey [N.J. Exec. Order No. 53 (Oct. 15, 1973) and Administrative Order No. 33 (August 1, 1973)]; Texas *(Policy for the Environment* adopted January 1, 1973), and Utah (Executive Order, August 27, 1974).

Bibliography

1.0 General Environmental Planning Requirements

1.1 General References on Environmental Management

Environmental Quality — 1974, 1975, and 1976, The Fifth, Sixth and Seventh Annual Reports of the Council on Environmental Quality, Washington, D.C.: U.S. Government Printing Office.

Forrester, Jay W. *Urban Dynamics.* Cambridge, Mass.: MIT Press, 1969.

Hines, Lawrence G. *Environmental Issues: Population, Pollution and Economics.* New York: W.W. Neston Co., 1973.

Hornebeck, Kenneth, et al. *Studies in Environment — Quality of Life.* Socio-economic Environmental Studies Series, U.S. Environmental Protection Agency. Washington, D.C.: November 1973.

International City Management Association, *An Anthology of Selected Readings for the National Conference on Managing the Environment,* U.S. Environmental Protection Agency, Office of Research and Monitoring, Environmental Studies Division. Washington, D.C.: 1973.

Robinson, Ira M. (ed.). *Decision-Making in Urban Planning: An Introduction to New Methodologies.* Beverly Hills, California: Sage Publications, 1972.

U.S. Environmental Protection Agency. *Environmental Management and Local Government,* EPA-600/5-73-016, February 1974.

U.S. Environmental Protection Agency. *Managing the Environment,* EPA-600/5-73-010, November 1973.

1.2 Planning Studies

Agreement for Coordination of Activities between Office of Community Planning and Development (701), Department of Housing and Urban Development and Federal Energy Administration, dated August 27, 1975.

Arthur D. Little, Inc. *Residential and Commercial Energy Use Patterns 1970-1990* (part of the FEA Task Force Reports for Project Independence). Washington, D.C.: U.S. Government Printing Office, 1974.

ASCE Urban Water Resources Research Program. "Urban Mathematical Model-
    ing and Catchment Research in the U.S.A.," Technical Memorandum
    No. IHP-1, June 1975.

Associated Universities. *Reference Energy Systems and Resource Data for Use
    in the Assessment of Energy Technologies.* Springfield, Virginia: NTIS
    PB 221 422.

Association of Bay Area Governments. *Land Capacity Analysis.* San Francisco:
    December 1975.

Baker, Earl J. and Joe G. McPhee. *Land Use Management and Regulation in
    Hazardous Areas: A Research Assessment.* Boulder: University of Colo-
    rado, 1975.

Beall, S.E. and M.M. Yarosh. "Status of Waste Heat Utilization and Dual Purpose
    Plant Projects," Oak Ridge, Tennessee: Oak Ridge National Laboratories,
    1973.

Borsky, Paul. "The Use of Social Surveys for Measuring Community Response
    to Noise Environments." In James Chapulnik (ed.), *Transportation Noise.*
    Seattle: University of Washington, 1970.

Center for Ecological Research in Planning and Design, University of Pennsyl-
    vania. *Medford: Performance Requirements for the Maintenance of
    Social Values Represented by the Natural Environment of Medford
    Township, New Jersey.* Philadelphia: 1974.

City of Dallas Department of Planning and Urban Development. *Dallas Ecologi-
    cal Study,* 1973; and Dallas Ecological Study, Phase 1, Data Storage
    System, 1972.

Council on Environmental Quality. *Sixth Annual Report.* Washington, D.C.:
    1975.

DeForest, J.D. *State Energy Information Systems.* Prepared by the National
    Governors' Conference for the Economic Development Administration,
    U.S. Department of Commerce, July 1975. Springfield, Virginia: NTIS
    PB 247-457.

Dukelow, G.G. "Energy Conservation in Current Power Plants." In *Energy
    Conservation Policy Options for Illinois: Proceedings of the Second
    Annual Illinois Energy Conference,* June 24-25, 1974. Springfield, Vir-
    ginia: NTIS PB 240 548.

Environmental Research Technology, Inc. *A Guide for Considering Air Quality
    in Urban Planning.* Lexington, Mass.: March 1974.

Fels, Margaret F. and Michael J. Munson. "Energy Thrift in Urban Transporta-
    tion: Options for the Future." In *The Energy Conservation Papers.* Cam-
    bridge, Mass.: Ballinger, 1975.

*The Fiscal Impact of a New Industry in a Rural Area: A Coal Gasification
    Plant in Western North Dakota,* modification of a chart from Leistritz.
    Paper for presentation at the Seventh Annual Meeting, Mid-Continent
    Section, Regional Science Association, Duluth, Minnesota, June 13-14,
    1975.

Gilmore, John and Mary Duff. *Sweetwater County Boom: A Challenge to Growth Management.* July 1974.

Gold, Raymond, et al. *A Comparative Case Study of the Impact of Coal on the Way of Life of People in the Coal Areas of Eastern Montana and Northeastern Wyoming.* Missoula, Montana: University of Montana, Institute for Social Science Research, 1974.

Haskell, Elizabeth H. *An Evaluation of Section 208 as a Model for Air Quality Planning and Management.* Prepared for the Office of Transportation and Land Use Policy, U.S. Environmental Protection Agency, July 1975.

Haule, Gregory. "Comment: Toward the Comprehensive Abatement of Noise Pollution." In *Ecology Law Quarterly* 4: 109 (Winter 1974).

Herendeen, Robert A. "Energy Cost of Goods and Services." Oak Ridge, Tennessee: Oak Ridge National Laboratory, 1973.

Hittman Associates, Inc. *Residential Energy Consumption: Multifamily Housing Final Report.* Washington, D.C.: U.S. Government Printing Office, 1974.

"HUD Helps Localities with Expected to Reside Data." In *Practicing Planner* 6:1 (February 1976).

Interagency Agreement between the Department of Housing and Urban Development and the Environmental Protection Agency, dated March 24, 1975.

Keast, David N. "Some Pitfalls of Community Noise Development." In *Journal of the Air Pollution Control Federation* 25:1 (January 1975).

Keifer and Associates, Inc. *Nationally Recognized Safe Land Use and Construction Practices.* January 1976.

Keyes, Dale. *Land Development and the Natural Environment: Estimating Impacts.* Washington, D.C.: The Urban Institute, 1976.

L.S. Goodfriend and Associates. *Urban Noise Survey Methodology.* New York: 1971.

Leistritz, Larry. *Will Bust Follow Boom? The Case of ABM Development in North Dakota.* Talk presented at the "Summit on Coal," a conference sponsored by the Rocky Mountain Center on Environment and Federation of Rocky Mountain States, Denver, Colorado, March 20, 1975.

Lewis, Philip H. *Study of Recreation and Open Space in Illinois.* Urbana, Illinois: University of Illinois. Department of Landscape Architecture and Bureau of Community Planning, 1964.

Litton, R. Burton, Jr. *Forest Landscape Description and Inventories — A Basis for Planning and Design.* U.S. Department of Agriculture, Forest Research Paper PS V-49, 1968.

Loewenstein, M. "The Impact of New Industry on the Fiscal Revenues and Expenditures of Suburban Communities." In *National Tax Journal* XVI:2 (1963), pp. 113-129.

Luken, Ralph. *Economic and Social Impacts of Coal Development in the 1970's for Mercer County, North Dakota.* Washington, D.C.: Old West Regional Commission, 1974.

Marks, David H., et al. *Evaluation of Policy Related Research in the Field of Municipal Solid Waste Management.* Cambridge, Massachusetts: Massachusetts Institute of Technology, Department of Civil Engineering, 1974.

Memorandum from the Secretary of Housing and Urban Development to HUD Administrators and Area Office Director, *Utilization of Regional Housing Planning in Department Programs,* March 5, 1976.

Metropolitan Washington Council of Governments. *Sound Cooperation: First Phase of an Areawide Environmental Noise Study,* June 1975.

Meyer, Alvin, Jr. "EPA's Implementation of the Noise Control Act of 1972." In *Sound and Vibration,* December 1975.

Minneapolis Department of Planning. *Problems in Downtown Minneapolis and Options for Downtown Problems.* Minneapolis, Minnesota: 1972.

National Park Service, U.S. Department of the Interior. *Guidelines for Local Surveys: A Basis for Preservation Planning.* Office of Archeological and Historic Preservation, Draft Report, 1976.

Roberts, James S. *Energy, Land Use and Growth Policy: Implications for Metropolitan Washington.* Chicago: Real Estate Research Corporation, 1975.

San Francisco Bay Conservation Development Commission. *San Francisco Bay Plan.* San Francisco: 1969.

San Francisco Department of City Planning. *The Urban Design of San Francisco,* May 1971.

Seattle Department of Community Development. *Seattle Urban Design Report No. 1: Determinants of City Form.* Seattle, Washington: January 1971.

Southeastern Wisconsin Regional Planning Commission. *Soils Development Guide.* Wankesha, Wisconsin: 1969.

State of Michigan. *Michigan Outdoor Recreation Study.* East Lansing, Michigan: 1966.

Steinitz, Carl et al. *Honey Hill: A Systems Analysis for Planning the Multiple Use of Controlled Water Areas.* Cambridge, Mass.: Department of Landscape Architecture Research Office, Graduate School of Design, Harvard University, IWR Report 71-9, October 1971. Prepared for the U.S. Army for Water Resources.

Steinitz, Carl, Peter Rogers, et al. *Urbanization and Change.* Cambridge, Mass.: Department of Landscape Architecture, Graduate School of Design, Harvard University, 1971.

Strong, Ann L., et al. *The Plan and Program for the Brandywine.* Philadelphia: Institute for Environmental Studies, University of Pennsylvania, 1968.

Szczepanski, Charles. "Air Quality Considerations in HUD Programs and the Relationship to EPA Activities. In John J. Roberts (ed.), *The Proceedings of a Specialty Conference on Long Term Maintenance of Clean Air Standards,* February 4-5, 1975.

Szczepanski, Charles. *Comments* on "Air Quality Management Using Land Use and Transportation" by Fred C. Hart. In *Proceedings*, op. cit., 1975.

Tampa Bay Regional Planning Council. *Shoreline Resource Development.* St. Petersburg, Florida: 1972.

Technology and Economics, Inc. *An Overview and Critical Evaluation of the Relationship Between Land Use and Energy Conservation*, submitted to the Federal Energy Administration, March 1976.

Thermo-Electron Corporation. *Potential for Effective Use of Fuel in Industry.* Waltham, Mass.: 1974.

U.S. Department of Housing and Urban Development. Circular 1390.2, *Noise Abatement and Control: Departmental Policy, Implementation Responsibilities, and Standards.* August 4, 1971.

U.S. Department of Housing and Urban Development in cooperation with the Federal Energy Administration. *Rapid Growth from Energy Projects: Ideas for State and Local Action.* Washington, D.C.: 1976.

U.S. Department of Transportation, Federal Highway Administration. Policy and Procedure Memorandum 90-2, *Noise Standards and Procedures.* February 8, 1973.

U.S. Department of Transportation, Federal Highway Administration. *Techniques for Incorporating Historic Preservation Objectives into the Highway Planning Process.* April 1974.

U.S. Environmental Protection Agency. *Coordinating 208 Planning and Air Quality Maintenance Area Planning.* Program Guidance Memorandum AM-14. October 30, 1975.

 . *Guidelines for Air Quality Maintenance Planning, Volume 4, Land Use and Transportation Considerations.* EPA-450/4-74-004. August 1974.

 . *Guidelines for Areawide Waste Treatment Management Planning.* August 1975.

 . *Land Use Implications and Requirements of EPA Programs.*

 . *Measuring External Effects of Solid Waste Management.* EPA-600/5-75-010. March 1975.

 . *Performance Standards for Sensitive Lands: A Practical Guide for Local Administrators.* EPA-600/5-75-005. March 1975.

 . *Promoting Environmental Quality Through Urban Planning and Controls.* EPA-600/5-73-015. February 1974.

 . *Report to Congress: Disposal of Hazardous Wastes.* 1974.

 . *State Program Implementation, Hazardous Waste Surveys.* Washington, D.C.: 1973.

 . 208-AQMA Program Guidance Memorandum AM-14.

VTN Consolidated, Inc. *Socioeconomic Impact Analysis, Sheridan County, Wyoming, Relative to Proposed Shell Oil Company and Decker Coal Company Projects.* Denver, Colorado: 1975.

1.3   Development and Evaluation of Plan and Policy Alternatives

Abel, Fred. "Project-by-Project Analysis vs. Comprehensive Planning." In *Evaluation of Techniques for Cost-Benefit Analysis of Water Pollution Control Programs and Policies.* Report of the Administration of the Environmental Protection Agency to the Congress of the United States. December 1974.

The American Institute of Planners. "The Comprehensive Plan and Environmental Quality." Prepared for the Environmental Statistics Division, ORKM, U.S. Environmental Protection Agency. Washington, D.C.: February 1974.

Ayers, Robert V. and Allen Kneese. "Production, Consumption and Externalities." In *American Economic Review* 59:4 (June 1969).

Baker, Earl J. *Toward an Evaluation of Policy Alternatives Governing Hazard Zone Land Use.* Boulder, Colorado: Institute for Behavioral Studies, University of Colorado, 1976.

Boyce, David, et al. *Metropolitan Plan Making: An Analysis of Experience with the Preparation and Evaluation of Alternative Land Use and Transportation Plans.* Monograph Series No. 4. Philadelphia: Regional Science Research Institute, 1970.

Cambell, Angus and Philip Converse. *The Human Measuring of Social Change.* New York: Russell Sage Foundation, 1972.

Churchman, et al. *Introduction to Operations Research.* New york: Wiley, 1951.

Council on Environmental Quality. "Preparation of Environmental Impact Statements: Guidelines," 40 CFR Part 1500, 38-FR 205550. August 1, 1973.

Dalkey, Norman C., Ralph Lewis, and David Snyder. "Measurement and Analysis of the Quality of Life." Santa Monica: The RAND Corporation, August 1970. Prepared for the U.S. Department of Transportation.

Day, J. "A Recursive Model for Nonstructural Flood Damage Control." In *Water Resources Research* 6, pp. 1262-1271.

Dee, Norbert, et al. *Environmental Evaluation System for Water Resource Planning.* Columbus, Ohio: Battelle Columbus Laboratories, 1972. NTIS No. PB-208-822.

Development of the Arizona Environmental and Economic Tradeoff Model. Planning Division, Department of Economic Planning and Development, Office of the Governor, State of Arizona, March 1973.

Dorfman, Robert and Henry Jacoby. "A Model of Public Decisions Illustrated by a Water Pollution Problem." In *The Analysis and Evaluation of Public Expenditures: The PPB System,* Volume I. Washington, D.C.: U.S. Government Printing Office, 1969, pp. 226-274.

        . *Models for Managing Regional Water Quality Management.* Cambridge, Mass.: Harvard University Press, 1973.

Executive Office of the President, Office of Management and the Budget. *Social Indicators 1973.* Washington, D.C.: U.S. Government Printing Office, 1973.

Fitzsimmons, Stephen, Lorrie Stuart, and Peter Wolff. *Social Assessment Manual: A Guide to the Preparation of the Social Well-Being Account.* Denver, Colorado: U.S. Department of the Interior, Bureau of Reclamation, July 1975.

Goals for Dallas: Submitted for Consideration by Dallas Citizens, 1966; *Goals for Dallas: Mutual Aims of its Citizens,* 1967; *Goals for Dallas: Proposals for Achieving the Goals,* 1969; *Goals for Dallas: Achieving the Goals,* 1970. Dallas, Texas: Cokesbury.

Hite, James C. *Environmental Planning: An Economic Analysis.* New York: Prager, 1972.

Houston-Galveston Area Council. *Region Simulation and Systems Control Model (ReSiSCM),* 1971.

Isard, Walter, et al. "On the Linkage of Socio-Economic and Ecologic System." In *Proceedings of the Regional Science Association* 21 (1968).

Isard, Walter and Tze Hsiung Tung. "Selected Non-Economic Commodities Definitions, and Speculations on Supply and Demand, Measurement and Utility." In *Proceedings of the Regional Science Association* 13 (1964).

James, L.D. "The Role of Economics in Planning Floodplain Land Use." In *Journal of the Hydraulics Division, Proceedings of the American Society of Civil Engineers* 98 (HY 5, #8935), pp. 981-992.

Kelly, Eric. "Impact Zoning: Concept for Growth Management." In *Colorado Municipalities* 51:5 (September/October 1975).

Keyes, Dale. *Land Development and the Natural Environment: Estimating Impacts.* Washington, D.C.: The Urban Institute, 1975.

Klarman, H.E., "Syphilis Control Programs." In Robert Dorfman (ed.), *Measuring Benefits of Government Investment.* Washington, D.C.: The Brookings Institution, 1965.

Klee, A.J. "The Role of Decision Models in the Evaluation of Competing Environmental Health Alternatives." In *Management Science* 18:2 (October 1971).

Langford, Thomas V. *Regional Input-Output Study: Recollections, Reflections and Diverse Notes on the Philadelphia Experience.* Cambridge, Mass.: The MIT Press, 1971.

Laurent, E.A. and J.D. Hite. "Economic-Ecologic Linkages and Regional Growth: A Case Study." In *Land Economics* 48 (Fall 1972).

Leontief, W. and W. Ford. "Air Pollution and the Economic Structure: The Empirical Results of Input-Output Computations" (mimeo.). Cambridge, Mass.: Harvard University, 1971.

Lichfield, Nathaniel, Michael Whitebread, and Peter Kettle. *Evaluation in the Planning Process.* Oxford, England: Pergamon Press, 1975.

Lin, Ben Chieh. *Quality of Life Indicators in the U.S. Metropolitan Area.* Kansas City, Missouri: Midwest Research Institute, 1975.

Loucks, Daniel, Blair Bower, and Walter O. Spofford, Jr. "Environmental Noise Management." In *Journal of the Environmental Engineering Division, Proceedings of the American Society of Civil Engineers* 99: EE6.

McHarg, Ian. *Design with Nature*. New York: The Natural Science Press, 1969.

Metropolitan Council of the Twin Cities Area. *Development Framework: Policy, Plan, Program*. St. Paul, Minnesota: 1975.

Muller Thomas. *Fiscal Impacts of Land Development: A Critique of Methods and Review of Issues*. Washington, D.C.: The Urban Institute, 1975.

Neea, R.N., et al. "Texas Coastal Zone Management." Austin, Texas: The General Land Office of the State of Texas, 1974.

Nehman, Gerald, et al. *Application of the Land Use Trade Off Model to Assess Land Use Capabilities of the Beaufort-Jasper County Area*. Two volumes. Columbus, Ohio: Battelle Columbus Laboratories, 1974.

New Jersey Department of Community Affairs, Local Assistance Planning Unit. *The Environmental Assessment Requirement: A Guidance Document for 701 Participants*. Revised January 13, 1975.

Pennsylvania Land Policy Project. *A Land Use Strategy for Pennsylvania: A Fair Chance for the "Faire Land" of William Penn*. Prepared for the Pennsylvania Office of State Planning and Development, Harrisburg, Pennsylvania. This is the main volume of a series of studies published by the Pennsylvania Land Policy Project. Other studies in the series are:

- *Laws which Regulate Land Use in Pennsylvania*, by Thomas M. Schmidt.

- *Potential Economic and Fiscal Impacts of a Land Use Policy for the Commonwealth of Pennsylvania*, by Benjamin H. Stevens.

- *State Land Use Programs: Issues and Options*, by Raymond R. Christmas.

- *The Pennsylvania Land Policy Survey: Expectations of the Land*

Pharis, Claudia. "Citizen Involvement in Comprehensive Planning. In *HUD Challenge* (January 1976), p. 22.

Rahenkamp, Sachs, Wells and Associates. "Duxbury Comprehensive Master Plan Statement." RSWA Planning Library Report Z-6, 1973.

　　　　　"Revised Impact Zoning Ordinances for Duxbury, Massachusetts." RSWA Planning Library Report Z-7, 1974.

Real Estate Research Corporation. *Business Prospects Under Coastal Zone Management*. Chicago: March 1976.

Regional Association. *Handbook on Public Participation in Regional Planning*. New York: 1974.

　　　　. "Metropolis Speaks," No. 95. New York: August 1974.

　　　　. *Listening to the Metropolis, An Evaluation of the New York Region's Choices for '76 Mass Media Town Meetings*. New York: 1974.

Schaenman, Philip and Thomas Muller. *Measuring Impacts of Land Development: An Initial Approach.* Washington, D.C.: The Urban Institute, 1974.

The Social and Economic Costs and Benefits of Compliance with the Auto Emission Standards Established by the Clean Air Amendments of 1970. Interim Report prepared for the Committee on Public Works, United States Senate, by the Environmental Studies Board, Commission on Natural Resources, National Research Council, National Academy of Sciences, December 1973.

State of California, Governor's Office. *Environmental Goals and Policies.* Sacramento, California: March 1, 1972.

Steinitz Rogers Associates. *The Santa Ana River Basin: An Example of the Use of Computer Graphics in Regional Plan Evaluation.* Cambridge, Mass.: June 1975. NTIS AD/A-013 404.

TRW Systems Group. *A Methodology for Floodplain Development and Management.* Institute for Water Resources Report 69-3, 1969.

U.S. Army Corps of Engineers, North Atlantic Division. *North Atlantic Regional Water Resources Study: Report.* Prepared for the North Atlantic Regional Water Resources Study Coordinating Committee, June 1972.

U.S. Environmental Protection Agency. *Guidelines for Air Quality Management Planning and Analysis,* Volume # 2: Plan Preparation. EPA-450/4-74-002, July 1974.

———. *Guidelines for Areawide Waste Treatment Management Planning.* Washington, D.C.: August 1975.

———. *Promoting Environmental Quality Through Urban Planning and Controls.* Op. cit., 1974.

———. *The Quality of Life Concept, A Potential New Tool for Decision-Makers.* Washington, D.C.: March 1973.

U.S. Water Resources Council. *Principles and Standards for Planning Water and Related Land Resources,* effective October 25, 1973.

Urban Land Institute. *The Economic Benefits of Coastal Zone Management.* Washington, D.C.: March 1976.

Weisbrod, B. "Collective Consumption Services of Individual Consumption Goods." In *Quarterly Journal of Economics* 78.

Whipple, William. "Optimizing Investment in Flood Control and Floodplain Zoning." In *Water Resources Research* 5, pp. 761-766.

Williams, D.L., et al. "Environmental Analysis for Development Planning." Houston, Texas: The Southwest Center for Urban Research, 1974.

Wise, Harold. "The Environmental Impact Statement and the Comprehensive Plan." In Robert N. Burchell and David Listokin (eds.), *Future Land Use.* Rutgers, New Jersey: 1975.

Woodcock, K.R. *A Model for Regional Air Pollution Cost/Benefit Analysis.* McLean, Virginia: TRW Systems Group, May 1971. Prepared for the Environmental Protection Agency, Contract No. PH 22-68-60.

1.4   Plan and Policy Implementation

Bosselman, Fred and David Callies. *The Quiet Revolution in Land Use Controls.* Washington, D.C.: Council on Environmental Quality, U.S. Government Printing Office, 1971.

Bosselman, Fred, David Callies, and John Banta.*The Taking Issue.* Washington, D.C.: Council on Environmental Quality, 1973.

Bucks County Planning Commission. "Plan for Implementation of Provisions of Act 515 of 1965." Doylestown, Pennsylvania: 1971.

Douglas Commission Report: Building the American City and "A National Public Works Investment Policy." Background papers for the U.S. House of Representatives Committee on Public Works, 1974.

Executive Office of the President, Office of Management and the Budget. *Catalogue of Federal Domestic Assistance.* Washington, D.C.: 1976.

Hershkowitz, Ronald M. "Local Environmental Protection: Problems and Limitations." In *Environmental Affairs* II:4 (Spring 1975).

Leon County, Florida. "Environmental Criteria for Erosion and Sedimentation Control." January 1975.

New Jersey State Soil Conservation Committee. *Model Municipal Land Disturbance Ordinance.*

Pennsylvania Department of Environmental Resources. *Soil Erosion and Sediment Control Manual.*

Sicard, Russell R. "Pursuing Open Space Preservation: The Massachusetts Conservation Restriction." In *Environmental Affairs* IV (Summer 1975), pp. 481-514.

State of Vermont, Office of the Governor. *Vermont's Policies and Procedures for Public Capital Investment.* Montpelier, Vermont: September 1975.

U.S. Department of Agriculture, Soil Conservation Service. "The Maryland Sediment Control Program." College Park, Maryland: 1971.

U.S. Department of Housing and Urban Development, Office of Small Town Services and Intergovernmental Relations. "Capital Improvements Programming in Local Government." Washington, D.C.: U.S. Government Printing Office, 1970.

U.S. Environmental Protection Agency. *Performance Standards for Sensitive Lands: A Practical Guide for Local Administrators.* EPA-600/5-75-005, March 1975.

1.5   Plan and Policy Management and Monitoring

Applied Decision Systems, Inc. *Small Area Model of the Houston-Galveston Area, Volume I, Summary of the Project.* Prepared for the Houston-Galveston Area Council, May 1973.

Bauer, Raymond A. (ed.). *Social Indicators.* Cambridge, Mass.: The MIT Press, 1966.

Boulder Area Growth Study Commission Citizen Survey. Boulder, Colorado: 1972.

Dalkey, Norman C., et al. "Measurement and Analysis of the Quality of Life." Santa Monica, California: The RAND Corporation, 1970. Prepared for the U.S. Department of Transportation.

"Environmental Indices and Interpretive Techniques." In *Environmental Quality, The Fifth Annual Report of the Council on Environmental Quality*, December 1974.

Graduate Research Center of the Southwest. *Goals for Dallas*. Four volumes. Dallas, Texas: 1966.

Gross, Bertram M. "The City of Man: A Social System Accounting." In William R. Ewald, Jr., (ed.), *Environment for Man*. Bloomington, Indiana: Indiana University Press, 1967.

Hysom, John L., Jr., et al. *A Handbook for Creating an Urban Development Information System*. Springfield, Virginia: NTIS, November 1974. Prepared for the U.S. Department of Housing and Urban Development by the Fairfax County, Virginia Office of Research and Statistics.

Regional Plan Association. *Handbook on Public Participation in Regional Planning*. New York: 1974.

———. *Listening to the Metropolis, An Evaluation of the New York Region's Choices for '76 Mass Media Town Meetings*. New York: 1974.

———. "Metropolis Speaks," No. 95. New York: August 1974.

Robinson, Ira M. (ed.). *Decision Making in Urban Planning: An Introduction to New Methodologies*. Beverley Hills, California: Sage Publications, 1972.

San Diego Regional Goals Committee. *Goals for the San Diego Region*, 1973.

State of Oregon, Office of the Governor. *Williamette Valley Attitude Survey*, 1970.

U.S. Environmental Protection Agency. *The Quality of Life Concept: A Potential New Tool for Decision Makers*. Washington, D.C.: March 1973.

1.6   Bibliographies and Information Sources for Environmental Management

Bestor, George C. and Holway R. Jones. *City Planning Bibliography: A Basic Bibliography of Sources and Trends*. New York: American Society of Civil Engineers, 1972.

Ehler, Charles. *Environmental Impacts of New Technology: An Annotated Bibliography*. Ann Arbor, Michigan: Michigan University Architectural Research Laboratory, 1969.

Environment Information Center. *Buyer's Guide to Environmental Media: A Directory of Books, Magazines, Films, and Information Sources*, No. 2. New York: 1974.

Grimes, Maria H. *Environmental Organizations*. Washington, D.C.: U.S. Library of Congress Congressional Research Service, 1972.

Holleb, Doris B. *Social and Economic Information for Urban Planning.* Chicago: Center for Urban Studies of the University of Chicago, 1969.

Meskenberg, Michael J. *Environmental Planning: A Selected Annotated Bibliography.* Chicago: 1970. American Society of Planning Officials Planning Advisory Service Report.

Onyz Group Inc. *Environment U.S.A., A Guide to Agencies, People and Resources.* New York: Bowker, 1974.

Shell, Joel C. and Gary R. Dean. *A Social Ecological Bibliography.* Exchange Bibliography No. 532. Monticello, Illinois: Council of Planning Librarians.

Smithsonian Institution. *Environmental Protection Research Catalog.* Washington, D.C.: Science Information Exchange, 1972. Prepared for the U.S. Environmental Protection Agency, Research Information Division.

Wolff, G.R. (ed.). *Environmental Information Sources Handbooks.* New York: Simon & Schuster, 1974.

2.0   Specific Environmental Concerns in Comprehensive Planning

2.1   Land Use

"A National Public Works Investment Policy." Background paper for the U.S. House of Representatives Committee on Public Works, 1974.

Agreement for Coordination of Activities between Office of Community Planning and Development (701), Department of Housing and Urban Development and Federal Energy Administration, dated Auguest 27, 1975.

Arthur D. Little Inc. *Residential and Commercial Energy Use Patterns 1970-1990* (part of the FEA Task Force Reports for Project Independence). Washington, D.C.: U.S. Government Printing Office, 1974.

ASCE Urban Water Resources Research Program. "Urban Mathematical Modeling and Catchment Research in the U.S.A." Technical Memorandum No. IHP-1, June 1975.

Associated Universities. *Reference Energy Systems and Resource Data in the Assessment of Energy Technologies.* Springfield, Virginia: NTIS PB 221 422.

Association of Bay Area Governments. *Land Capability Analysis.* San Francisco: December 1975.

Beall, S.E. and M.M. Yarosh. "Status of Waste Heat Utilization and Dual-Purpose Plant Projects." Oak Ridge, Tennessee: Oak Ridge National Laboratories, 1973.

Bosselman, Fred, David Callies, and John Banta.*The Taking Issue.* Washington, D.C.: Council on Environmental Quality, 1973.

Bucks County Planning Commission. "Plan for Implementation of Provisions of Act 515 of 1965." Doylestown, Pennsylvania: 1971.

Candlestick Properties, Inc. v. *San Francisco Bay Conservation and Development Commission.* 89 Cal. Rptr. 897 (Cal. App. Ct., 1970).

Center for Ecological Research in Planning and Design, University of Pennsylvania. *Medford: Performance Requirements for the Maintenance of Social Values Represented by the Natural Environment of Medford Township, New Jersey.* Philadelphia: 1974.

City of Dallas Department of Planning and Urban Development. *The Dallas Ecological Study,* 1973; and *Dallas Ecological Study, Phase 1 Data Storage System,* 1972.

Construction Industry Association of Sonoma County vs. *City of Petaluma.* United States Court of Appeals for the 9th Circuit, Docket No. 74-2100, August 13, 1975.

Council on Environmental Quality. *Sixth Annual Report.* Washington, D.C.: 1975.

DeForest, J.D. *State Energy Information Systems.* Springfield, Virginia: The National Governors' Conference for the Economic Development Administration, U.S. Department of Commerce, July 1975. NTIS PB 247 257.

Development of the Arizona Environmental and Economic Tradeoff Model. Planning Division, Department of Economic Planning and Development, Office of the Governor, State of Arizona, March 1973.

Douglas Commission Report: Building the American City. Background paper for the U.S. House of Representatives Committee on Public Works, 1974.

Euclid vs. *Ambler Realty Co.* 262 U.S. 365 (1926).

Fels, Margaret F. and Michael J. Munson. "Energy Thrift in Urban Transportation: Options for the Future." In *The Energy Conservation Paper.* Cambridge, Mass.: Ballinger, 1975.

The Fiscal Impact of a New Industry in a Rural Area: A Coal Gasification Plant in Western North Dakota. Modification of a chart from Leistritz. Paper for presentation at the Seventh Annual Meeting, Mid-Continent Section, Regional Science Association, Duluth, Minnesota, June 13-14, 1975.

Gilmore, John and Mary Duff. *Sweetwater County Boom: A Challenge to Growth Management.* July 1974.

Gold, Raymond, et al. *A Comparative Case Study of the Impact of Coal Development on the Way of Life of People in the Coal Areas of Eastern Montana and Northeastern Wyoming.* Missoula, Montana: Institute for Social Science Research, University of Montana, 1974.

Golden vs. *Planning Board of Ramapo.* 30 NY2d,359, 355 NE2d,291, appeal dismissed, 409 US1007 (1972).

Herendeen, Robert A. "Energy Cost of Goods and Services." Oak Ridge, Tennessee: Oak Ridge National Laboratory, 1973.

Houston-Galveston Area Council. *Region Simulation and Systems Control (ReSiSCM).* Houston, Texas: 1971.

　　　　. *Environmental Decisions Assistance System (E.D.A.S.).* Houston, Texas: 1973.

Hysom, John L., Jr., et al. *A Handbook for Creating an Urban Development Information System.* Springfield, Virginia: Fairfax County Office of Research and Statistics for the U.S. Department of Housing and Urban Development, November 1974. NTIS No. PB-238 815.

Just vs. *Marionette County.* 201 N.W. 2d.761 (Wisconsin, 1972).

Keyes, Dale. *Land Development and the Natural Environment: Estimating Impacts.* Washington, D.C.: Urban Institute, 1975.

Laurent. E.A. and J.C. Hite. "Economic-Ecological Linkages and Regional Growth: A Case Study." *Land Economics* 48 (Fall 1972).

Leistritz, Larry. *Will Bust Follow Boom? The Case of ABM Development in North Dakota.* Talk presented at the "Summit on Coal," a conference sponsored by the Rocky Mountain Center on Environment and Federation of Rocky Mountain States, Denver, Colorado, March 20, 1975.

Leon County, Florida. "Environmental Criteria for Erosion and Sedimentation Control." January 1975.

Lewis, Philip H. *Study of Recreation and Open Space in Illinois.* Urbana, Illinois: Department of Landscape Architecture and Bureau of Community Planning, University of Illinois, 1964.

Lifton, R. Burton, Jr. *Forest Landscape Description and Inventories — A Basis for Planning and Design.* U.S. Department of Agriculture, Forest Research Paper PS V-49, 1968.

Loewenstein, J. "The Impact of New Industry on the Fiscal Revenues and Expenditures of Suburban Communities." In *National Tax Journal* XVI:2 (1963), pp. 113-129.

Luken, Ralph. *Economic and Social Impacts of Coal Development in the 1970's for Mercer County, North Dakota.* Washington, D.C.: Old West Regional Commission, 1974.

Maine Shoreline Zoning and Subdivision Control Law, P.L. 1971, Chap. 535.

Marks, David H., et al. *Evaluation of Policy Related Research in the Field of Municipal Solid Waste Management.* Cambridge, Mass.: Department of Civil Engineering, Massachusetts Institute of Technology, 1974.

McHarg, Ian. *Design with Nature.* New York: The Natural Science Press, 1969.

Minneapolis Department of Planning. *Problems in Downtown Minneapolis* and *Options for Downtown Problems.* Minneapolis, Minnesota: 1972.

Morris County Land Improvement Campaign vs. *Parsippany-Troy Hills Township.* 40 N.J. 539, 193A2d.232 (1963).

Nehman, Gerald, et al. *Application of the Land Use Trade Off Model to Assess Land Use Capabilities of the Beaufort-Jasper County Area.* Two volumes. Columbus, Ohio: Battelle Columbus Laboratories, 1974.

New Jersey Statutes Ann. 15: 8A-20 (d) (Supp. 1973).

New Jersey State Soil Conservation Committee. Model Municipal Land Disturbance Ordinance.

Pennsylvania Coal Company vs. *Mahon.* 260 U.S. 393 (1922).

Pennsylvania Department of Environmental Resources. *Soil Erosion and Sediment Control Manual.* January 1974.

Rahenkamp, Sachs, Wells and Associates. "Duxbury Comprehensive Plan Statement." RSWA Planning Library Report Z-6, 1973.

———. "Revised Impact Zoning Ordinance for Duxbury, Massachusetts." RSWA Planning Library Report Z-7, 1974.

Rules and Regulations of the Pennsylvania Department of Environmental Resources, Title 25, S102.23.

San Francisco Bay Conservation and Development Commission. *San Francisco Bay Plan.* San Francisco: 1969.

San Francisco Department of City Planning. *The Urban Designs of San Francisco.* May 1971.

Seattle Department of Community Development. *Seattle Urban Design Report No. 1: Determinants of City Form.* Seattle: January 1971.

Sicard, Russell R. "Pursuing Open Space Preservation: The Massachusetts Conservation Restriction." In *Environmental Affairs* IV (Summer 1975).

Southeastern Wisconsin Regional Planning Commission. *Soils Development Guide.* Wankesha, Wisconsin: 1969.

State of Michigan. *Michigan Outdoor Recreation Study.* East Lansing, Michigan: 1966.

State of Vermont, Office of the Governor. "Vermont's Policies and Procedures for Public Capital Investment." September 1975.

Steel Hill Development, Inc. v. *Town of Sanborton.* 469F2d.956. (CA 1st, 1972).

Steinitz, Carl, et al. *Honey Hill: A Systems Analysis for Planning the Multiple Use of Controlled Water Areas.* Cambridge, Mass.: Department of Landscape Architecture Research Office, Graduate School of Design, Harvard University, IWR Report 71-9, October 1971. Prepared for the U.S. Army Institute for Water Resources.

Steinitz, Carl, Peter Rogers, et al. *Urbanization and Change.* Cambridge, Mass.: Department of Landscape Architecture, Graduate School of Design, Harvard University, 1971.

Tampa Bay Regional Planning Council. *Shoreline Resource Development.* St. Petersburg, Florida: 1972.

Technology and Economics Inc. *An Overview and Critical Evaluation of the Relationship Between Land Use and Energy Conservation.* Submitted to the Federal Energy Administration, March 1976.

Thermo-Electron Corporation. *Potential for Effective Use of Fuel in Industry.* Waltham, Mass.: 1974.

Turnpike Realty Co. v. Town of Dedham. 284NE2d.891 (Mass., 1972).

U.S. Department of Agriculture, Soil Conservation Service. "The Maryland Sediment Control Program." College Park, Maryland: 1971.

U.S. Department of Housing and Urban Development, Office of Small Town Services and Intergovernmental Relations. "Capital Improvements Programming in Local Government." Washington, D.C.: U.S. Government Printing Office, 1970.

U.S. Department of Housing and Urban Development, in cooperation with the Federal Energy Administration. *Rapid Growth from Energy Projects: Ideas for State and Local Action.* Washington, D.C.: 1976.

U.S. Environmental Protection Agency. *Performance Standards for Sensitive Lands: A Practical Guide for Local Administrators.* EPA-600/5-75-005, March 1975.

        . *Promoting Environmental Quality Through Urban Planning and Controls.* EPA-600/5-73-015, February 1974.

        .*Measuring External Effects of Solid Waste Management.* EPA-600/ 5-75-010, March 1975.

VTN Consolidated, Inc. *Socioeconomic Impact Analysis, Sheridan County Wyoming, Relative to Proposed Shell Oil Company and Decker Coal Company Projects.* Denver, Colorado: 1975.

Wolfe, M.R. and R.D. Shinn. *Urban Design Within the Comprehensive Planning Process.* Seattle: 1970.

2.2   Water Quality

Houston-Galveston Area Council. *Environmental Decisions Assistance Systems (E.D.A.S.).* Houston, Texas: 1973.

Interagency Agreement between the Department of Housing and Urban Development and the Environmental Protection Agency, dated March 24, 1975.

Strong, Ann L., et al. *The Plan and Program for the Brandywine.* Philadelphia: Institute for Environmental Studies, University of Pennsylvania, 1968.

U.S. Environmental Protection Agency. *Coordinating 208 Planning and Air Quality Maintenance Area Planning.* Program Guidance Memorandum AM-14, October 30, 1975.

        . *Guidelines for Areawide Waste Treatment Management Planning.* August 1975.

        . *Land Use Implications and Requirements of EPA Program.*

        . *Performance Standards for Sensitive Lands: A Practical Guide for Local Administrators.* EPA-600/5-75-005, March 1975.

. *Promoting Environmental Quality Through Urban Planning and Controls.* EPA-600/5-63-015, February 1974.

. 208-AQMA Program Guidance Memorandum AM-14.

2.3 Air Quality

Environmental Reserach & Technology, Inc. *A Guide for Considering Air Quality in Urban Planning.* Lexington, Mass.: March 1974.

Haskell, Elizabeth H. *An Evaluation of Section 208 as a Model for Air Quality Planning and Management.* Prepared for the Office of Transportation and Land Use Policy, U.S. Environmental Protection Agency, July 1975.

Interagency Agreement between the Department of Housing and Urban Development and the Environmental Protection Agency, dated March 24, 1975.

Keyes, Dale. *Land Development and the Natural Environment: Estimating Impacts.* Washington, D.C.: The Urban Institute, 1976.

Szczepanski, Charles. "Air Quality Considerations in HUD Programs and the Relationship to EPA Activities." In John J. Roberts (ed.), *Proceedings of a Specialty Conference on Long Term Maintenance of Clean Air Standards,* February 4-5, 1975.

Szczepanski, Charles. *Comments* on "Air Quality Management Using Land Use and Transportation," by Fred C. Hart. In *Proceedings,* op. cit., 1975.

U.S. Environmental Protection Agency. Guidelines for Air Quality *Maintenance Planning, Volume 4, Land Use and Transportation Considerations.* EPA-450/4-74-004, August 1974.

U.S. Environmental Protection Agency. 208-AQMA Program Guidance Memorandum AM-14.

2.4 Noise Abatement and Control

Borsky, Paul. "The Use of Social Surveys for Measuring Community Response to Noise Environments." In James Chapulnik (ed.), *Transportation Noise.* Seattle: University of Washington, 1970.

Haule, Gregory. "Comment: Toward the Comprehensive Abatement of Noise Pollution." *Ecology Law Quarterly* 4:109 (Winter 1974).

Keast, David N. "Some Pitfalls of Community Noise Measurement." *Journal of the Air Pollution Control Federation* 24:1 (January 1975).

L.S. Goodfriend and Associates. *Urban Noise Survey Methodology.* New York: 1971.

Metropolitan Washington Council of Governments. *Sound Cooperation: First Phase of an Areawide Environmental Noise Study.* June 1975.

Meyer, Alvin, Jr. "EPA's Implementation of the Noise Control Act of 1972." *Sound and Vibration,* December 1975.

U.S. Department of Housing and Urban Development. Circular 1390.2. *Noise Abatement and Control: Departmental Policy, Implementation Responsibilities, and Standards.* August 4, 1971.

U.S. Department of Transportation, Federal Highway Administration. Policy and Procedure Memorandum 90-2, *Noise Standards and Procedures.* February 8, 1973.

2.5   Flooding and Other Hazards

Baker, Earl J. and Joe G. McPhee. *Land Use Management and Regulation in Hazardous Areas: A Research Assessment.* Boulder, Colorado: University of Colorado, 1975.

Houston-Galveston Area Council *Environmental Decisions Assistance System (E.D.A.S.).* Houston, Texas: 1973.

Keifer and Associates, Inc. *Nationally Recognized Safe Land Use and Construction Practices.* January 1976.

U.S. Environmental Protection Agency. *Report to Congress: Disposal of Hazardous Wastes,* 1974.

        . *State Program Implementation, Hazardous Waste Surveys.* Washington, D.C.: 1973.

2.6   Historic Preservation

National Park Service, U.S. Department of the Interior. *Guidelines for Local Surveys: A Basis for Preservation Planning.* Office of Archeological and Historic Preservation, Draft Report, 1976.

U.S. Department of Transportation, Federal Highway Administration. *Techniques for Incorporating Historic Preservation Objectives into the Highway Planning Process.* April 1974.

Index

AICUZ. *See* Air Installation Compatible Use Zone
ALI. *See* American Law Institute
AQMA. *See* Air Quality Maintenance Area
ATOM. *See* Arizona Tradeoff Model
Abt Associates, 137
Adirondack Park (N.Y.) Agency, 192
Aerial surveys, 69-70, 214-215
Affirmative action, 79, 194
Air Force, 61, 198
Air Installation Compatible Use Zone, 61-62
Air quality, 6-7, 27, 50-58, 221
 alternatives, 106
 cost-benefit analysis, 131-132
 regulations, 195-197
Air Quality Maintenance Area, 46, 47, 49, 52, 54-58
Aircraft Noise Abatement Policy Studies Program, 65
Airports, 49, 63, 64-65, 198
American Law Institute: Model Land Development Code, 189-190, 204
Aquifers, 42
Areas of Critical Concern, 190, 192-193
Areawide Waste Treatment Management, 11, 38-40
 and 701 Program, 46-50
Arizona Tradeoff Model, 117
Army Corps of Engineers, 23, 50, 69, 180
Authorities and special districts, 165
Ayres and Kneese model, 113

Baker, Earl J., 133-134
"Balancing of public good vs. individual loss" theory, 175, 176
Battelle Memorial Institute, 117, 119, 136
Beaufort County, S.C., 119
Bonds, 164

Boston, 167
Boulder, Colo., 179, 216
Branch, Melville, 211-212
Brandywine (Pa.) watershed, 47-48
Bucks County, Pa., 96-97
Bureau of Economic Analysis, 83
Bureau of Reclamation, 136, 137, 139
Bureau of the Census, 82

CAASE. *See* Computer-Assisted Area Source Emissions Gridding Procedure
CDBG. *See* Community Development Block Grants
CEQ. *See* Council on Environmental Quality
CIP. *See* Capital Improvements Program
COG's. *See* Councils of Governments
CZM. *See* Coastal zone management
California, 189, 202
 Coastal Plan, 130
 Environmental Goals and Policies Report, 94-96
Canada, 159
Candlestick Properties, Inc., vs. *San Francisco Bay Conservation and Development Commission,* 177-178, 179, 181
Capital-gains tax, 202-203
Capital improvements financing, 164-165
Capital Improvements Program, 160-161, 162-165
Carrying capacity analysis, 110-112
Census data, 82-83, 135
Charleston, S.C., 114-115
Chemical hazards, 70-71
Chicago, 197, 203
CHOICES FOR '76, 149
Circular A-95 (OMB), 147, 205-206

Circular 1390.2 (HUD), 61, 62, 63, 65, 198, 248-249
Citizen participation, 147-149, 216-217
Civil Rights Act (1964), 79, 206, 254
Clean Air Act amendments (1970, 1977), 50, 51, 131, 142, 195, 246-248
Cluster development, 173, 174
Coast Guard, 23
Coastal zone management, 21-26, 130, 187-188
Coastal Zone Management Act (1972), 22, 188, 234-238
Community Development Block Grants, 74, 79, 81-82, 139, 141, 159, 167, 194-195
Compensable regulations, 203-204
Comprehensive planning: air quality, 51-56
  noise control, 64-65
  social equity, 79
  water quality and land use, 46-50
Comprehensive Planning Assistance Program, 11, 34, 148
  and air quality, 54, 56
  and coastal zone management, 22-23, 24
  and environmental assessment, 139-140, 141-142, 143
  and historic preservation, 73-74
  and housing, 81-83
  and water quality-land use integration, 46-50
Computer-Assisted Area Source Emissions Gridding Procedure, 55
Computer graphics, 104, 220, 221
Computerized data-storage and retrieval systems, 217-221
Conditional use, 173
Connecticut, 181, 202
Conservation easements and restrictions, 157-158, 170-171
Constitutional issues, 156, 168, 170-172, 175, 193
Construction Industry Association of Sonoma County vs. City of Petaluma, 161
Corte Madera, Marion Co., Calif., 189
Cost-benefit analysis, 110, 123-134
Council on Environmental Quality, 23, 130, 140, 142

Councils of Governments, 56, 62
COZMOS computer model, 24-26

DOE. See Department of Energy
DOT. See Department of Transportation
DRI. See Development of Regional Impact
Dallas, 35, 37
  Ecological Study, 17-18
  Goals for Dallas, 99-100, 216-217
Data base, 213-215
  use of computers, 217-221
Dayton, Ohio, 82, 84, 193
DeKalb County, Ga., 184-185
Demonstration Cities and Metropolitan Development Act (1966), 167, 205-206
Department of Agriculture, 13, 50
  Soil Conservation Service, 69, 183
Department of Energy, 34
Department of Housing and Urban Development, 11
  and air quality, 54, 56
  and citizen participation, 148, 149
  and coastal zone management, 22-23, 24
  and energy, 34
  and environmental assessment, 117, 139-140, 141-142, 143
  and flood insurance, 23, 67-68, 69, 180
  and historic preservation, 73-74
  and housing equity, 78-79, 81-83
  and new towns, 166
  and noise control, 61, 62, 63, 65, 198, 248-249
  and rent subsidies, 167
  and water quality-land use integration, 46-50
Department of Interior, 11, 23, 50, 159
Department of Transportation, 56, 61, 72
  Historic and Cultural Resources Inventory, 77-78
Design with Nature (McHarg), 111
Developers, 174-175, 201-202
Development, timing of, 160-161
Development and evaluation plan alternatives, 9, 91-149
Development assistance, 166-167
Development incentives, 204-205

Development of Regional Impact, 190, 191-192
"Diminution of value" theory, 175, 176
Disaster Relief Act (1974), 66, 180-181, 251-252
Discount rate, 126
Due process, 170-172
Duxbury, Mass., 123-205

EDAS. *See* Environmental Decision Assistance System
EES. *See* Environmental Evaluation System
EIS. *See* Environmental impact statements
EIU's. *See* "Environmental Impact Units"
EPA. *See* Environmental Protection Agency
Easements, 157-158, 170-171
Economic models, 111, 113-116
Eminent domain, 156
Emission density zoning, 106
Emission inventory and projections, 57-58
Emission regulation, 195-196
Energy conservation, 30-34, 106
Environmental assessment, 91, 117, 139-146
Environmental Assessment Requirements (N.J. Dept. of Community Affairs, 143
"Environmental corridors," 17
Environmental Decision Assistance System, 116-117
Environmental Evaluation System, 136
Environmental impact statements, 139-143
"Environmental Impact Units," 136
Environmental Protection Agency:
    and air quality, 49-52, 56, 57, 58, 131, 195-196
    and hazardous wastes, 71-72
    and monitoring, 221
    and noise control, 197-198
    and quality of life concept, 134-135
    and Section 208, 11, 38-40, 41, 130
    and water quality-land use integration, 46-50

Environmental systems analysis, 18-20
Equal protection doctrine, 171-193
Erosion and sedimentation, 44-45, 182-185
ERTS-1 satellite, 69-70
Euclid vs. *Ambler Realty Co.*, 172
Euclidean zoning, 172
Evaluation methodologies, 91, 109-139
Excess condemnation laws, 159
Executive orders: and historic preservation, 73-74
    and social equity, 255

FAA. *See* Federal Aviation Agency
FHWA. *See* Federal Highway Administration
Fair Housing Act (1968), 255
Fair-share allocations, regional, 193-195
Fairfax, Va., 205
Fairfax County, Va., 217-220
Federal-Aid Highway Program, 140
Federal Aviation Agency, 198
Federal Highway Administration, 50, 61, 63, 198
Federal Water Pollution Control Act amendments (1972), 30, 38, 142, 179-180, 240-245
    Section 208, 11, 38-40, 46-50
Fee simple, 157
Fels and Munson study, 33
Fiscal policy, 200-204
Floating zones, 173
Flood Disaster Protection Act (1973), 66, 67, 250-251. *See also* Disaster Relief Act.
Flood Insurance Program (HUD), 23, 67-69, 180
Floodplain management, 7, 65-72
    alternatives, 107-109
    cost-benefit analysis, 133-134
    regulations, 179-181
Florida, 191, 192-193

Galveston Bay water-quality model, 116-117
"General welfare" concept, 161, 175, 176, 194
Geographic Priority Area Identification System, 83-84
Geological Survey, 69

Golden vs. *Planning Board of Ramapo*, 160-161
Government expenditures, 156-167
"Grandfather clauses," 186
Great Britain, 196
Griggs vs. *Allegheny*, 198
Guidance framework plans, 91, 92-100

HAP's. *See* Housing Assistance Plans
HCRI. *See* Historic and Cultural Resources Inventory
HGAC. *See* Houston-Galveston Area Council
HPO. *See* State Historic Preservation Officers
HUD. *See* Department of Housing and Urban Development
Hackensack (N.J.) Meadowlands Area, 165, 191
Hartford, Conn., 82, 195
Hawaii, 186, 190-191, 202
Hazardous areas, 67-72, 108-109, 179-180. *See also* Areas of Critical Concern
Highways, 63, 77-78
Hillside development, 188-189
Historic and Archeological Preservation Data Act amendments (1974), 73
Historic and Cultural Resources Inventory, 77-78
Historic preservation, 7, 72-78, 109, 167
Historic Sites Act (1935), 73
Hite, James, 111
Hite and Laurent, 114-115
Holmes, Justice, 176
Home rule provisions, 169
Housing, low-income, 193-195, 205
Housing Act (1949), 166
    amendments (1954), 166-167
Housing and Community Development Act (1974), 5, 14, 148, 167, 180, 194, 228-231, 256
    and historic preservation, 73-74
    and social equity, 8, 78-79
Housing and Urban Development Act (1968), 255
Housing Assistance Plans, 81-83, 167, 194-195
Housing density, 32, 173, 174, 203, 205
Houston-Galveston Area Council, 116-117, 220

Impact zoning, 122-123, 204-205
Incentive zoning, 205
Incentives and disincentives, indirect public, 199-205
Incinerators, 27
Industry: energy use, 32
    hazardous wastes, 70-71
Information needs, determination of, 213-214
Input-output models, 33, 113, 220
Intergovernmental Cooperation Act (1968), 205, 206, 232-234
Investment policy, public, 199-200
Iowa, 181
Isard, Walter, 111, 113

Jasper County, S.C., 119
Joint financing, 165
"Just compensation," 156, 170, 175
Just vs. *Marionette County*, 177, 178-179, 181

Kneese and Ayres model, 113

Lake Tahoe (Calif.-Nev.) Regional Planning Agency, 192
Land acquisition, public, 156-159
Land and Water Conservation Fund Program, 159
Land-based planning systems, 83-85
Land capability analysis, 14-16
Land development, effects of, 118-119
Land speculators, 201
Land suitability studies, 12-21
Land use, 6, 12-37
    alternatives, 101-105
    and energy conservation, 30-34
    regulations, 172-195
    and solid waste management, 26, 186-188
    and water quality, 41-46, 221
Land-use districts, 172
Land-use models, 20-21
Land-use restrictions, 157-158, 170-171
Land Use Tradeoff Model, 119-122
Landfills, 26-30, 186-188
Landscape analysis, 13, 17-18
Large-lot zoning, 174, 179
Leachates, 26-27, 45-46
Lease-purchase, 164-165
Lewis, Phillip H., 17
Litton, R. Burton, 13
Local governments: regulatory powers, 168-198 *passim*

MPO's. *See* Metropolitan Planning Organizations

MRI. *See* Midwest Research Institute

McHarg, Ian, 18-19, 110, 111-112

Madison, N.J., 194

Maine, 188, 190

"Mandatory dedication," 175

Mapping, 67-70, 111-112, 119, 120

Marine Protection, Research and Sanctuaries Act (1972), 22

Marionette County, Wis., 178-179

Martha's Vineyard (Mass.) Land Use Law, 191

Maryland, 167, 183, 203

Massachusetts, 157-158, 159, 194, 200-201, 204

Medford Township, N.J., 19-20

Memphis, Tenn., 83-84

Methane, 27

Metropolitan Planning Organizations, 56

Metropolitan Washington Council of Governments: TRIMS model, 34

Miami Valley (Dayton, Ohio) Regional Planning Commission, 82

Michigan RECSYS simulation model, 20-21

Midwest Research Institute, 135

Minneapolis, 35, 97-99, 165

Minnesota, 97

Model Cities Act, 148

Model Code, 189-190, 204

Montgomery County, Md., 193, 205

Mount Laurel, N.J., 194

NAAQS's. *See* National ambient air-quality standards

NASA, 214

NASQUAN. *See* National Stream Quality Accounting Network

NEPA. *See* National Environmental Policy Act

NOAA. *See* National Oceanic and Atmospheric Administration

NRDC vs. *EPA*, 196

NWQSS. *See* National Water Quality Surveillance System

Nassau-Suffolk (N.Y.) Regional Planning Board, 24-26

National Academy of Sciences, 131

National Aerometric Data Bank, 221

National ambient air-quality standards, 50, 51

National Environmental Policy Act (1969), 73, 139, 141, 206, 226-228

National Flood Insurance Act (1968), 180

National Historic Preservation Act (1966), 73, 167, 252-254

National Oceanic and Atmospheric Administration, 11, 23, 24, 50, 69

National Park Service, 73, 74, 159

National Register, 73, 74, 75, 76, 77

National Stream Quality Accounting Network, 221

National Trust for Historic Preservation, 73

National Water Quality Surveillance System, 221

Natural gas pipelines, 72

Natural Resources Defense Council, 51

Negotiated life tenancy, 159

New Jersey, 158, 194

New Orleans, 167

New towns, 166

New York City, 149, 203

New York State, 192, 193-194

Noise control, 7, 27, 58-65, 107, 132

Noise Control Act (1972), 59-61, 197-198, 249

North Atlantic Regional Water Resources Study, 94

"Nuisance abatement" theory, 175-176

OCZM. *See* Office of Coastal Zone Management

OMB. *See* Office of Management and Budget

Oak Ridge energy input-output model, 33

Oakwood at *Madison* vs. *Madison*, 194

Ocean County, N.J., 49

Ocean Dumping Act, 22

Office of Coastal Zone Management, 24, 130

Office of Management and Budget: Circular A-95, 147, 205-206

Open space, 175, 201-202, 203, 205

"Option demand," 126

PUD. *See* Planned Unit-Development

Pay-as-you-go financing, 164

Pennsylvania, 158, 167, 182, 183

Pennsylvania Coal Co. vs. *Mahon*, 176
Performance standards, 173, 196, 214
Petaluma, Calif., 161
Photography, aerial and satellite, 69-70, 214-215
"Physical invasion" theory, 175
Planned Unit-Development, 173-174
Planning agencies: cooperation and coordination of activities, 48-50, 205-207
Planning studies, 9, 11-85
Plans and policies: alternatives, 91, 100-139
    implementation, 9, 155-207
    monitoring, 9, 211-221
    selection, 91, 146-149
Police power, 161, 168-198
Policy-analysis techniques, 129-134
"Policy evaluation," 129
Preferential assessment, 200-201
Private sector development, public assistance to, 166-167
Project impact analysis, 110, 117-123
Project-level vs. regional analysis, 127-128
Public facilities, construction of, 159-162
"Public good" concept, 161, 175, 176, 194
Puerto Rico, 203

Quality of life concept, 134-136, 137

RAPA. *See* Regional Air Pollution Analysis
RES. *See* Reference Energy System
ReSiSCM. *See* Regional Simulation and System Control
Rahenkamp, Sachs, Wells and Associates, 122, 123
Ramapo, N.Y., 160-161
"Reasonable use" theory, 177
Recreational planning, 20-21, 66, 126, 159
RECSYS simulation model, 20-21
Reference Energy System, 33
Regional Air Pollution Analysis, 131-132
Regional land-use controls, 189-192
Regional Plan Association, 149
Regional Simulation and System Control, 116, 117
Regulatory authority, 168-198

Rent subsidies, 167
Reserve-fund financing, 164
Resource Conservation and Recovery Act (1976), 30, 238, 240
Revenue sharing, 165
Review procedures, 146-147, 205-207
Rhode Island, 204
Riverside, Calif., 189
"Roll-back" charge, 202

SCORP. *See* State Comprehensive Outdoor Recreation Plan
SIP's. *See* State Implementation Plans
SWB. *See* Social well-being account
SWRPC. *See* Southeastern Wisconsin Regional Planning Commission
Safe Drinking Water Act (1974), 50, 245-246
San Diego County, Calif., 216, 221
San Francisco, 35, 37
San Francisco Bay, 15, 24, 177-178, 192
Sanbornton, N.H., 179
Santa Ana (Calif.) River Basin, 104-105
Satellites, use of, 69-70, 214-215
Scavengers, 187
Seattle, 35, 37
Section 208 Plan (EPA). *See* Area-wide Waste Treatment Management
Sensitive areas, 179-180
Septic tanks, 187
701 Program (HUD). *See* Comprehensive Planning Assistance Program
Shorelands. *See* Coastal zone management
Sierra Club, 52
Single-purpose vs. comprehensive analysis, 128-129
Site location planning, 27, 29-30, 162
Social-cultural factors, 134-139
Social equity, 8, 78-85
    alternatives, 109
    legislation, 254-256
Social Indicators 1973, 135
Social well-being account, 136-139
Socioeconomic baseline data, 79-81

Soil conservation districts, 183-184
Soil Development Guide (SWRPC), 13
Solid waste management, 26-30, 186-188
South Carolina Port Authority, 119
Southeastern Wisconsin Regional Planning Commission: *Soil Development Guide*, 13
Southern Burlington County NAACP vs. Township of Mount Laurel, 194
Space heating and cooling, 32
Special assessments, 165
Special-use zoning, 173
"Spillover" effects, 128, 199
St. George, Vt., 203
St. Paul, Minn., 97, 99, 165
Standard State Zoning Enabling Act (1926), 172
State Comprehensive Outdoor Recreation Plan, 50
State Historic Preservation Officers, 73, 74-75
State Implementation Plans, 51, 195-196
Staten Island, N.Y., 111-112
States: coastal zone management, 23, 130, 188
    land-use controls, 189-191
    regulatory authority, 168-169
    solid waste management, 30
Steel Hill Development, Inc., vs. *Sanbornton*, 177, 179
Steep slopes, 43-44, 188-189
Steinitz Rogers Associates, 21, 104-105
Streams and creekbeds, 41-42, 221
Subdivision regulations, 174-175
Suffolk County, L.I, N.Y., 24-26, 203
Surface and subsurface pollution, 45-46

TDR. *See* Transfer of development rights
"Takings," constitutional, 156, 170, 175-179, 204
Tax base revenue sharing, 165
Tax deferral, 201-202
Tax policy, 200-204
Technology, 29, 32-33
Television, use of, 149
Texas, 220

Time-phased development, 160-161
Tradeoff analysis, 110-117
Transfer of development rights, 203
Transportation planning, 29-30, 32-33, 34, 51, 56, 106
TRIMS model, 34
Turnpike Reality Co. vs. *Town of Dedham*, 176
Twin Cities Metropolitan Area, 165
    development guide, 97-99

UDIS. *See* Urban Development Information System
Urban design, 34-37
Urban Development Information System, 217-220
Urban Growth and New Community Development Act (1970), 166, 231-232
Urban Institute, 118, 119
Urban redevelopment, 166-167
U.S. vs. *Causby*, 198

Variances, 173
Vermont, 199-200, 202-203

Washington, D.C., 49
Washington County, Md., 184
Washington State, 202
Waste disposal, 26-30, 186-188
Waste heat, use of, 32
Wastes, hazardous, 71-72
Water quality, 6, 38-50
    alternatives, 106
    cost-benefit analysis, 130-131
    and land use, 41-46
    monitoring, 221
    and solid waste management, 26-27
Water Resources Council: *Principles and Standards*, 136-137
Water Resources Development Act (1974), 66, 180
Willamette Valley, Ore., 216
Woodlands, 43

Zoning, 122-123, 160, 161, 196
    as development incentive, 204-205
    and land-use regulation, 172-175
    and low-income housing, 193-194